LISTENING
TO THE
BIRDS

LISTENING
TO THE
BIRDS

A Nez Perce Woman's Journey of Self-Discovery and Healing

ROBERTA TAWLIKITSANMAY' PAUL

Washington State University Press
Pullman, Washington

Washington State University Press
PO Box 645610
Pullman, Washington 99164-5610
Phone: 800-354-7360
Email: wsupress@wsu.edu
Website: wsupress.wsu.edu

Publication of this book is supported by the Rupert Costo Endowment,
University of California, Riverside

The Washington State University Pullman campus is located on the homelands of the Niimíipuu (Nez Perce) Tribe and the Palus people. We acknowledge their presence here since time immemorial and recognize their continuing connection to the land, to the water, and to their ancestors. WSU Press is committed to publishing works that foster a deeper understanding of the Pacific Northwest and the contributions of its Native peoples.

Interior design by Tracy Randall
Cover design by Jeffry E. Hipp

Roberta Paul tells about her regalia in the cover image: "I had made [it] to meet Archbishop Desmond Tutu when attending the Truth and Reconciliation Conference hosted by University of Cape Town, Cape Town, South Africa, in November 2006. Created together with Raynel Olney Begay (Yakama) and myself, in October 2006. The buckskin dress is smoked deer hide, made to be white of color. Cornhusk hat and purse by Rose Frank. Braid medallions and medallion necklace, moccasins, and otter furs by Raynel Begay. Raven fan and blue shawl with red fringe made by Roberta Paul."

Dedication

For my ancestors and their descendants, known to me or not.
Especially to my grandparents, Black Raven and Tawlikitsanmay,
whose voices guided me in dreams.
And to my family, that we all might continue our healing journey.

Contents

Foreword

REVEREND DR. MARY JANE MILES

Dr. Roberta Paul, whose nickname "Robbie" captures her effervescent nature, has written her family's experience of historical trauma that so many Native American families have walked through silently.

As a scholar writing a doctoral thesis of my own, I read Dr. Paul's thesis before I actually met her.

Many Native American families do not speak about what their ancestors might have endured. Often there has been positive recall of what they were taught in boarding school life. In my own family, it was at an advanced age that I realized three childless aunts had attended the same boarding school known for sterilizing the young girls arriving from various tribes, as a procedure that was prioritized. A sinking feeling of truth as to why they were childless brought tears that burned my face: to think how one had raised me since my natural mother died giving birth to my younger sister. All these aunts showered their brothers' children with beneficent acts to assure a comfortable lifestyle for their family's offspring.

In the boarding school they had learned cooking, housekeeping, and personal cleanliness habits that made them exemplary citizens in their neighborhoods. Negative talk of boarding school days was not theirs in visitation with family, friends, and neighbors. Usually, it was romantic talk of how their mother went to school with Jim Thorpe. Nothing was shared about any negative experiences.

My thought processes during my years of pursuing higher education always seemed to want to dig into our history of being patronized and then subordinated to genocidal acts of the government that was so obvious and that I really did not want to believe. But our inability to move upward in our societal lifestyle seemed to come from what we did not want to talk about. So here it is, I was saying to myself as I read how Dr. Paul boldly told her family's story as a path to wellness she charted for her people.

The actual research that Dr. Paul has done comes through loud and clear in the old tribal names the family members carried as well as the

English names they later assumed. The connection to the revered leaders of the Nimiipuu, the Nez Perce word for themselves, is recorded humbly and matter of fact. The dates are included to authenticate the ancestral family tree. The events that the family went through are described in a manner that nuances watching a video of what they were experiencing at the time. Describing winter scenes makes the reader shiver as if they were part of the action. The writing style is vivid. It makes the reader want to finish the story in one sitting or to get back to the action as soon as can be. It feels as if the thesis itself was the prelude that would lead to the writing of a book that needed to be for the pleasure of the public.

After I actually met and visited in person with Dr. Paul, I felt I could now use her nickname Robbie because I knew her better. I felt emboldened to accept that tribal peoples needed to acknowledge that historical trauma needed exposure in our circles of life. She had opened that door and we could all come through it because of her work. I owed her a debt of confidence to claim my own background of insecure family life that was not all of my own making but what our people were made to endure because of the advent of colonialism.

Tribal people are unique in this country. It feels as if the dominant cultures want us to be invisible. This is our home, our homeland, and we are not going anywhere. We are spiritual because we are tied to the land we live upon. The creatures of this land provide for our livelihood so we revere them. Our legends glorify these animals that used to talk with us and now we speak for our brothers who cannot, or will not, talk for themselves. Robbie's rural upbringing adds to the hard work that was normal during the times we grew up in. These times recorded in writings tend to come off as romantic, as if we grew up like in the Laura Ingalls Wilder "Little House on the Prairie." Work was from dawn to nighttime. Playtime was with homemade toys usually or swing sets out of old tires. Relatives who joined were cousins who would be close the rest of our lifetimes. The extended family was revered because many families actually lived out the truth of "it takes a village to raise a child." Robbie's writing style gives you that feel of community being enjoyed regardless of what the circumstances might be.

Although the book brings nostalgia to our heads and hearts, the raw truth of living under perilous times of subordination simply because of who we are comes through clearly. Times when movies came out in the so-called "spaghetti western" times, under the auspices of Ted Turner, there was a personal uncomfortable feeling that persisted in me, that cried out "how does the public feel going to these movies?" Even the recent movie *Killers of the Flower Moon* details how the dominant society used marriage by Anglo men to marry Native women to gain control over the oil fields that could made them rich. A visit to the Red-Black Museum several years back made me hang my head because it focused on how tribes practiced slavery as well. Some had even intermarried, so their tribal roots display the practice. Even though I am proud of our peculiar Indian humor, it is used amongst ourselves in teasing how dark we can be, so are we really and truly authentic enrolled tribal members. Although the remarks seem innocent enough, they are racial. A bumper sticker caught my eye that professed "rez-neck." All tribal nations have legends that teach tribes they are "the people." So, we are proud.

My present position as Minister of the Word and Sacraments of the Presbyterian Church (USA) on the Idaho Nez Perce reservation leads me to look for healthy ways to own the past and be grateful for the strength our ancestors had that surely was passed on. My reading of Dr. Paul's doctoral thesis was in preparation for writing my thesis on how to be a Christian Indian. I wanted to be able to keep my cultural self and still serve our Lord Jesus Christ. There has been a noticeable division in our tribe that separated the Christian from the traditional religion. It has lessened and surely the ways and culture of our tribe glorify the Creator.

Listening to the Birds: A Nez Perce Woman's Journey of Self-Discovery and Healing is a seminal work by a woman warrior who wants to gently show us a path we can follow for our own self-discovery and healing journey. I feel she has humbly left her legacy in her work. I am grateful to come to know the author and to admire her grit in writing on how she describes her walk towards good health in understanding her circumstances of the life she was dealt. Her strength is found in the generation of her family. She is not through, but she is enjoying where she is now and waves to us to come along with her. I am thankful for what she has done.

Preface

Listening to the Birds is timely, as it deals with racial justice, personal empowerment, and the healing of intergenerational wounds. The book opens with me, Dr. Roberta "Robbie" Tawlikitsanmay' Paul, experiencing an emotional shock that led me and my family to uncover five generations of our family's stories. From a Nez Perce chief who met Lewis and Clark in Idaho, to a warrior who died fighting alongside Chief Joseph in the Nez Perce War of 1877; from surviving Indian boarding school assimilation to an Irish American woman who, at age 16, decided she was going to marry a handsome young Indian boy, *Listening to the Birds* is a family saga told with the intimacy of a memoir, the heart of a woman warrior, and the intensity of a woman on a mission to heal the soul of her people.

In my talks to survivors of intergenerational trauma, I say that telling stories is a Native way to heal wounds—but if you don't know the story, you can't heal. Finding my family's stories was my first step toward healing the wounds of racism, relocation, and assimilation. After much research, I wrote versions of this history for my master's and doctoral degree programs. Now, my ancestors have given me permission to tell this story to a wider audience and, working with a professional editor, I have transformed my doctoral dissertation into a lively, richly informative and illustrated, and heartfelt narrative that draws on memoir, psychology, and history to tell a compelling story that will appeal to anyone who has dealt with psychological trauma, especially those who have experienced intergenerational trauma.

Matriarchal Lineage

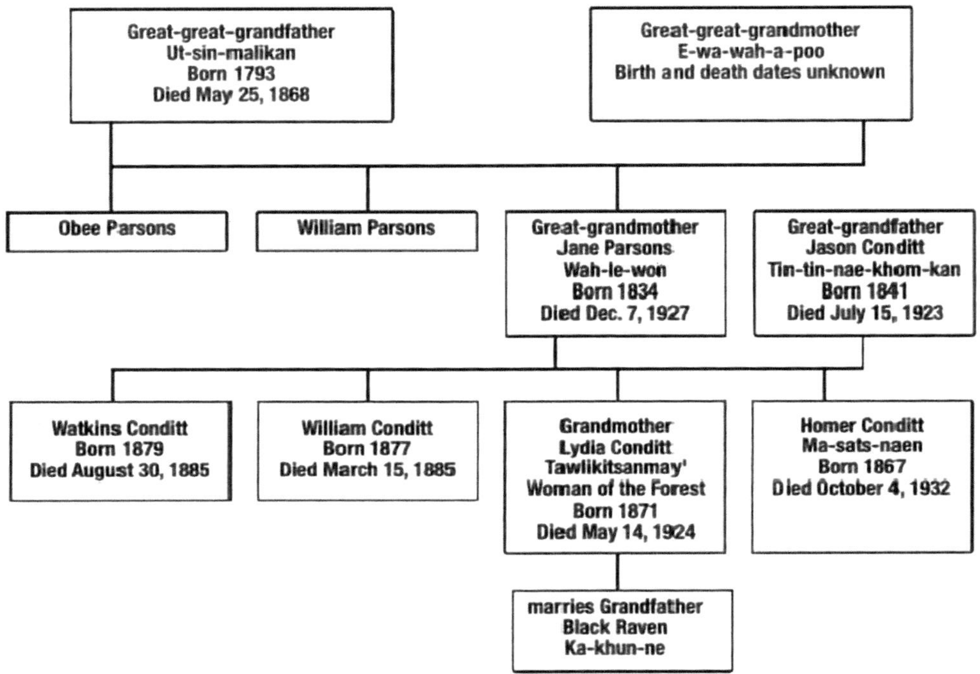

Patriarchal Lineage

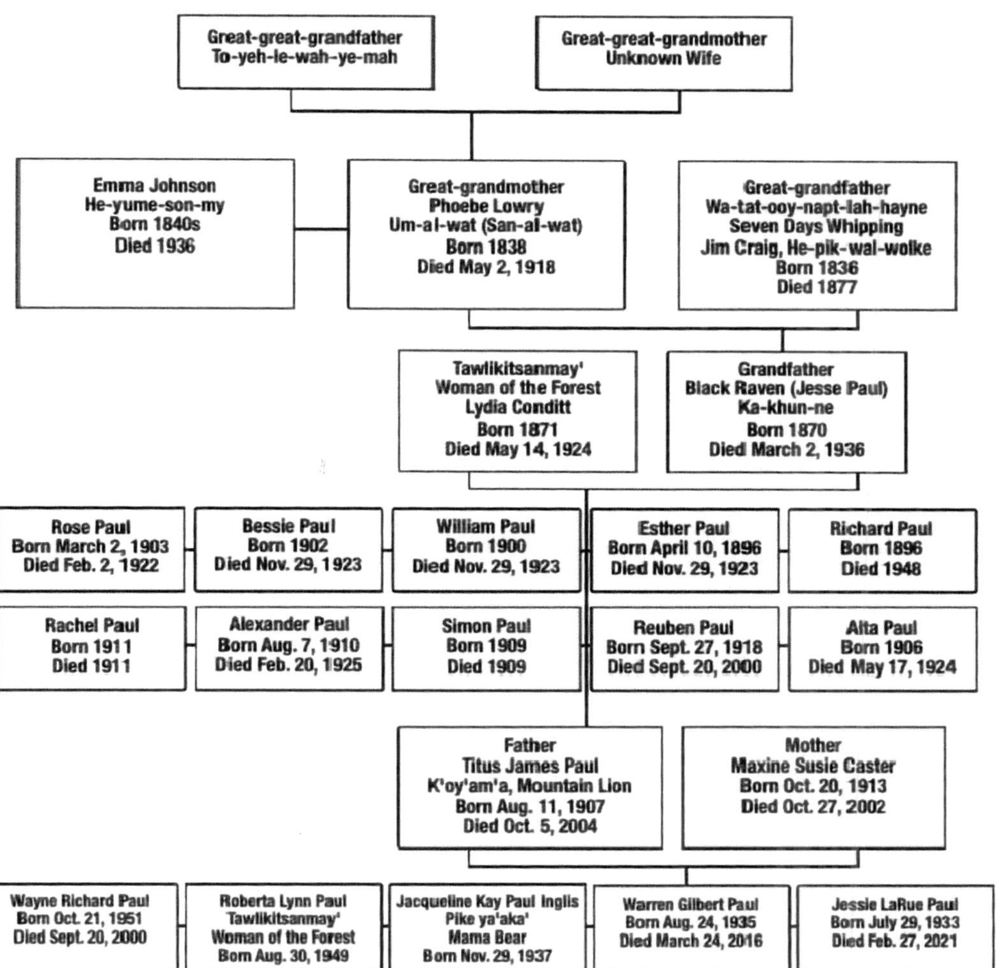

CHAPTER 1

Happy Birthday

*"Obey the Creator; it is good medicine, healing your
wounds and easing your pains."*
—Anonymous

On my 39th birthday in 1988 my husband announced he no longer loved me and walked out the door. He'd been cheating on me for years, a fact I'd been trying to ignore in the interest of keeping our marriage together. Two days later, I dropped my daughter off at the school where she would get her college education. After twenty years of marriage, I felt dejected, discarded, and not very loveable. I sank into a deep depression.

One night this feeling was so intense I tried to kill myself by taking pain pills. It started with a headache. I couldn't stand the pain any longer. I wanted to die. I believed nobody cared and I wouldn't be missed. My son, 11, was in his room in the basement that night. I don't think he could hear me crying, but I don't really know for sure.

Earlier in the evening, I had been on the phone with my daughter. She heard the despondency in my voice. I hung up on her, saying I didn't want to be here anymore. Concerned, she called the counselor I had been seeing and asked him to call me. I didn't want to talk with anyone, so when the phone rang, I picked up and then immediately hung up again. But the phone kept ringing, and something was nudging me: answer the phone!

When the phone rang again, I picked up. I was surprised to hear my counselor's voice. At first, I was angry at the intrusion—why couldn't people just leave me alone, let me disappear? But then he asked me a question that jolted me: "What are you afraid of?"

Gasping, I realized suddenly that I was afraid of being single. "I'm afraid of being alone. It's scary out there"—I was terrified of being single in a world of couples. "It's okay to feel afraid," my counselor replied. A huge sigh escaped my chest. This was the first time I had ever heard it was okay to feel afraid—and that seemingly tiny bit of information began to free something long trapped inside me.

My counselor made me promise to come in and see him in the morning. At first, feeling foolish for trying to take my life, I was reluctant, but I did agree. My counselor also spoke with my son, who had heard the phone ringing. I don't think he knew I had taken the pills, but he could see that I had been crying. He was concerned and ended up sleeping upstairs with me in my king-size bed.

Later in the night, I felt another stirring inside me. Something I had buried and denied for over twenty years began to make itself heard. I cried out, "Who am I? Am I Indian—or am I White?" I heard a voice, and it told me, *Go home.* "Home? Do you mean the reservation, the ranch?" *Yes.*

I had not heard my inner voice for a very long time, not since I was a child. On the ranch, we were isolated from the outside influences. Back then, I didn't recognize the voice, but I associated it with being a free spirit, with a feeling of joy. When I started elementary school, though, I realized how different I was from the other children. I also started feeling the pressure of having to look and act like a White kid. The voice of freedom and joy became quiet for a very long time.

That night, I welcomed the voice, a voice connected to the Creator, the inner voice that hears, feels, and speaks to my spirit and the spirits of my ancestors. I have since come to believe the voice nudging me was my Nez Perce grandfather, Ka-khun-ne Black Raven. At the time, though, I was confused, devastated, and grasping for a sense of direction and purpose.

My gut was telling me I needed to obey the command, and within a month I was back home on the ranch.

My family's ranch is on the Camas Prairie, near Craigmont, Idaho, an hour's drive or so southeast of the Lewiston-Clarkston valley at the confluence of the Snake and Clearwater rivers. My Nimiipuu father and White mother had raised a big family on this spread, but now, no one had lived here for 31 years, and I hadn't visited for several. It was late March and snow, still on the ground, was just starting to melt.

I'd been warned about getting stuck if I tried to drive all the way up to the ranch house, so I parked at the old mailbox and pulled on my high-top boots. It was a quarter mile walk up the old grass-covered road to the ranch house. As I was walking the old road up to the house, many memories came to mind. But I also felt fearful—my knees were wobbly and I was shaking. It had been so long: what was I going to find here after all these years? Grandfather Black Raven's voice kept nudging me along, saying, "Go ahead, you'll be okay."

My senses were numb—by depression, by the trauma of separation and impending divorce as well, it turned out, as a whole host of other things. But my sense of smell suddenly woke up to the wonderful scent of the pine trees that surrounded me.

I neared the place where the barn used to stand and remembered that as a young girl a horse had taken off with me astride, galloping toward the feed in the barn. As the horse turned the corner, I flew off into a patch of nettles. Remembering that made me itch!

Up the hill was the now weather-beaten house where I was born nine months after an unusually cold and snowy winter. I longed to go in and felt as if the house itself were daring me to enter. But, at the same time, I sensed an even stronger nudge from Grandfather. "No, not now, there are too many memories," he told me. "You are not yet ready to meet them." I think what he meant was that I wasn't ready to confront the historical trauma of the violence perpetrated on my Native American family.

Paul Ranch House, 1993: what the house looked like when I first went to the ranch in March 1989. The house looked ominous, and Grandfather was saying to me, "Don't go in there yet, you are not ready yet." *Paul Family Photo Collection.*

I walked by the two pine trees next to the house. These were the trees where my brother and I had held competitions to see who could climb to the top the fastest. The pine trees had grown very tall. I moved towards the back of the ranch house, where there stood a very large old Ponderosa pine tree that, as a child, I had called the Grandfather Tree.

Grandfather Tree had been there for hundreds of years. There was a hollow in the trunk from a fire, which the tree had survived. When my brother and I were small, we used this hollowed out place for games of hide-n-seek. Now I tried to step inside the hollow, but I was too big, and only my leg would fit in. I hugged the tree, recalling what my father had told me so long ago, that trees give strength. I felt the tree's strength. Was this why Grandfather wanted me to come back to the ranch, so I could feel again, so that my numbness would thaw? So that I could feel, smell, touch my roots, the roots of my ancestors?

I wanted to find the creek that ran through the bottom of the ranch, land allotted to my grandfather in the federal government's efforts to subdue Indians, to get them to settle down and farm.

Thorn bushes had overgrown much of the path to the bottom of the hill. I hesitated, but then started down the slope through the snow. I heard a loud screech, and froze, suddenly frightened. It had been so long; I did not recognize the sound. Was it a cougar, a bobcat, or what? I didn't see anything, but then it came again: *skreeeech!* I looked up. A red-tailed hawk circled and soared above me. I sighed and chided myself for being so afraid.

Drawing of Red Tail Hawk by the author.

I finally found the creek at the bottom of the hill. The snow was so deep I had to be careful where I walked for fear of getting stuck. I found the big rock where I used to sit when I was a child. Sitting, resting, listening: the gentle rushing and gurgling of the creek was a joy to my ears. Above me, the red-tail screeched at me again. He circled away but then came back again. *Skreeeech!* This hawk was telling me to move on.

I had to find a narrow place to jump across the creek. This had been easy when I was a child. Now, though, the banks of the creek were buried under snow, and I was far from a child anymore. I found a place where there was a rock I could step on as I hopped across. I made it across without getting wet and started up the hill to where the grain fields had been.

At the top of the hill, I found the farm machinery my grandfather had used, now old and rusty. I clambered up into the seat of the thresher and looked around at the ranch. It was so quiet. I could yell or scream and no one could hear me. The sun was peeking through the clouds. I sat and breathed in the scents of trees, grasses, soil.

Suddenly, that same hawk circled around again, screeching, startling me from my reverie. I looked up at the bird circling above me and calling, seeming to say to was time to move on. I wondered, *Is that you, Grandfather?*

Train tracks used to run through the middle of the ranch, dividing the grain fields from the forest and pasture. My older brother Warren used to run the train from the sawmill at Winchester to Craig Junction, hauling logs to be taken onto Lewiston. As he passed through the ranch, he would slow the train, reach down and lift my brother Richard and me by our arms and give us a ride to Craig Junction and back, about a 20-mile round trip. The tracks had been removed long ago; all that remained were the rotting railroad ties. Rich and I would race on the tracks to the back forty. I was older and nimbler on my feet. I would beat him on a regular basis, which irritated my younger brother.

When I got to the back forty, I found the old rock quarry. This, I thought, would be a good place to stop and eat my lunch. Hundreds of chipmunks were scurrying over and around the rock wall of the quarry. I realized this must be where they wintered—but I've been back at the same time of year again and never saw such a congregation of chipmunks. How cute they were. Some of the chipmunks approached me. They sat up on their hind legs and sniffed at me. When I sniffed back at them, off they scurried. They came back, though, staring at me. I sat very still and let them come close. It dawned on me that these guys were curious about the world around them. They were taking pleasure in the warmth of the sun, exploring this new creature in their midst. I had not been living but had been drowning myself in sorrow because my husband had left me. These little animals were teaching me a lesson: Have fun and be curious. The hawk soared over me and screeched. This time I didn't hesitate but got right up and moved on.

An old road ran across the back of the ranch. Rich and I had once found a baby deer here, and we brought it back to the ranch house to nurse. Father would not let us keep it very long and told us we had to return it to the wild. That we did, only to find out later that it had been run over on the very same road where we had found it. That was sad for us, but Father told us it was part of the cycle of life.

As I walked down the road, I recalled that Father had farmed green peas. To harvest the peas, combines cut the vines while the peas were still attached. The pea vines were brought to a machine that would strip the peas off the vines. The pea vines that were left behind had a strong smell as they rotted. As I was standing in the road, I could smell them as if they had just been harvested. Red-tail swooped around again, screeching at me to move on.

Time to return to the ranch house, I thought. Instead of backtracking, I decided to cut across a neighbor's field that abutted our property. I picked out a path that kept me to high spots so I wouldn't get stuck in the rich, dark, wet, plowed ground. That was the theory.

Soon I was sinking up to the top of my boots with each step. I had to pull my leg up and then take another step. I came to a very muddy spot, and when I put my foot down, I couldn't raise it back up. I yelled, "No, I can't get stuck, no one will find me!" I struggled, and the more I struggled the deeper I sank.

"Stop struggling," I told myself. As I stood there thinking how I was going to get out of this mess, it came to me how my own life had been stuck: stuck in a marriage where I was not myself, stuck in not enjoying life, stuck with not being happy. Stuck. "So how do I get unstuck?" The answer to the question would come in time, but now I had to figure out how to get myself out of the middle of the field. I slowly picked up my leg, but my boot stayed in the mud. I pulled the boot out and put my foot back in it and placed my foot a little farther ahead. I kept moving across the hill until I reached drier ground and was able to walk freely.

I clambered over the fence and plopped down on a log where I took a moment to rest and cool down; I had worked up quite a sweat. I had to laugh at myself, a deep laugh that made my sides hurt. I had not laughed that hard at myself in a long time. I heard a woodpecker, who seemed to be laughing at me, too. I thought of the Woody Woodpecker's crazy laugh. I learned another lesson: Laugh at yourself; don't take yourself so seriously. Red-tail circled back around, and I walked on to the back side of the ranch house.

I found another log to sit on. I listened to the sounds of the trees and the birds. This is the place where I was created. Then Grandfather Black Raven spoke to me. "You are beautiful," he said, "you were created for a reason, and must not give up. You have a lot of life yet to live." Tears streamed down my face as I heard these words. I sat for a long time, soaking in the good memories of childhood, reflecting on the lessons I had learned that day. I must feel, smell, listen, and connect with earth. I knew I would be coming back here, soon. There were more lessons to be learned.

I did return, many times, and each time I visited I became stronger. Slowly, I could feel my broken heart healing. I began to realize there was far more than a divorce to heal from—I had ignored my Native culture's traditions for many years. The Christian culture I grew up in told me, You are born anew in Christ—so forget about all that "heathen" Indian stuff.

Grandfather and Grandmother were with me on these visits—I could feel their spirits. It's hard to describe such an intuitive feeling: there is a stirring, a sensation of being nudged, of something touching my inner being. Sometimes the hair on the back of my neck stands up and I get goosebumps. Especially at first, when I started to become aware that I was connecting with my ancestors, I felt a sense of eeriness, of being out of the normal stream of time. Grandfather and Grandmother didn't grab on to me, but I could feel them, their sorrows, their hopes. They encouraged me to lie on the ground and feel the earth, and said to me, "Let the earth heal you."

On one visit to the ranch, I had a vision. Grandfather told me to have a naming ceremony and that I was to share the ceremony with my friends. But first, Grandfather said, I had to ask for my parents' permission. That requirement frightened me—I thought for sure they would say no. But my mother, a White woman from Kansas, and my father, a Nez Perce from the wilds of northern Idaho, said yes. I asked Father if I could take his mother's name. He agreed.

My immediate concern was finding buckskin to make a dress. My father must have read my mind. That night, from in my old room across the hallway from my parents' room, I heard Father ask, "Where is Roberta going to get a buckskin dress?" Mother replied that we had an elk hide that my brother Richard had recently shot and tanned. That and another she'd been given would do the job. Overhearing my parents, I felt so loved and was thrilled that they too wanted to honor the tradition of making a buckskin dress for the naming ceremony.

My naming ceremony marks the beginning of my family's process to reclaim the traditions of our people, the Nimiipuu or Nez Perce. For centuries, Christians called us heathens and tried to destroy our culture, including ceremonial family practices like naming's. The Euro-American colonists and settlers were determined to have our land and systematically sought to wipe us out. The Nimiipuu, like many other Indigenous peoples, are still here, keeping alive what has been so long suppressed. It was August, 1989 and healing was beginning for my family.

To prepare for the ceremony, the first thing I had to do was make a buckskin dress. No one in our immediate family had ever had one but Grandfather and my other ancestors were telling me it was time to reclaim tradition. A lot of Native people my age were doing the same and we ended up sharing knowledge about healing and reclaiming tradition. This naming ceremony would be the first in the family since before Father was born.

There was a woman in Lewiston, Idaho, who sold beads from her home. I visited her to get the beads I needed to make my dress. While I was there, another Native woman came in. She said, "I need to sell my dress because my pastor says it's heathen"—that was in 1989! I didn't say anything, but I wanted to. *You don't have to do that*, I very much wanted to tell her. It hurt to hear her deny her traditions. I've often wondered if she was ever able to leave that kind of thinking behind.

I made my buckskin dress largely on intuition, using the skills I'd acquired as an undergrad at the University of Idaho studying textiles. My parents helped, as did my older brother Jesse. He had already begun to attend ceremonies. He owned a buckskin outfit tailored for him and knew a lot of what should be in the ceremony.

The most important part of a naming ceremony is gift giving. The parents honor with gifts all who have been played a significant role in their child's life. The presents are made for each significant person either by the parents or by the child to be named. I loved making all the presents, as each gift represented a reclaiming and honoring of self, and the presents were given in honor and love to all who had supported me through the transition of divorce and being a single mother. I made blankets—I found Native designs that I could applique on polar fleece. I made aprons, too, and did more beadwork. I bought key chains for the men, figuring they wouldn't want an apron. I made a wall hanging for the winner of the best pronunciation contest—that is, whoever could say my new Nimipuutímt name most accurately would win a prize! The winner was an old friend of the family, Jim Willis.

The ceremony, attended by about 75 people, was held on my 40th birthday in a grove of pine trees at my home in Spokane. A traditional Nimiipuu dinner was served, then everyone gathered in a large circle. Our family history was shared. Jesse did a traditional dance, with the recorded drummers blasting from a boom box, that honored our ancestors. Next was a friendship round dance, where we all gathered into a circle and shook each other's hands while going around the circle. The song ended, and in the silence, all were seated. Father escorted me to the center of the circle. He told a story of his mother, of how she lived her life. The thing I remember best is that my father said she always made things for the family, including pemmican— "it was really good!" he said. Pemmican is dried meat with mixed berries pounded into the meat. He placed his hand on my head and he gave me my grandmother's name: Tawlikitsanmay, Woman of the Forest.

That first year after my first husband left was about merely surviving. It took me several years to heal from the divorce. But even as I was becoming stronger, I felt sad, especially at certain times of the year. The source of this sadness wasn't my broken marriage. "So," I asked myself, "what is this?"

I was ignoring an old tape, one imprinted in my brain by a teacher years ago, a tape that told me, "You're a dumb Indian." I was about seven years old, at school. I still remember the day in detail: I had been trying to read out loud in class and couldn't pronounce some of the words—and the teacher told me I was dumb. Those words stung me at the time, and strangled me for a long time after. That day, the bus ride home felt extra-long.

Throughout my remaining school years, I often heard that tape replaying in my mind: I was a "dumb Indian."

That tape had long kept me "in place," and held me back from realizing what I could really do in the world. That first year or so after the divorce, what I had to do was support myself and my two children. I had picked up an AA degree in early childhood education, which was required to get licensed as a daycare provider—but daycare was not going to pay the bills. I took in boarders to supplement the limited maintenance and childcare income from my ex. Despite my previous degree in textiles, I didn't want to become a home seamstress—dealing with clients was too demanding.

I figured I needed to return to college for a master's degree. I enrolled at Eastern Washington University and started a class, but I was scared I might still be that "dumb Indian." While I had managed to earn both a bachelor's as well as the associate's degree that enabled me to start a day-care center, which gave me a little confidence, academia was still a mental and emotional challenge.

Sometime in 1990, my father could see that I was struggling. He asked me to take a walk with him—something we had not done together since I was a child. On those walks, Father would point out things of interest, such as the wolves, mountain lions, and elk that crossed the ranch on their way to Craig Mountain. He was often accompanied by wolves and mountain lions as he walked the country road up to the ranch. Instead of fear, he said he respected these predators.

Father taught us children how to identify the sounds of the birds. He could predict when it was going to rain. When I asked him how he did that, he replied, "I can hear a bird sing and understand if it's predicting rain. I can bet money that it's gonna rain within two days. I'd never lose. There's a certain song they sing, and they have another one they sing when we've had enough rain. They're different." He said the bird that predicted the rain was the robin. When I pushed him to tell me more about how he was able to predict the weather and other predictions, he answered, "I have a strong way-a-kin [spirit guide]—a lot of people are that way," by which he meant that listening to your way-a-kin was a traditional way of being in the world for the Nimiipuu.

He often reminded us that you must learn to listen and listen to learn. He also said: "You have to listen so quietly that you are able to hear a bird take a drink of water on the other side of the mountain."

Unfortunately, none of us children learned how to predict rain by listening to the way the robins sing. There is still time to learn, though! Years later, however, I had a dream about needing to draw birds. Not really understanding why I should make such drawings, I obeyed the dream and trusted that its meaning would someday become clear. I drew a black eagle, a red-tail hawk, a meadowlark, a red cardinal, and a black raven. Now, my father's ability to listen to the birds makes a lot more sense to me. I've been guided by hawks and eagles, from whom I have learned important lessons.

My father taught us about the strength of trees, and how they have been here since time immemorial. He taught us to respect the land we walk on, to protect and honor the earth. If we were ever caught littering, we would get a scolding. He taught us to honor our elders and how to greet them when meeting them: we were always to greet the oldest first and give a slight handshake, with a slight bow of the head. Even though his Nimipuutímt was rusty, he was able to teach us a few words, which we all still use.

In 1990, when I was at my lowest, he pointed out the Ponderosas, trees that can live hundreds of years, trees that have witnessed so much in their lifetimes. The Ponderosa has a deep-delving root system, and they grow tall and majestic. My father said, "You know, I used to walk along the streets of Lewiston, Idaho, and I would see signs in the windows saying, 'No Indians or Dogs Allowed.'" Then he told me how the Ponderosa can withstand winds, rain, snow, and bitter cold. "As I was walking along the streets of Lewiston," he continued, "I would figure I was just as good as they were, and I walked right on past them." Father would then return to describing how we Nimiipuu and the Ponderosa are strong, with deep roots in this land that go back thousands of years.

As we were out walking, Father called me by the nickname he had given me when I was a child, one that only he used. "Burr Bear, what is your creation story?"

"Dad, you know it, tell me."

"No," he said firmly, "it is time for you to go and find your creation story."

Did he mean the Nimiipuu legend about Coyote killing the Monster? Our tribe has preserved many of our legends and history and has published a book titled *Nimiipuu Legends* by Allan Slickpoo, a Nimiipuu historian. In this book, I found the story of Coyote and the Monster of Kamiah.

I showed Father the story, and asked him, "Is this the story?" "Well," he responded, "only if you now learn the story and learn to tell it from your heart and head."

It had been many years since I first heard the story. As I began to read it, I felt a little silly—I always thought this was a child's story. I read on, though, and before I knew it, I was engrossed.

That day my father taught me that, if I did not understand or know how to do something, I should go study and learn. I've been listening and studying ever since. Sometimes alone, but often with my family, friends, colleagues, even with strangers I've met along the way. I want you to walk and listen with me, so let me tell you a bit about where we're headed.

I'm going to tell you the story of my people, the Nimiipuu, of my ancestor Ut-sin- malikan who met Lewis and Clark, of my ancestor Seven Days Whipping who fought in the dreadful War of 1877 that nearly ended us, of my ancestor Black Raven who went to the first government boarding school where my people were ripped from their roots in the advancing storm of Euro-American colonists and settlers. I'll tell you of my mother and father, a White woman who defied her family to marry a brown-skinned Native man. I'll tell you how I found myself in all this, a woman in a forest surrounded by life and history and family and love.

And along the way, I want to tell you how I found my ancestors in archives and cemeteries and ceremonies, sometimes by diligent searching and occasionally by seemingly random chance. This journey I and my family have been on has, I think, always been guided by our ancestors.

On that day in 1990 when I walked with my father, he also gave me an instruction: don't just walk on the path of our ancestors but listen to them. Let's start right where my father told me to start: at the very beginning with the Nimiipuu creation story.

CHAPTER 2

Hardworking, Brave, and Intelligent

I figured the best way to honor my father's request was to learn our creation story so I could tell it from the heart and head. At first, I thought I'd simply memorize the version I found in Nimiipuu historian Allen Slickpoo's book, *Nu Mee Poom Tit Wah Tit*.[1] As I became more and more familiar with the story, I felt it becoming a part of me. I could hear, feel, see, and touch these ancient characters, beings, and I felt a part of what they were up to. As if for the first time, I heard things about how the Nimiipuu came to be and why we are where we are. I was beginning to answer my own question, "Who am I?" I began to understand that, because I was created from the Heart of the Monster, I too am strong, brave, and intelligent. The following story is based on the one in Slickpoo's book modified, as is done in the oral tradition, with minor additions to make the story my own.

Coyote and the Monster of Kamiah

Once upon a time, Coyote was busy tearing down the waterfall at Celilo and building a fish ladder so salmon could go upstream for the people to eat. He was so busy doing this that he almost didn't hear someone shout to him, "Coyote! Why are you doing that? All the people are gone now because the Monster has eaten them!"

"Well, I'll stop doing this, because I was doing it for the people. I will go find out what has happened to them."

Coyote traveled upstream by way of the Salmon River Country. He was looking around and not noticing where he was walking when all of a sudden, he stepped on the leg of Meadow Lark. Meadow Lark cried out at Coyote, "Lima, lima, lima! What business do you have going around breaking people's legs?"

Coyote replied, "Oh, Aunt Meadow Lark, please forgive me! If you will tell me what has happened to all the people, then I will fix your leg."

Meadow Lark thought for a moment and then said, "Oh, alright, Coyote. Did you know the Monster has swallowed all the people? And what are you going to do about it."

Coyote answered, "Well, Aunt Meadow Lark, you know the Creator gave me special powers to kill the Monsters, and to prepare the animals for when the la-te-tel-wit (Human Beings) come. I will find the Monster and kill him."

So, Coyote fixed the leg of Meadow Lark with a chokecherry branch, and off he went to prepare himself to meet the Monster.

"Hm! What should I do first? I know, I will take a bath." He jumped into the creek and spruced himself up. He then looked into the creek at his reflection and said to himself, "My, I am handsome!" (Humility was not one of his attributes.) Then he tied himself with a rawhide rope to three great mountains, Tuhm-lo-yeets-mekhs (Pilot Knob), Se-sak-khey-mekhs (Seven Devil's Mountain), and Ta-ya-mekhs (Cottonwood Butte). This is where the young people would go to seek their wey-a-kin (spirit guide) when the la-te-tel-wit (Human Beings) come.

Then Coyote packed five flintstone knives, a flint fire-making set, and some pure pitch, which he strapped to his back in a pack. Now he was ready to hunt for the Monster. Coyote thought to himself, "Where would this Monster live?" He started traveling and looked in the Seven Devils, in the valleys, and all along the rivers, when all of a sudden, he saw the monster. He saw the huge head, and the biggest longest, sweatiest body he had ever seen behind it.

Coyote said to himself, "I'm supposed to kill that?"

As he hid himself in the grass, Coyote talked with the Creator, reminding him he was to make Coyote brave to kill the Monster. After this talk with the Creator, Coyote got a little bit brave, and ever so softly said, "Oh Monster, let us inhale each other."

The Monster heard but couldn't find Coyote hiding in the grass. Coyote again talked with himself, saying, "I am going to have to trick the Monster into swallowing me, so I will cover myself with clay, so he won't vomit me up."

Then he told the Creator, "Okay Creator, you promised me I would have special powers to kill the Monster."

Coyote closed his eyes, as if in prayer to receive his powers. Then he opened his eyes and paused to take a deep breath, and then he jumped up and waved to the Monster, calling out, "Oh Monster, here I am! Let us inhale each other!"

Monster laughed, "Oh no, you trickster you, you swallow me first!"

Coyote thought for a moment and then replied, "Okay, I will!" He powerfully and noisily drew a big breath and let out a howl. But not a hair on that Monster's head moved.

Then Coyote said to the Monster, "Now you inhale me. You have already swallowed all the people, so you should swallow me too, so I won't be lonely. I am lonesome. You have to swallow me too, yes you do, yes you do, and yes you do!"

Monster said, "Oh Coyote, be quiet, you are too noisy."

The Monster thought for a bit, and then in a weak moment said, "Okay, Coyote, I will swallow you too." The Monster did not know that Coyote had carried a backpack holding five flintstone knives, a flint fire-making set, and some pure pitch.

The Monster inhaled like a mighty wind, and brought Coyote towards him, but as Coyote approached, he left along the way great kehm-mas (camas bulbs) and service berry fields, saying, "Here the people will find them and will be glad, for soon is the coming of the la-te-tel-wit (Human Beings)." Coyote almost got caught up on the ropes, but he cut them with his knife as he tumbled into the Monster's mouth.

Coyote looked around and began to walk down the throat of the Monster where he saw many bones lying around. Coyote noted, "So it is true that the Monster has eaten the people." He went a little further and he saw some boys. He asked them, "Do you know the way to the Monster's Heart? Come, show me."

As they were going along, Grizzly Bear rushed out at them, roaring, and Coyote said, "So, you make yourself scary only to me!" and he kicked Bear on the nose. Thus, the bear has only a short nose today.

They traveled on when Rattlesnake rattled at them in fury. "So, only towards me you are vicious? We are nothing but dung to you." And Coyote stomped on Rattlesnake's head, and thus it was flattened out and is so to this day.

And they continued on to find the Heart of the Monster. They were almost there when Coyote met Brown Bear, who said, "Coyote, you can't do anything, hah! I'd like to see you try and save your people!"

Now, Coyote had been known to get in trouble with his BIG mouth and was just about to say something to Brown Bear, when along the way, people began to greet Coyote and talk to him. His close friend, Fox, greeted him from the side and said, "The Monster is so dangerous. What are you going to do to him?"

Coyote replied, "Oh Fox, I am here to kill the Monster." He then turned to Brown Bear, saying, "Off with you, I have important business to do!"

Finally, they arrived at the Monster's Heart, and Coyote told Fox, "You and the boys go find wood or anything that will burn and bring it here." Coyote then cut off slabs of fat from the great heart and threw them to the people, saying, "It's too bad you are hungry. Here, eat this."

When the boys returned with the wood, Coyote started a fire with his flint, and smoke drifted up through the Monster's eyes, ears, nose, and anus.

The Monster said, "Oh, you Coyote! That's why I didn't trust you. Let me cast you out!"

Coyote said teasingly, "If you do, people will later say, 'He who was cast out is giving salmon to the people.'"

"Well, then, go out through the nose," the Monster said.

Teasingly again, Coyote said, "But then they will say the same thing… Nana, nana, nana!!!"

"Well, then, go out through the ears," the Monster said.

"If I do," answered Coyote, "they will say, 'There is old ear-wax, giving food to the people.'"

"Hn, hn, hn! Oh you Coyote! This is why I didn't trust you. Then, just get *out*," and the Monster began to wilt.

The fire was burning near the Monster's heart, and the Monster began to feel pain. Coyote took his first stone knife and sliced into the heart until that knife broke. He brought out his second stone knife, and that knife broke too. Right away he took his third knife and kept cutting, but soon that one broke. Then Coyote said to the people, "Now gather up all the old women, men, and children, along with the bones here, and carry them to the eyes, ears, mouth, and anus of the Monster, for when the Monster dies, they may get out quickly."

He then continued to cut on the heart with his fourth knife until that one broke. He brought out his last knife and continued to cut on the Monster's Heart, and as it was hanging by one muscle strand, the knife broke.

Coyote told the people, "All right, get yourselves ready, because I am going to throw myself onto the Monster's Heart, and as soon as he falls dead, each one of you must go through the opening that is closest to you."

Coyote threw himself onto the Monster's Heart, just barely tearing it loose with his hands. When the Monster died, all the openings immediately cleared and everybody got out. The people kicked the bones out, and then they left. Coyote left, too.

Coyote turned around and saw Muskrat pulling on his tail, and said to him, "Muskrat, you must have thought of something to do at the very last minute; you're always behind in everything." So, just as the big hole was closing, Muskrat pulled on his tail and all the hair was pulled off, and that is how his tail is today.

Then Coyote told the people, "Gather up all the bones and arrange them well." They did as they were instructed. Then Coyote said, "Now let us cut up the Monster and fling him to the four directions. Wherever a body part lands a new nation shall be born. Thus, Coyote smeared blood on his hands and sprinkled the blood on the bones. Suddenly, all those who had died while inside the Monster came to life again. Everyone eagerly helped to carve up the great Monster. Coyote began flinging the parts of the body to different areas of the country all over the land, toward the sunrise, toward the sunset, toward the north, and toward the south. Where each part landed, he named a tribe and described what their appearance would be. The Cayuse were formed, and they became skillful horsemen. The Blackfeet became mighty warriors. The Coeur d'Alene and their neighbors to the north became skillful gamblers. The Yakama became good fishermen.

Coyote used up the entire body of the Monster in this way. Then Fox came up to Coyote and asked, "Coyote, you have given everything away and forgotten here. What are you going to do about it?"

Coyote replied, "Well, why didn't you tell me before? Very well then bring me some water with which to wash my hands." The water became bloody, and Coyote sprinkled it about himself, saying, "You may be small, because I did not give you enough of the Monster's body, but you will be brave, strong, and intelligent, and you will work hard, for I give you the heart. In only a short time, the La-te-tel-wits (Human Beings) are coming. And you will be known as the Nimiipuu (later referred to as Nez Perce), or Tsoop-nit-pa-lu (People Crossing over into the Divide)."

The Nimiipuu are hardworking, brave, and intelligent? Wow! This realization caused me to reframe my perception of myself. Finally, I was able to erase the "dumb Indian" tape. This reframing enabled me to continue with my college education and earn a master's degree. I completed my master's in psychology in 1994 with a cumulative GPA of 3.7. My father Titus K'oy'am'a'(Mountain Lion) always said that one is always learning, you are never too old to hear the legends of the Nimiipuu and learn and then apply to your life. You may not hear the lesson until you are ready to receive the

Roberta Paul standing in front of Heart of the Monster. *Paul Family Photo Collection.*

lesson. When my father told me to go and learn the story of Coyote and the Monster of Kamiah, I was ready to receive the story and begin to learn lessons. As I began to tell the story I soon realized that telling the story from the heart resulted in the power of head and heart coming together.

Learning to tell a story from the heart inspired me to search out more of my family history. I was hungry to learn, to listen, to explore. I began to reconnect with the Nimiipuu communities at Lapwai and Kamiah. I started to attend meetings of the Native American Student Association at Eastern Washington University. Still, something was missing. I began to wonder about the history of the Nimiipuu and how that history intertwined with my family's stories. I knew bits and pieces and that our tribe had been in a war, but I was not fully aware of what all of this meant.

I continued the practice I had started with my master's thesis, of reading, taking notes and, when the ancestors moved me, making drawings and writing down thoughts, feelings, and stories I recalled from childhood.

When I was born in the late summer of 1949, I was a "surprise." Apparently, my mother thought she was through with having children—I am 12 years younger than my sister, Jackie. Years later when I asked Mother why there were so many years between my three older siblings and me. I asked her: Were you mad at Dad for 12 years, Mom replied, "No it was the depression and WWII and we were careful," well, then what happened? "It was a cold winter," she chuckled. "We were snowed in." Curious, I checked the weather history and, sure enough, there had been record snow falls that winter, with road and schools all closed for a couple weeks.

Soon after I was born Father installed indoor plumbing—we now had running water, a toilet, bathtub, and sink. Before that, my family had used an outhouse. To take a bath, they heated water on the woodstove, then poured it into a tub in a small room just off the kitchen.

I was given many a bath in that wash tub. In the summer, if warm enough outside, my sister would bathe me and my younger brother, Richard, in a tub on the front porch. Richard and I had a lot of fun splashing and getting everything wet.

As an infant, I slept in a bassinet in my parents' room. For a while I was the center of attention for my older siblings. But when Richard came along about two years later, I got demoted and was put just outside my parent's bedroom door. I have been told I cried a lot about that exile, as I was probably a little jealous of this new baby taking my place as the favored one. When all five children were home, we all slept upstairs. There were only three bedrooms, with a foyer alongside the staircase that made a little room for a small bed for me. One night, when I was probably three or four, I somehow fell out of bed and went tumbling down the stairs, waking everyone with my frightened crying. The first to come see what happened was my brother Warren. He checked me over to make sure nothing was broken. I was mostly just scared from the tumble. My mother comforted me and made sure I was tucked back into bed. I must have gained new respect for those stairs, as I don't recall ever falling down them again.

My sister Jackie often had the responsibility of babysitting me and Richard. Outside in the yard, we would have tea parties with my dolls and the kitties. I had a calico and a white cat; I didn't really name them as they were barn cats, so they were all called Kitty. The cats weren't allowed in the house, but I would hold them in my arms and pretend to give them tea and cookies. I thought Jackie was pretty cool. She was in high school and could twirl a baton. She was a majorette, leading the band as they marched in parades. I wanted to be like her, so I tried to twirl a baton, only to end up bonking myself in the head. Try and try as I might, I never did learn to twirl a baton.

I was free to roam over the ranch, at least the grounds not planted in crops. Tall Ponderosa pines were scattered across the property, and a small creek ran across the ranch, which we always just called the ranch creek. My younger brother Richard and I spent hours climbing trees and playing in the creek. During the hot summer months, we dammed the creek enough so we could cover our legs. It took lots of rock moving and piling, big engineering jobs for a couple of 6- and 4-year-olds to manage.

Richard and I loved to play hide and seek. We each had our favorite hiding places. One of mine was the old grandfather Ponderosa just at the back of the pantry building. Someone had tried to burn the inside years earlier and left a nice cubby hole just big enough for a small child to hide in. My brother Richard liked to hide in the old garage or woodshop. It never took us long to find each other.

Northern Idaho winters can be long and cold, and we were often snowed in. Because Mother did not like being snowed in, a few times she had the family move into town for the coldest months to avoid being isolated on the ranch. When I was in the first grade, we even spent the winter in Clarkston, Washington, across the Snake River from Lewiston, Idaho and 40 miles from Craigmont. To get to the Lewiston-Clarkston Valley meant traveling down a very winding two-lane road from the top of the Camas Prairie, a trip that usually took about an hour and a half. Mother liked that the valley was a lot warmer and received much less snow.

One spring my parents ordered a batch of chicks which we picked up down in Lewiston. We brought them home to the ranch and raised them during the summer so we could slaughter them in the fall for food. My mother told us *not* to name the chicks and not to handle them too much. I would watch them for hours out in the garage, where they were kept under a heat lamp so they'd stay warm.

Then it came time to kill the chickens. Father started a fire and placed a tub of water over the fire to heat. Mother and Father had a system. Mother would grab a chicken by its feet and place its head on a large stump with a flat top. Father would chop off the chicken's head with a hatchet. Mother would let go of the chicken, which would flop around for a while. At first, this was scary. Mother would then dunk the chicken into the tub of hot water, and my brother and I would have to pluck the feathers off the dead chickens. I thought this was a very smelly job.

When I was old enough to start school, I would walk the quarter-mile dirt road to the county road where the bus would pick me up. I was the first student to be picked up in the early morning on the bus route and the last one to be dropped off at the end of the day. It made for a long day. On my return trip in the afternoon, I would sometimes stop along the way and play with rocks, weeds, or whatever other interesting distractions I could find.

I started piano lessons in the first grade. I would walk from school down to my piano teacher's house for my lessons. On these days my mother would come to town and pick me up. This was also the time my mother and three other mothers decided their girls needed dance lessons. The lessons were in Grangeville, Idaho, a 40-mile trip one way. This only lasted one year as it was difficult to maintain the schedule, plus farming always took precedence over extra activities that involved money and time away from the ranch. But because we four girls were the only ones who had formal dance lessons, we were asked to perform for the annual Christmas talent play. I was a holly tree; Mother sewed real holly onto my dress. I had to be careful when sitting down so as not to poke myself or anybody close to me.

I was in the third grade when my parents moved from the ranch to the town of Craigmont. We lived in a corner section of town on about seven acres. The house was an older one-bedroom. Father remodeled the back porch into a bedroom for my brother and me. His welding skills came in handy when he built a bunk bed for the two of us. I now walked to school instead of taking the long bus ride of the previous two years. But somehow to me it felt longer to walk to school than it did to walk from the mailbox to the ranch house. I missed the ranch terribly. I remember a teacher commenting, "Aren't you glad you don't live out in the country anymore?" I shrugged it off but felt hurt inside.

This was about the time when I discovered there were other Indian tribes. I had always known I was Nimiipuu. One of the first oral lessons I learned from my father was that even though the name "Nez Perce" means pierced nose, we did not pierce our noses. In fact, no one knows where the name came from. It might be a sort of literal translation of Plains Indian Sign Language: in that language, the sign for Nez Perce is the right forefinger pushing left under the nose. I can imagine a French fur trapper, fluent in Sign, seeing that gesture and saying to others that it means "Nez Percé." But that's just a guess!

One day the teacher was talking about Indians, and I realized she was talking about a different tribe of Indians. I thought to myself, "There are other Indians!" I ran home and asked Father, "How come you didn't tell me there were other Indian tribes?" He just shrugged his shoulders, "I thought you would figure it out someday."

I was also becoming more aware of being an Indian. I realized my skin was darker than that of my classmates. And I began to hear the racial slurs used during that time. I heard Indians were "dirty, lazy, good for nuthin', fat, drunk, heathen, superstitious, and dumb." I would hear these comments from peers, teachers, and community members. There were well-meaning teachers who told me my race was going to die out, and Sunday school teachers asked me, "Aren't you glad you aren't 'heathen'?"

Sometimes I was teased at school for being Indian—I was the only one. Most other Native families weren't farming and lived down in the valley near Lapwai and Kamiah. Classmates sometimes called me a "dirty, lying Indian" even though I hadn't lied. Another told me, "I don't think of you as Indian," a statement that confused me. When I looked in the mirror, I still saw my skin as being dark—not White. I also would hear sneers behind my back, "Oh there's an Indian, *phew!*" My mother and father would always say to me, "Be proud of who you are." I tried, but the words still hurt. I tried to push them out of my mind.

When I was about ten, my mother gave me a handmade Indian doll with a beaded dress of soft buckskin. It was beautiful. I took it to school to show but was teased for having an Indian doll and not a new Barbie doll. I never took the doll to school again. It sits now in a place of honor in one of my display cases.

If my parents had not told me again and again to be proud of who I am, I do not think I would have graduated. I'm not sure I even knew the word "racism" back then but that is certainly what I was being subjected to.

We owned a large trunk which belonged to my grandfather Black Raven when he was at boarding school. I would later learn how the boarding school system in the United States and Canada worked to strip my people of their names, languages, cultural practices, of our very identities. But when I was a child, I was thrilled by the contents of the trunk, which was full of Indian beadwork, baskets and other heirlooms and keepsakes. I would sometimes sit beside it to study and touch the wonders within. Who had made these beautiful things? Where did the wampum beads and all the other things come from?

My father had a photo album, a collection of pictures of his family. "Who were these people?" I wondered. Father wouldn't talk about them very often. When I looked at the pictures, I would get a strange feeling inside, a sort of melancholy or sadness that seemed to soak through me. I couldn't understand it at the time. The pictures were of Father's siblings who had died suddenly. Sometimes this strange feeling came around Thanksgiving time or right before Christmas.

I think I was always somehow sensitive to the ebb and flow of life forces that were part of my family, both in my generation as well as past generations. When I was 13, my maternal grandmother died of breast cancer. She lived with us off and on during her illness. Mother was anxious during this time. I vividly recall the feeling of death hovering over Grandmother. I don't know why I felt it, but I did—I'd had this "death hovering" sensation before. When I was seven, I got the "hard measles," also known as German measles. According to my mother, I was very sick, with a high fever. Lying on the couch, Mother placed cool cloths on my forehead, trying to break the fever. I must have passed out, believing I was never going to wake up—I remember the sensation of death being very nearby. Finally, the fever broke. I was lying on my mother's lap. I asked her to make the woodpecker stop pecking on the porch post just outside the living room window. Woodpecker was waking me up; it was not my time to leave.

Soon after Grandmother's death, Mother decided to move us to Lewiston, Idaho. She had inherited her mother's home and wanted to enroll in a nursing program at the college there. At first, Father didn't want to move, but Mother said, "Okay fine. The children and I are moving and if you want to join us, you can." Father stayed in Craigmont for a while. Soon, though, he started coming down for visits, and he eventually moved in with us. Father now commuted to Craigmont so he could continue to farm our land. The whole family would stay in Craigmont during the busy times of planting and harvesting.

At school, I went from a class size of 20 in Craigmont to one of 400 in Lewiston. The move was exciting to me: in this larger place I figured everybody wouldn't know everybody, meaning I could leave my racist tormentors behind. It also meant that I could—even if only to a limited extent—reinvent myself. In one of my classes, a teacher asked me what I liked to be called, and I saw this as an opportunity to change my name to Robbie. At the time, I had no idea that I was echoing an ancient Native practice of taking new names at significant moments in life. My family members called me Berta, which I thought was too childish. I wanted a "cool" name. Today, while my friends call me Robbie, my family still calls me Berta.

High school was both fun and painful. Even more than in Craigmont, people in Lewiston were more openly racist. I began dating, but sometimes when I brought a boy home to meet my family, he would not call me or look at me at school after meeting my father. I also dated Indian boys, but that too was painful, because I wasn't "Indian enough." A part of me did not want a close relationship with an Indian boy, because then I would have to face being Indian.

I was struggling with identity issues, constantly asking myself, "Am I Indian, or am I White?" I didn't wear any Indian jewelry. I cut my hair short and streaked it blonde. I was trying to fit in. Short, blonde, and petite: that's what I thought my peers and society wanted me to be. In the mid-1960s, sexism and racism must have been in the water: we heard Dean Martin crooning "five foot two, eyes of blue" on the radio, watched Gidget going to Hollywood at the movies, and every fashion magazine had the super-skinny Twiggy or her clone on the cover.

My academic skills were so-so. I tried to study and do the best I could, yet in the back of my mind I could still hear that teacher saying I was a "dumb Indian." I did manage mostly B's, a few C's, and a few A's. The old message was reiterated by an English teacher who told me I would not do well in college because of my writing skills. I graduated with a 3.1 GPA which, while not great, did allow me to enter college at the University of Idaho.

Before I left for college, the tribe was notified of a bridge program for Native Americans. It was at the Haskell Institute in Lawrence, Kansas. Haskell was one of the government boarding schools modeled after the famous and notorious Carlisle Indian Industrial School in Pennsylvania. My father volunteered me to go, and told me, "It will be good for you." I didn't think so, but I obeyed my father.

A girlfriend went with me. Her grandmother had been at the Chilocco boarding school in Oklahoma with Father back in the 1920s. My friend and I traveled by bus, a three-day and two-night ordeal on the cramped bus. This was the first time I had left my family—a little scary, but also an adventure.

At Haskell, I enjoyed meeting the other Indian students from the different tribes. We shared many social activities—we'd play games like charades, have scavenger hunts, and dance to the radio. We saw *My Fair Lady* at an outdoor theater, as well as the then Kansas City Athletics pro baseball game. I didn't care for the regimentation. Haskell was still run in military style, much like the boarding schools that Father and Grandfather Black Raven attended. Up by 6 in the morning, clean my room, shower, and dress before breakfast. Then classes for the morning, followed by lunch. In the afternoon, I worked as a janitor, cleaning the student union building. We were not allowed to leave the campus after 5 p.m. unless chaperoned. After dinner, we had study table and then it was lights out at 10. At age 17, I thought this was restrictive and demeaning. I had never adhered to a routine like this in my life.

Although the classes were good for me, and did help prepare me for college, all the restrictions gave me the feeling I was not capable of taking care of myself; it felt like I couldn't be trusted. There was that tape again, playing the "dumb Indian" routine. I tried not to hear those messages, but still they crept in.

When I returned from Haskell, I headed to the University of Idaho. Although Moscow is only 32 miles from Lewiston, I was homesick and went home every weekend for the first two months of classes. I wasn't convinced I could succeed in college, and the first semester was a struggle. I barely passed my classes.

But the social part of college life was great. I discovered I could date and the young men would never have to meet my parents. The question of me being Indian didn't really arise. Dating was fun—so much so that I failed the second semester and had to petition for readmission, which was granted.

I met my future first husband, a Euro-American man, during my second semester. I'm not going to name him because, even after all this time, there is too much trauma associated with him and his family. Our relationship was an exciting whirlwind. By early spring of my sophomore year, I was pregnant. We became engaged and were married that August 1969. Our daughter, Kimberly Ann, was born the following January. Several jobs and several moves later, we had our second child, Michael Paul, born in 1977.

My 20-year marriage had many ups and downs. I struggled with low self-esteem. I didn't feel I was White enough, but neither did I want to be Indian, not after the racism I had experienced during my youth. Besides, I was raised in a kind of Christian dogmatism that stressed being born anew in Christ, which meant I could and should reject all the "heathenism" that being Indian represented.

I buried myself in volunteer work, Bible studies, and sewing. I was constantly dieting, trying to mold myself into that petite blonde image. I thought this would keep the marriage together. But my husband kept having affairs, and I kept denying my Native heritage. I thought I put on a good front and that everything was fine—but clearly, that was not the case. Something had to give, and it finally did. In the fall of 1988, my husband left, and I fell apart. Happy birthday to me.

Around 1980, my older brother Jesse went to work for the Indian Health Service in Washington, DC. Jesse was curious about our Native ancestry. His girlfriend at the time said she could help him do research in the National Archives in Washington. He soon discovered we had a great-great-grandfather, Ut-sin-malikan, who had met Lewis and Clark on the Weippe Prairie when he was a boy. Jesse also learned we had a great-grandfather, Seven Days

Whipping, who had fought in the Nez Perce War of 1877. This war devastated the Nimiipuu with much loss of life, fracturing the survivors, and making Chief Joseph one of the most famous Native Americans in the world.

Jesse's excitement was catching, and in 1988 he and I began to research our family history collaboratively. My other motivation to learn about being Nimiipuu was to try to figure out why I felt haunted and sad around certain dates of the year.

My parents had several books about the Nimiipuu, but I had not previously been interested in reading them. But as my identity crisis intensified, I wanted to know more about who I was and where I came from. One day I was exploring a bookshelf at my parents' home and discovered *Yellow Wolf: His Own Story*. Yellow Wolf, a Nimiipuu, had told his account of the Nez Perce War to writer L.V. McWhorter.

I found I could only read one chapter at a time before having to take a break. Why was this book being so hard to read? Each time I picked up the book I felt something, but I couldn't quite figure out what the feeling was. Then I came to the chapter about the surprise attack at Big Hole, Montana. American cavalry forces killed about 80 Nimiipuu. Yellow Wolf says only 12 warriors were killed; the rest were women and children. The Nimiipuu had fled Idaho thinking they would be safe and could live in peace in Montana. Now they knew they would not find a haven anywhere.

With a cold shudder, I realized that this was the attitude of the dominant culture toward Native peoples: from the East Coast to the West, we were hunted down and exterminated. The verbal microaggressions I'd been on the receiving end of in school were nothing compared to this. Reading McWhorter's book was especially difficult because I now knew that at least one child of my great-grandparents—my grandfather, Black Raven—had somehow survived the Big Hole slaughter.

As I read, I kept breaking into tears. In my heart, I asked Grandfather Black Raven, "What happened to you that day? Where were Great-grandmother and Great-grandfather during this battle?" When I finished reading Yellow Wolf's story, I knew I had to visit the battle site, which is now called Big Hole National Battlefield, to find answers to some of my questions for myself.

A friend told me about an upcoming ceremony at Big Hole on the anniversary of the battle in August 1990. Although I was nervous about what I might encounter there, I had to go. I called my father and told him of the commemoration ceremony the tribe would be hosting at Big Hole. I invited him to come with me. "No," he simply replied. Disappointed, I continued to make plans to attend with my son, Michael, my daughter being away at college. A few days later, my parents called and told me: "Yes, we will go to Big Hole with you."

Michael and I picked up my parents at their home in Lewiston and traveled over the Lolo Pass through the high crags of the Bitterroot Mountains. Yellow Wolf had told McWhorter that the Nimiipuu crossed through the mountains here. I was dazed, wondering how they managed to cross the rugged, steep terrain with all their belongings, their children, their horses—all the while fearing they were being chased by American soldiers. I asked Father if he knew how they would cross over into Montana. He explained that the Nimiipuu had crossed the Bitterroots many times, as our people had been avid buffalo hunters and knew how to travel with their belongings.

After spending the night in Hamilton, Montana, where the fleeing Nimiipuu had probably camped, we arrived at Big Hole National Battlefield the next morning. The Nimiipuu campsites had been preserved, with plaques indicating where each family had camped. We silently walked among the sites. I could feel the spirits of those who had gone before. At the campsite of Chief Joseph, my father placed a hand on the tepee pole and looked up with a prayer-like expression, an honoring of his ancestor. We were not able to identify the campsite of our ancestor Wa-tat-ooy-napt-lah-hayne, Seven Days Whipping, but it would have been one of the tepees that had been set up near Chief Joseph's, since we knew Seven Days Whipping was a member of Joseph's band. Father, Mother, Michael, and I paused there for a good while, not speaking, just feeling and listening. At first, I was overwhelmed with sadness, which was gradually replaced by emotional numbness. It was a lot to take in.

Up at the park building there were army tents and other displays. We went inside to watch a video interpretation of the battle. When the video was over, my father stated, "That was murder." It was the first time I had ever heard my father express anything about the war.

About a dozen Nimiipuu were present, along with approximately 100 or so other visitors. Otis Halfmoon, a Nimiipuu park ranger, began the commemoration with the introduction of a Native group called the Nez Perce Drum. This group of six or seven men drummed and sang an honor song. Halfmoon described the battle in detail. I sat there numb, wondering how Grandfather Black Raven and his parents, Seven Days Whipping and Um-al-wat, survived this battle, but survive I think they did. I was in awe of their stamina to fight, their ability to carry on. At that point, though, I didn't know a fraction of what they'd been through. I had a lot more crying to do.

Father sat in silence most of the way home. I asked him if his father had ever spoken about the war or about Seven Days Whipping's wife, who came to be called Phoebe. "No," he replied, "it was not spoken of." He was trying to process something deep, and I now suspect this must have been our family's soul wound. Of such wounds, I will soon have much more to say but, at the time, I had no idea how deep wounds cut, even across many generations.

But I was done with silence. That visit to Big Hole gave me insight about why I felt sad on certain days: somehow memories of a past I did not know were haunting me. I had to learn more.

In 1992, I went to a conference in Spokane to gather information for my master's thesis. At the conference, called Suicide Prevention for Native Americans, a PBS *American Experience* documentary called "In the White Man's Image" was shown. The documentary was about the first Indian boarding school, the Carlisle Indian Industrial School in Pennsylvania. My grandfather, Jesse Black Raven Paul, had been sent to Carlisle, but I had no idea what had happened there nor the treatment to which they were subjected. The PBS documentary showed images of the newly arrived Native American youth wearing tattered clothing. They were forced to take lye baths, their hair was shorn, and they were put into surplus clothing: scratchy wool uniforms for the boys, dresses for the girls. They were forced to take English names and were punished if they spoke their Native languages.

I started feeling anxious. That's when it hit me: this is what my grandfather had gone through. My guts started heaving. I felt my heart rate accelerate and I felt like I needed to get out of the room to get fresh air. I dashed out of the screening room and ran the short distance down to the Spokane River, where I threw up. I have since learned that this is secondary post-traumatic stress disorder, also known as compassion fatigue. I managed to return to the conference but had a hard time focusing on what the speakers were saying—another symptom of secondary PTSD.

The shock of discovering the horrible truth about the boarding school Grandfather Black Raven had been sent to stuck around that evening at home. I lay on the couch in the fetal position, dazed and bewildered, a blanket over me and my thumb almost in my mouth. On the wall were the photos of my Nez Perce family. One of them was a photo of the five Nez Perce children who were at Carlisle in 1880. For the first time, I really noticed that my grandfather had a hand inside his uniform.

I asked the photo, "Grandfather, why do you have your hand inside your uniform?" Later that night, as I slept, Grandfather came to me in a dream. In the dream, I learned he was holding a medicine bag hidden in a pocket inside his uniform—medicine his mother had given him to keep him safe and sane. There was great power in that medicine: when he came home eight years later, he still spoke Nimipuutímt, despite the punishments meted out for speaking Native languages at the boarding school.

In the dream, Grandfather declared, "You may capture the outward appearance of me, but you will not get all of my Indianness." I knew he was speaking to the boarding schoolers and the assimilators, the ones who wanted to strip him of his culture and his land, and he meant for me to hear the spiritual power in his words so that I, too, might draw on that power to help heal myself and my family.

In 1993, I attended a conference called Native American Women and Wellness that changed the way I look at myself, my people, and the world. This is when I first began to understand the sources of my sadness, and about what we now call historical trauma. The term was first used by Maria Yellow Horse Brave Heart, a Native mental health expert who, in the 1980s, was working with Lakota people. She coined the term to describe the cumulative emotional harm to Natives caused by 500 years of genocide by Euro-Americans.[2] We now use the term to describe the trauma of any group that has suffered from genocide, including Jews and Black Americans, the Indigenous peoples of Australia, and many others. We Natives survived, a few of us, true, but every new trauma was piled on top of the previous and was passed on to the next generation as depression, substance addiction, and all manner of physical ailments that Billy Rogers called the "baggage that Native people have had to carry for generations that led to feelings of hopelessness, external loss of control, and acting-out behavior."[3] Rogers was, at the time, the director of the Native Wellness and Healing Institute at the University of Oklahoma.

Inspired by what I heard, I began reading a lot. I became a sponge. I couldn't read fast enough. The pressure of keeping my Native identity bottled up gave way to an explosion.

I started reading history books, and I began plotting out the timeline of the Nez Perce War and filling in the genealogy of the Nimiipuu side of my family. I discovered that the dates of certain battles coincided with the times when I felt overwhelming sadness. I struggled to deal with all this information, with the increasing awareness that brought more pain.

I continued visiting the Paul ranch and connecting and listening to the spirits of my grandfather and grandmother. I began to sense I was being told I needed to go on a vision quest. But how? I knew of no one who had done this before. Grandfather's spirit kept nudging me, and I began to pray for the time and place to go. I dreamed I was with friends near a beautiful blue lake surrounded by lush forest and snow-covered peaks. I asked others to pray for me to help prepare my heart to go, and for a place to go. It took two years, but then a friend offered me her cabin on a lake in Canada, accessible only by boat. I began to release my anger at my ex-husband, which I had to do before I went. Anger blocks healing and leaves us stuck in a spiral of recrimination.

Finally, the day arrived, and I drove north into beautiful Canada. My friend had told me how to contact the people who would take me across the lake to the cabin. The men took me across in early evening. When I arrived at the cabin, I had to ask them for help in lighting the lantern and igniting the wood stove. I could see by their expressions they were thinking, "How is this woman going to survive by herself for five days if she can't even light a lantern and stove?" I questioned myself as well, but I had faith I could do it—but I did experience fasting for the first time.

During my first two days at the cabin, it poured rain. It was raining so much I thought the cabin might slide down into the lake. I also cried. I cried the deep cry of letting go of my marriage, remembering the good times and the bad. My inner spirit was telling me to let go and move forward. The rain finally stopped, and the brilliant sun showered the landscape with light.

Outside, I walked on moss glistening in the sun. It was a beautiful green, and so soft to the touch. I walked along the beach. At a certain point, I looked up and goose bumps rose on my arms and neck; my hair stood on end. Before me was the place where I had dreamed—nearly two years before—my vision quest would take place. I was where I needed to be.

My remaining three days were spent in meditation and deep thought. One such thought brought to light the meaning of rebirth after the death of a marriage, which I recorded in my journal, dated May 23, 1991:

> Peace, harmony, and love, a vision of rebirth. I am of the earth in the forest. I have been reconciled to you! A male deer is waking me up and uncovering me. I am covered with leaves and pine needles. The buck is saying to me, "Wake up." He helped me up, and then I noticed that a female mountain lion was also present at my side. They were motioning me to follow them, saying, "We're going deep into the forest." I followed them, and we then came to a clearing, I saw an Appaloosa horse waiting for me. I had dreamt of this horse before and had named it Tew-le-ka. In the clearing was an Indian Chief in radiant white buckskin. I thought I recognized him as Christ.
>
> I was nudged by the buck and the mountain lion to kneel before him. He placed a hand on my head, saying, "You are Woman of the Forest, raised from the forest floor of the earth. You are woman. I give you the spirit of the forest, to love, nurture, and be compassionate with life around you. You are to live in peace, harmony, and balance. The female mountain lion is a symbol of power, strength, cuddly, purring, huntress, territorial, playful, yet she knows her boundaries and her enemies. The female mountain lion likes napping in the sunshine, cleanliness, and is beautiful in motion. The male white tail buck is alert, sees all around, head held high, and is agile, quick, graceful, warning of danger by waving his white tail. He is handsome and strong. The eagle that soars above you has keen eyesight, and the ability to soar with the wind. Tew-le-ka, your Appaloosa horse, is your spirit personality, which allows you to move and ride with the wind. It gives you spunk, strength, and swiftness to work hard and be spirited.

With this vision I recognized the spirits who were helping me on my life journey. The female mountain lion represented all my female grandmothers, and the white tail buck represented all my male grandparents. They were all with me. There were other spirits present, but I am not able to tell of them because they are the ones that became my way-a-kin, my spirit guides. This time of being renewed and reborn helped me to let go of the marriage and release the anger.

I did not want to go home but return I must. My ancestors and spirit guides told me to move on, let go, forgive. Back in Spokane, I invited my ex-husband to dinner. I bought a dozen roses and explained to him that four of the roses represented my part in the marriage and forgiveness of self; the next four roses represented his part in the marriage and hope for his forgiveness of self; and the remaining four roses represented our lives moving forward separately.

I also worked to complete the timelines and genograms of my family. I wanted to identify the wounds caused by unresolved grief passed down through the generations. I came to realize that a healing process was taking place, a process that had begun when my father told me to find my creation story.

One way to visualize the healing process is as a set of concentric circles: "self" is in the center surrounded by "family," which is in turn nested within "culture." The healing begins with self, and when healed, the self can help heal the family; as the family heals, it can help heal the culture. I had so removed myself from Nimiipuu culture that I had become confused and lost. If I had not had a father who knew of his culture through the Nimiipuu stories, I could not have connected with my Nimiipuu culture. The family had been here all along, wounded, but they were still here, as were the Nimiipuu. With members of my Nimiipuu family wounded, the culture of the Nimiipuu was also wounded. To heal, we must know the story of how we are wounded, and then healing can begin.

Over the years, my family and I have made lots of discoveries as we've researched our history and retraced the steps of our ancestors. We've learned about ourselves, our family history, and the history of our tribe. One of the things I've discovered about myself is that I have become a storyteller. This role has helped me to lead workshops for people recovering from historical trauma, in which I talk about the power of stories and how they can heal us, and about recovering history to reclaim self and identity. My purpose with this approach to healing is to give participants the strength they need to discover and tell their own stories.

While my primary tool is storytelling, that's not always an easy thing to do for people just setting out on their own healing path. Over the years, I've developed a model or method for healing, which I offer towards the end of this book. It's not complicated or esoteric, but it does require patience. Healing takes time! It also requires that we take responsibility individually for our own healing. While we take individual responsibility, that doesn't mean others aren't involved. We often need to involve others in order to forgive and understand—and, again, this process requires patience, as forgiveness and understanding have many layers, like an onion.

In leading people onto and along the healing path, I use stories from my own culture but urge individuals to learn their own creation and culture stories, to find and participate in their own ceremonies, and to visit (as they have the strength) those places that are the sites of trauma. In these workshops, we not only listen attentively to stories, but we also draw, journal, craft with modeling clay and other media, sing, and dance—all these are ways of breaking the silence and gaining access to the stories of our wounds.

What follows now is the story of my family, as far as we have been able to know it. I'll tell the story in chronological order, starting with our great-great-grandfather, Ut-sin-malikan, and ending with myself. That's only a convenience, though, as healing doesn't happen chronologically—it happens a little here, then a little there, before the story of a wound weaves itself into a tapestry.

Initially, my family knew very little about Ut-sin-malikan—who he was, how he died in Washington, DC, or where he was buried. In 1984, my brother Jesse found our great-great-grandfather's grave in the Congressional Cemetery in Washington, DC, officially known as the Washington Parish Burial Ground. Located on the west bank of the Anacostia River, the cemetery is the final resting ground of some 65,000 individuals—23 of whom are Native American.

In 1988, the Association for the Preservation of Historic Congressional Cemetery sponsored a Celebration of Native American Life. Descendants of the Indians buried there were invited to the celebration and asked to lead a ceremony at their ancestor's grave site. Many descendants of Chief Ut-sin-malikan went and had the largest group there. This group included my parents, Titus and Maxine Paul; my brother Jesse; his son Greg; my father's nephew, Bill, and niece, Jessica; and sister-in-law, Harriet Skye Paul.

Newly separated from my husband, I was not ready to participate in the ceremony. I was too wounded, too hurt to be able to appreciate anything ceremonial. In addition, my sister had just had throat surgery and was not able to travel. But my family reported events back to me when they returned from Washington. The ceremony began with a Native drum group playing a traditional flag song which honored warriors who have returned from battle. My brother Jesse spoke about how we found Ut-sin-malikan's story of the trip to Washington in a diary, how he had died and came to be buried at the Congressional Cemetery.

In 2004, I travelled to visit Ut-sin-malikan's grave site with my sister, both of our daughters, and my new husband, Phil. We held a short ceremony to honor our ancestor who had faced many difficult decisions in his lifetime. We thanked him for his leadership and coming to Washington to confront the President. Many in our family thought we should take Ut-sin-malikan back to Idaho and rebury him there. But now, after many journeys and much healing, we no longer feel that way. Even though his headstone was in bad shape, with the engraving barely readable, and the whole thing crumbling away, we knew he is where he is supposed to be. We were grateful to be able to come here, stand beside his grave, and discover his story. At some point in time, we knew we would have to replace that headstone—but not before we preserved his story.

CHAPTER 3

Finding Ut-sin-malikan's Story

My father, grandfather, and ancestors had been telling me to learn our story and to tell it from the heart and head. "It is when the two come together that will give you the power to heal self," they all said. I have often wondered how my ancestors spoke to me long before I was more certain of my own identity, long before I was aware of their spirits. Looking back, though, I realize that they were with me all along.

I learned the story of Ut-sin-malikan by ferreting out bits and pieces of his life from books written by White people. While they often wrote with a colonialist-settler bias, favoring the exploitation of our lands, its animals, minerals, and peoples, they were also more thorough than any other histories I have found. Much of what follows is based on my reading of books by Alan Slickpoo and Deward Walker, Clifford Drury, Alvin Josephy, and L.V. McWhorter.

When the *Roots* miniseries aired in 1977, I had just given birth to my son, Michael. My new son and the drama of the show moved me to think about my own roots. Hearing the name Kunta Kinte made me realize I didn't know my own father's Indian name. I was determined to give my son my father's Nimipuutimt name. Completing Michael's birth certificate was held up until I could find out. With a few exceptions—such as learning to do cornhusk weaving from some ladies at a local park around 1975—I had very little awareness of myself as Native. In fact, in a lot of ways, I had actively suppressed that awareness. Too painful. Too many aggressive, racist words. Too many assumptions about "Indians."

But this was an era—the mid-1960s through the 1970s—when many Native peoples were actively trying to reconstruct a history that had been buried, lost, and otherwise blown to the four winds. The American Indian Movement (AIM), founded in 1968, and other activist groups were making us aware of the centuries of injustice Native peoples have experienced. Father thought AIM was too radical—they were occupying the abandoned Federal penitentiary on Alcatraz Island in the San Francisco Bay—but my brother was more sympathetic to their cause, as he, too, was working on who he was.

I suspect my father knew all along that we had a chief in our ancestry, but he never mentioned it because, as Christians, we were told our history didn't matter. Christianity, boarding schools, and the allotment process forced us to forget or erase our history in order to survive and hold on to what little we could by assimilating into the dominant Euro-American culture. But even as our history was assimilated into a story of White people "improving" the land by destroying the environment, bits and pieces of our Nimiipuu culture survived. My father always "heard" the land and its creatures; as I mentioned, he could listen to the birds to know the weather. He also attended sweats where such things as genealogies were discussed.

The Nimiipuu practiced sweats for thousands of years, and still do to this day. The sweat lodge is a domed structure usually made from willow branches woven and tied together. In the old days, the structure would then be covered with hides. Today, we use cotton canvas cut with a flap to make a door. Heated rocks are piled in a small pit dug just inside the door, over which cold water is poured to make steam. Only certain kinds of rocks are used, as they must withstand being heated in a fire. (We don't want exploding rocks in the sweat lodge!) As we sweat, we use body scrapers to scrub away old skin and cleanse our bodies. Not just hygienic, sweats were used to cleanse before hunts, and are still used today for that purpose as well as to help cleanse the spirit. Women and men sweat separately, each at their own appointed times. Once nice and hot and clean, we leave the lodge to rinse with cold water, in a nearby creek or in an outdoor shower.

My brother Jesse learned of Chief Ut-sin-malikan from an old family friend, Gene Wilson, while they were at a sweat. Gene was my dad's age. At some point, probably in the early or mid-1980s, Gene and Jesse connected and started going to sweats together. That's when he learned we had a chief as an ancestor.

It wasn't long after that when, during a visit to the Nez Perce National Historical Park, I found a booklet with a flimsy vinyl record bound in. You don't see these records anymore, but back then they'd be bound into magazines, or even come in cereal boxes. The record was a collection of Nez Perce songs recorded years before by Sol Webb, a Nimiipuu elder and so a source of wisdom and history. One of the songs was about Ut-sin-ma-likan. A fierce joy ran through me, a kind of ecstasy. Here, on this floppy piece of vinyl, was evidence of my past. My great-great-grandfather really did exist—and was celebrated in song! I felt rededicated, empowered, and more determined than ever to continue this healing journey.

At the time, I was a mother with a son at home while also working as the director of the daycare center I had started at the Whitworth Presbyterian Church in Spokane. I started the center because of a dream I'd had—so much of my life has been guided by dreams! But at the time, there simply wasn't enough daycare capacity on the north side of Spokane to meet the need. After dreaming that there would be a center at the church, I asked the church administrators what they thought. "Go for it!" they said. Although my involvement has long since ended, the daycare was active until the COVID-19 pandemic caused the closing of the daycare center in 2020.

I was also a full-time master's student in psychology, working on a thesis about historical trauma and approaches to healing multigenerational wounds. I began researching not only my family (including my White mother, who, at 16 years of age, declared she was in love with and would marry the Nez Perce man who became my father) but my Nimiipuu people as well.

During my three-year graduate program, I worked at the daycare full-time. I would go to class, to my son's sporting events, and in the evenings, to my friend Randy's place to write papers for school. Randy had been one of my daughter's high school teachers. He had Microsoft Word, which was a luxury once I learned to use it. He had a better computer than I did, which I struggled to learn to use. It was at Randy's that I wrote my master's thesis. That 100-page thesis would years later grow to a 500-page doctoral dissertation, again on family history and historical trauma.

Late one night, I was struggling to put the story of my family into the finicky American Psychological Association format required for my thesis. It was frustrating enough to have to write about myself in the third person, in that supposedly objective academic voice, but then, too, I had to somehow prove and document my own family's oral history. At that time, oral history was not an acceptable form of academic discourse. Finally, in frustration, I shoved my chair back from the computer and sat down in the middle of the room. I was crying, but soon I felt a warmth surround me. I could feel them place their hands on me as they encircled me. "It's OK," I heard them say. "It is time to tell our story."

Fortunately, my two main professors agreed that my people's oral history had value. I am grateful to them to this day, especially for being in a sense on the cutting edge. These days, oral traditions are much more accepted and valued for their contributions to the historical record. My ancestors are part of my DNA, my spirit and being. They are alive within me and my relatives if we choose to listen. Even in the histories of my people authored by Whites, I can still hear my ancestors. All along, I have never stopped listening to them. Recently, when my ancestors started telling me that I needed to take my family's stories out of academia and offer them up to the wider world, I began to write this book. Here's what I've learned (so far!) about my ancestor Ut-sin-malikan.

In 1805 a few White explorers, their Native guides, and an enslaved Black man owned by William Clark arrived on the Oo-yipe Prairie near what is today Weippe, Idaho. My great-great-grandfather Ut-sin-malikan was 12 when the advance party from the Lewis and Clark Expedition made it over the Bitterroot Mountains onto the Prairie, where they found a band of open-hearted Nimiipuu. The starving "explorers" found respite among the bands gathered there. The Lewis and Clark party stayed in the area for two months. On the brink of manhood, Ut-sin-malikan may well have felt that this appearance of White men was of special significance for him and his people. Looking back, it certainly feels that way to me: Ut-sin-malikan's entire life, from this point on the Prairie to his death decades later in Washington, DC, was one of tumultuous change. What he went through amazes me, humbles me, and certainly gives me perspective on the events of my own life.

The arrival of these White explorers was indeed a pivotal moment in the long history of the Nimiipuu. Although this region had been Nimiipuu country for many millennia, starting in the late 18th century it was also caught in a global power struggle between the newly born United States, Britain, and, to a lesser extent, France and Russia. All vied for control of the resource rich region known to White Americans as Oregon Country and that the British called the Columbia District, a vast territory comprised of modern-day Washington, Oregon, Idaho, and the western parts of Montana and Wyoming. At that time, our people were unaware of the global competition about to impinge on their homelands, competition driven by desire for the luxurious warmth and softness of beaver fur.

In 1805, our people still lived as they had since Coyote made us. But desire for the luxurious warmth and softness of beaver fur was about to change all that. Ut-sin-malikan and his people already knew or had heard about White fur trappers. We called them soyapuu, a Nimipuutimt word meaning "people [puu]" from "across the water [soya]"[1] and which the Nimiipuu and other tribes of the Columbia Plateau used to refer to Europeans and Americans. On the heels of the trappers would soon come Christian missionaries and tens of thousands of White settlers, travelling from the eastern and midwestern states on the Oregon Trail. Ut-sin-malikan himself, once he became chief of his village, would be a key leader in the Nimiipuu adjustment to this influx of soyapuu. He would travel around the Pacific Northwest, meeting with other tribal leaders and, eventually, make the journey to Washington, DC, to meet with White leaders.

But in 1805 he is still a boy on the cusp of adulthood. His name is not yet Ut-sin-malikan. We don't know what his childhood name might have been, so I'll continue to call him by the only one of his Nimipuutimt names that has been preserved. A Nimiipuu child often had several nicknames. I've known children named for their antics and the impression they make on their elders: Talks-too-much and Earthquake are two that come to mind. Father called my sister Jackie Talks-too-much when she was a child. He called my son Earthquake because of a "minor incident." One day, my five-year-old son was with his father, grandfather, and uncles shopping at an REI outdoor equipment store. My son managed to stop the escalator, tumble a clothing rack, and knock a pile of shoe boxes over.

My great-great-grandfather lived in a village in the Clearwater River basin in the Kamiah Valley in what is now Idaho. His village was near a fishing place long used by our family.

Ut-sin-malikan's family lodge would have been made of heavy driftwood logs, which were placed in the ground in the middle of an area that had been dug out to a depth of two to three feet and twelve by sixteen feet in area. The logs were used as posts in the middle and along the sides. The posts in the middle supported an A-shaped roof. Cross timbers were lashed to the upright posts to support the rafters, and the roof was covered with large tule mats made by sewing together stalks of cattail or teasel.[2] These mats were light and easy to assemble and take down. They would swell up and seal when it rained, but would contract and shrink when it was dry to let in air. The lodge grew in length as each new family was added, until it was a hundred feet or more long. Then another lodge would have been started for additional family members.

A village had many other buildings, too: the young boys' lodge, the women's menstrual lodge, a birthing tipi, a sweat lodge, and others. I have been taught how to sew together the tulles to make a small mat. It took me two hours to make. I suspect it would have taken his wife several days to sew together enough mats to make a whole tipi.

As part of his morning ritual, Ut-sin-malikan would take his turn with the duty of heating rocks for the sweat lodge. In the sauna-like lodge, boys and adult men would sweat and then jump into the nearby stream, icy cold due to snow melt from the surrounding mountains. This community of men would talk and play around as they jumped into the cool stream. Sweats were used both for cleansing as well as for purifying, for we believe that purifying is a necessary part of preparation for any dangerous or important undertaking, or as a means of counteracting the evil consequences of some past mistake.[3] The men and boys would sweat first, followed by the women and girls.

Ut-sin-malikan lived according to the seasons. He had been taught when to hunt, gather, and fish, and how to prepare for winter. He would move with his village to spring and summer camps, such as the one of the Oo-yipe Prairie, where they'd gather roots and other edible plants, and to fish and hunt. Their summer-weather tule mat lodges were shaped like tepees. He would also take part in the first feasts of the spring to thank the Creator for bringing back our staple foods. We relied on lots of plants, especially Pacific Northwest natives such as khouse, bitter root, wild onion, wild carrot, and camas, as well as many other plants with hearty roots. Along with many kinds of berries, our people had drying techniques that ensured long-term provisions. The practice of gathering roots is still honored today. I haven't dug for roots in many years, although I enjoy eating them.

In the spring, after the snow melted, salmon would return from the ocean and fight their way up the then-wild Columbia River and its tributaries. One favorite fishing spot was Celilo Falls. Now tamed by dams, Celilo was a meeting place for people of many tribes for thousands of years. With huge boulders strewn across the rapid waters of the Columbia, fishers could claim strategic access points. Native people also built piers that jutted even farther out over the river, giving them precarious access to the rich bounty running just beneath their feet.

Ut-sin-malikan was taught many skills, including dip netting, spearing, and trapping salmon. His female relatives were skilled in cleaning, splitting, and placing the fish on drying frames over smoking pits. This collaboration with his female relatives would supply the food they needed to survive the winter months, 80 to 90 percent of their entire food supply. The dried salmon and other winter foods would be stashed in a reed-and-hide lined cache pit dug by the women. My son and his cousins still use the skills of dip netting at Rapid River when the salmon return in spring. I help by cleaning fish and cooking them on a barbeque.

My great-great-grandfather would have pitched in from the time he was three years old, helping his family and community collect and process foods. By age six, these youths made substantial contributions to the family's livelihood. Special ceremonial feasts were held to honor a boy's first kill or a girl's first root digging and berry picking. Our people thought that if a renowned hunter or fisherman ate the boy's first game, the boy would also become a good provider. The girls likewise would become good providers if their first roots and berries were eaten by an expert.[4]

Grandfathers instructed the young boys' first endeavors in hunting, fishing, horse riding, and sweat bathing. Grandmothers helped their granddaughters with their first root digs as well as making baskets, cooking, and sweat bathing. The children were treated equally by both sides of the family. The uncles, aunts, cousins, and older siblings all took part in a youth's training. According to Nez Perce historian Allen Slickpoo, "Children were rarely disciplined as infants, but when older, they were whipped in groups by special whippers when a member of their group misbehaved or disobeyed."[5]

Life wasn't all work. Play helped reinforce some of life's essential lessons and skills. Playing games helped prepare a young person for real-life situations, much like when Coyote prepared himself to meet the monster. Like other Nimiipuu youths, Ut-sin-malikan played games that helped develop hunting skills. They might play the pinecone game, which involved pitching pinecones through a reed hoop a foot or two in diameter. That same hoop might also be used in another game. The hoop would be rolled along a prescribed path and a shaft thrown so that it passed through the hoop as it rolled or hit the earth at the same time as the hoop fell flat. Then, too, there were mock battles, a perennial favorite of children everywhere. The battles might be conducted from horseback, sometimes reenacting a famous conflict with another tribe. Horseracing and all manner of athletic feats on horseback were popular.[6]

The young Ut-sin-malikan would have learned to train, ride, and breed horses, too. No one knows exactly how the Nimiipuu first acquired horses, but some have speculated that we were aware of them first by observing our neighbors, the Cayuses, from whom we may have either traded for or stolen horses.[7] Historian and friend of the Nimiipuu Francis Haines tells a trading story as the origin of horses among our people:

> Several villages combined their resources and gathered up a large amount of trade goods, including strings of dentalia [a kind of seashell] then used as money in the Northwest. Several *Nimiipuu* took this wealth south along the old war trail to buy horses. On their return, they distributed the horses among the various villages participating in the venture. To a village at the mouth of Asotin Creek went the prize of the lot, a white mare heavy with foal. The Indians of the valley, attracted by the strange animal, spent hours at a time watching it graze on the hills. Tradition has it that this white mare and the colt born to her were the foundation stock for all the *Nimiipuu* herds of later times.[8]

Our people started obtaining horses in the early 1700s. By 1750 the Nimiipuu were considered a "mounted tribe." We were one of the few tribes on the northern continent to breed horses for swiftness and intelligence. Many of the horses were marked with large spots of white mixed with black, brown, gray, or some other dark color. These beautiful animals, which the Nimiipuu often decorated with elaborate trappings made from rawhide decorated with porcupine quills and beads, were probably the ancestors of the modern Appaloosa.[9]

Band leaders might have herds of several hundred horses, wealth that represented prestige and could be used to give gifts, sold for goods, and to mount warriors. There were three types of saddles: one for the men, one for the women, and one for carrying packed belongings. Young Nimiipuu would have begun to learn how to manage horses and pack a travois. The travois, made of two long poles connected with a hide that formed a hauling bed, was dragged behind a horse to carry possessions.[10]

The boys would sit near the council fires and listen (but only listen!) to the men discuss the happenings of their village and the surrounding villages. There was talk of the soyapuu, the beaver trappers, but also traders eager to exchange iron pots, guns, and glass beads for beaver pelts. The Nimiipuu already knew of the existence of many soyapuu in the east. They had also heard of the explorers who had landed in big canoes on the west coast near present day Astoria, Oregon, and up north along the coast of present-day Washington. These explorers brought disease from other parts of the world, and by the late 1700s many villages had already suffered from smallpox, measles, and other afflictions, which drastically reduced our population.

There was something else being discussed around the council fire just before William Clark and his advance party of the Corps of Discovery appeared on the Oo-yipe Prairie near the present-day town of Weippe, Idaho. The men were discussing whether to go south on a vengeance war party against the Te-wel-ka (the Snakes, now called Shoshone-Bannock), enemies of the Nimiipuu. Earlier in the summer, there had been a peace-seeking journey by three Nimiipuu from the Hahahts-il-pilp village to the Te-wel-ka. The hope was that they would smoke the peace pipe, but instead, all three were killed. Chief Hahahts-il-pilp wanted to seek revenge for these deaths. He sought help from the men of his village as well as those from nearby villages. Several agreed to go to the land of the Te-wel-ka in southeast Idaho to avenge the killings.[11]

A small war party led by Chief Hahahts-il-pilp, Neesh-ne-park-ke-ook (Cut Nose, from the Ya-ho-tin Potlatch Creek), Chief Tunnachemootoolt (Broken Arm, from the Tee-e-lap-a-lo region near Kamiah), and one-eyed Chief Yoom-park-kar-tim (Fierce Five Hearts, from Lah-mah-ta near White Bird, Idaho), left just three days prior to Clark's arrival. With them went almost all the men from these various bands.[12]

Listening to all this, the young Ut-sin-malikan may well have wished he could accompany the war party as a warrior. The departure of the warriors left my great-great-grandfather's band without the manpower needed to defend itself against intruders. My people have long speculated what might have happened if the warriors had not gone south. Some Nimiipuu, such as Slickpoo and Walker, have speculated that if the Lewis and Clark Expedition had met a group of warriors rather than women, children, and the elderly, their journey might have ended there on the Oo-yipe Prairie.[13]

Although he probably wasn't yet of an age to join the warriors of his band, Ut-sin-malikan might have been old enough to live with other pubescent boys in an adjunct lodge called a la-we-ta. The boys' lodge was underground, with a flat roof of split timber covered with a heavy layer of rye grass on which dirt was piled several inches thick. The lodge was so well insulated that the young men could sleep on dried grass matts with little covering even in the middle of winter.[14]

When a Nimiipuu boy or girl entered adolescence, he or she was sent out alone on a vision quest to seek their way-a-kin, their spirit guide. When they returned, they were no longer a child and this transition to adulthood was honored with a special ceremony where the new adult received a new name. The family of the newly named individual would give gifts to honor those who had contributed to the child's upbringing.

Ut-sin-malikan's people had been preparing him all his life for this critical step into adulthood. His way-a-kin would assist him in his journey through life as he prepared himself to become a village chief and lead his people through the changes already arriving due to the Euro-Americans.

According to family oral tradition, Ut-sin-malikan's name means "Great Hunter of Grizzly Bear." He was a handsome, well-respected man. Ut-sin-ma-likan had two brothers, probably younger. One was Kipkip Pahlekin, and the other Yootim-malikin, who is referred to as a sub-chief several times along with Ut-sin-malikan. The meaning of both brothers' names has been lost.

According to Slickpoo and Walker,[15] when a girl reached puberty, an elaborate and formal ceremony was held. Adolescent girls were isolated from the community in a special house called El-we-tas, where they were attended by an older female matron. The girls' relatives and friends were notified of their impending transition into adulthood.

During their isolation, the girls were urged to keep busy and think good thoughts. Our people believed that anything a girl did during this time would influence her life as an adult. The girls could only come outside after dark, for short periods of time. Their meals were cooked on a separate fire.

This isolation lasted for about a week after a young woman's first menstruation ended. She was then welcomed back to the community as a woman ready for marriage. She was given gifts by friends and family, such as new clothes, hair ties, wampum necklaces, and moccasins. She created a new hair style to reflect her changed status as a young adult woman. Soon after, she would go on her vision quest. When she returned, she would receive a new name.

After receiving their adult name, an individual's name could change any number of times, often because of some significant milestone: important accomplishments, guardian spirit visions, or outstanding personal characteristics. One example is Watkuweis, whose name means Returns from a Far Land or One Who Was Lost but Returns Home.

One day, a group of Nimiipuu were hunting in buffalo country. The women were out gathering when a group of Blackfeet raided the party and captured a young girl. The Blackfeet raiders enslaved the Nimiipuu girl and sold her to a White man who, apparently, treated her well. They had a baby together. They lived in present-day Canada near the Great Lakes. One day the White man decided to take her across the Big Water to England. She did not want to go, did not want to leave this land, so she escaped, probably with help from friendly Whites. She carried her little boy with her, but the way back to the Nimiipuu was hard. The baby died during her journey and was buried in a shallow grave along the trail. Just as she had given up hope, a band of Salish found her. When she spoke to them, they replied in her language. They took her back to her village of Hahahts-il-pilp, Red Grizzly Bear, near Kamiah, Idaho. Her people, who must have been amazed and joyous at her return after so many years, listened to her stories and now called her Watkuweis. Watkuweis was the first Nimiipuu to see Euro-Americans, according to historians Slickpoo and Walker.[16]

CHAPTER 4

Meeting Lewis and Clark

After spending the spring and summer of 1805 on the camas prairie, the Nimiipuu, as usual, headed for Celilo Falls on the Columbia River near present-day The Dalles, Oregon. There they would fish and trade with the other tribes of the region. At this annual gathering, Ut-sin-malikan would marvel at the soyapuu trade goods and hear stories of the White people. I wonder if they were things he wanted. Perhaps he had trade goods to offer, things he had made such as braided buffalo rope or a bow and arrows.

One day a group of three Nimiipuu men wanted to learn more about the soyapuu in the east and trade for guns, called timuni[1] in our language. They traveled east to the country of the Mandans, who lived along the Missouri River in what are now the Dakotas. There they heard that a party of White men was traveling west seeking peace and friendship. These soyapuu were saying there was a new Great White Father and he wanted no more wars among the people. These soyapuu sought a river route to the big salt water in the west. The Nimiipuu men returned home before these White men arrived in our lands.

This group of soyapuu was the Lewis and Clark Corps of Discovery Expedition, which had started out in 1803 from St. Louis, Missouri. When the three Nimiipuu men returned, a council was held, and surely as many as possible gathered round to hear the stories. Among them would have been a curious young Ut-sin-malikan.

There was likely a lot of discussion about what action should be taken when this group of soyapuu came to Nimiipuu lands. Some wanted to kill the White men as soon as they arrived in our territory, while others spoke of the many trade items that could be had, such as metal pots, beads and, more importantly, guns. Even though a group of Nimiipuu men had just acquired six guns, they didn't have the black powder that would make them shoot. As they were discussing what to do, they remembered the story of Watkuweis, the woman who had lived among the Whites and had returned to her people a few years earlier.

According to tribal tradition, Watkuweis, now old and near death, said, "These are the people who helped me." White people had helped her escape captivity in the east, so she instructed, "Do them no harm."[2]

The Euro-Americans arrived at the Oo-yipe Prairie on a fall day. Ut-sin-malikan's band and family were there gathering camas, but his father might have been in the group of warriors who had gone south to the country of the Te-wel-ka.

Three Nimiipuu boys were out venturing when they saw seven strange men approaching on horses. One of the boys was Alle-oo-ya, the son of Tsap-tsu-kelp-skin. He was just a few years younger than Ut-sin-malikan. Alle-oo-ya would later become an important and controversial leader called Chief Lawyer.

What the boys saw was the expedition's advance party. The main body of the expedition was still making the treacherous journey over the Bitterroot Mountains. The boys ducked down and thought they were hidden, but

Weippe Prairie Camas Fields, in Weippe, Idaho. These are the fields where Lewis and Clark happened upon the Nimiipuu gathering camas on September 20, 1805. *Paul Family Photo Collection.*

William Clark saw them and got off his horse. He approached the boys, giving them red and blue ribbons. Using sign language, he told them to go to their village and tell the people that they were coming. (The sign language of the western Plains Indians was well known to both the Nimiipuu and their neighbors, the Flatheads.[3])

The boys ran back to their families as fast as they could, yelling, "People coming, strangers with hair on their faces, like pieces of buffalo robes stuck on!"[4] The women and children out in the camas fields soon saw the strangers riding into the encampment. At first everyone was hesitant to greet the strangers, but then Clark raised his right arm, calling "Peace, peace, we come in peace."[5]

That must have been a confusing thing for the Nimiipuu to hear. The word "peace" was heard in our language as "peese," which means the sinew of an animal used for sewing clothing and other material. So, according to Nimiipuu oral tradition, Clark and his men were given sinew. After more sign language it was understood that Clark wanted food. Several women brought the strangers dried camas, dried salmon, and other foods. The strange men ate as if they had not eaten in a long while. After Clark and his men had been fed, he sent one of them back with provisions for the remainder of the expedition and with the information that they had found a group of friendly Indians. The entire expedition then arrived and spent several weeks at the Nimiipuu encampment.

Meeting these men likely raised questions for Ut-sin-malikan and his fellow Nimiipuu. How could these men look so different? What was their purpose? The two lead men of the expedition had different color hair than our own black straight hair. Lieutenant Clark had red hair and a very furry red face, while Captain Lewis had blond hair and furry blond facial hair. To the Nimiipuu, facial hair was unusual. They plucked their facial hair, what little they had. (I remember watching my father pluck his facial hair every evening, looking into a mirror. He did this until his death.) Many thought it might be buffalo fur stuck on—but how? One youth got brave and close enough to reach out and tug on the man's beard. Much to his surprise, the hair didn't come off.[6]

Then there was the matter of the man with the black skin. His name was York, an enslaved man owned by William Clark. At first, many thought his black color was painted on, much like the Nimiipuu used war paint—but after an attempt to rub the color off, they soon realized it was indeed the color of his skin.

Soon after the meeting at Oo-yipe, the expedition asked for directions to the big water in the west. The chief who had this knowledge was Tsap-tsu-kelp-skin (Chief Twisted Hair), whose village was near present-day Kooskia, Idaho. When the expedition arrived at Tsap-tsu-kelp-skin's fishing camp, the word was sent out that the strangers were there, and all could come and see. This fishing camp is close to Kamiah and Ut-sin-malikan's village. Ut-sin-malikan and his family would have been among the first to arrive. Eager for another glimpse of the strangers, Ut-sin-malikan raced ahead. He wanted to see what was in the packs the strangers brought with them. Lewis and Clark brought out many items no one had ever seen before. For the first time the Nimiipuu saw spyglasses, compasses, magnets, and burning glasses. For the first time, they heard the blast from the long sticks—the rifles that eventually replaced the bow and arrow.[7] The three Nimiipuu men who had earlier traded for six rifles were now able to trade for gun powder.

After spending several days with Tsap-tsu-kelp-skin, Lewis and Clark needed to make canoes for passage to the big water via several rivers they had yet to navigate. Several Nimiipuu men showed the expedition party how to burn out a tall pine's core to make a canoe. Tsap-tsu-kelp-skin agreed to watch over their horses while the Expedition made their way to the Pacific. For this action, he received an American flag and a Jefferson Indian Peace medal, a medallion with the bust of the President on one side and a pair of hands shaking beneath crossed pipes on the other. Tsap-tsu-kelp-skin and a few of his men accompanied the expedition to Celilo Falls.

Many questions remained in the wake of the departing expedition. Why had they come? Could they be trusted? Was it true that many more soyapuu would be coming? Who was this Great White Father they spoke of who lived in the land where the sun comes up? How were they going to enforce peace among the many different tribes? How were these men able to make rifles, spyglasses, and glass fire makers? The Nimiipuu up until this time thought their way-a-kins brought them great power. Now they weren't so sure.

As Ut-sin-malikan himself would ultimately conclude (at great cost to himself), the question of trust had to be answered with a resounding *No*. It's not that there wasn't a certain cultural logic at work, so perhaps from the Euro-American point of view their continual taking of land and resources was perfectly consistent with what they thought (or said they thought) God wanted. As soon as they "discovered" our Turtle Island—which the Europeans called a new world—the takings began. Even before Columbus began the European exploitation of the Americas, the Catholic Pope issued the first of many papal bulls (or edicts) in 1452, sanctifying the taking of land and removal of resources from non-Christians. These bulls were modeled on the Catholic Church's brutalities of the past, such as the Crusades, and would shape future ones, including the genocidal Inquisition, which ravaged Europe from the Middle Ages until the early nineteenth century, erasing perceived heresy by eradicating entire populations.

These papal decrees have for centuries been used to justify violating the sovereignty and humanity of Indigenous peoples all over the world and are collectively referred to as the Doctrine of Discovery. They are the legal backbone of settler-colonialism.

Thomas Jefferson was quite clear about how the Doctrine applied to the newly established United States of America. "Whites," he wrote, had the "right of pre-emption of their [Native] lands." If another White nation were to try to claim the same land, that would be considered an act of war, of invasion. Native peoples had "no right of soil."[8]

The Doctrine of Discovery is still in use: An 1823 U.S. Supreme Court case that cites the Doctrine has long been the basis of modern international property law. The philosophy behind the Doctrine's legal offspring—Manifest Destiny, the Dawes Allotment Act, and the Homestead Act are the most relevant examples here—are based on the notion of "improvement." According to John Locke, the seventeenth century English Enlightenment philosopher whose thinking was so influential in Britain's role in the slave trade and colonialism, the value of property must be measured in how it is "improved." Living according to the seasons and managing landscapes sustainably was pretty much the opposite of what Locke had in mind. He called Indigenous peoples "barbarians"—while the vaunted Declaration of Independence says that Native Americans are "merciless Indian Savages" who live by the "Rule of Warfare" and are as much an enemy of Americans as the British. Locke argued that agrarian capitalism was the way of superior races: improvement meant mining the soil for crops, timber, minerals, and other resources, and selling them in an already globalizing market.[9] So Locke steered the Doctrine of Discovery, at least in his part of the world, towards a new foundation based on economics rather than divine right.

Economics was the motivation for President Jefferson to send Lewis and Clark on their journey, and it was these agents of a globalizing economy who straggled out of the mountain two centuries ago in the form of the Corps of Discovery.

Fur traders came to Nimiipuu country hot on the heels of Lewis and Clark. The desire for beaver pelts for fashionable hats and coats, and the profits that came from trapping, brought more and more soyapuu to the Pacific Northwest. Conflict erupted frequently between the two cultures. Great Britain and the United States wanted to establish trade among the tribes of the Northwest. Agents for the two countries vied with one another to offer the best prices for pelts, in hopes of gaining the loyalty of Native peoples and peaceful access to the region's riches.

The first trading post in Nimiipuu territory was established by Donald McKenzie on the north bank of the confluence of the Snake and Clearwater rivers, near the present-day city of Lewiston, Idaho. McKenzie worked for John Jacob Astor's Pacific Fur Company.

The enterprise got off to a shaky start. The Nimiipuu wanted what the fur trader had to offer: guns, ammunition, blankets, pots and pans, steel knifes, and more. McKenzie expected to trade for beaver pelts, but the Nimiipuu, for the most part, weren't trappers. They told McKenzie that taking up beaver trapping would mean taking time away from fishing, hunting, and root gathering.[10]

That first trading post lasted less than a year. McKenzie, frustrated, finally had to trade with the Nimiipuu for food. The Nimiipuu got the better part of trade, charging high prices for their horses, which the hungry trappers devoured. The fur traders had little choice: it was either trade on Nimiipuu terms and eat horse meat, or die of hunger.

Guns and ammunition magnified the conflicts between traditional enemies. The traders wanted peace so that all tribes would do business with them. The traders asked that the Nimiipuu, the Shoshone, the Blackfeet, and other area tribes smoke the peace pipe with the goal of establishing a climate of profitable stability. Gradually, tribal enemies came to terms: if their warring ways kept traders from coming, then no one would have guns and ammunition or any of the other desirable trade goods.[11]

The fur traders also brought liquor. After snow melt, in late spring or early summer, horse-drawn wagons loaded with goods and supplies started arriving from the east. These annual rendezvous brought out the mountain men, the White trappers who came to the meeting locales with their beaver pelts. After solo trapping all winter, they were at the end of their supplies and probably hungry for a little social interaction. There was a lot of gaiety, noise, dancing, music—and lots of alcohol was consumed. The records of some of the fur traders note that the first time the Nimiipuu attended a rendezvous was 1827. They'd been invited by trappers and entered the trading grounds "cautiously, with guns and lances aloft, riding with stiff dignity and prepared to trade or not, depending on the behavior of the 'Bostons'," as Native people referred to White Americans. Terms were apparently acceptable, as soon the Nimiipuu were "learning to swear in mountain-man English," dancing, racing, gambling—and drinking.[12]

Tribal people from the eastern bands were also trapping and trading with the Euro-Americans. Many were Iroquois, driven out of New York and forced west after the Revolutionary War. Most of the Iroquois had been christianized by the "Black Robes"—the Catholic priests. When the Catholics saw the religious ceremonies of our people, they insisted we were not worshipping the "One True God."

Some of the mountain men, too, were practicing Christians. Noticing that the mountain men acted like they were stronger and more skilled than the Indians caused many Nimiipuu to ask where this strength and skill came from. Was it really a spiritual power, as the traders claimed?

CHAPTER 5

Seeking the "Book of Heaven"

Incorporated by the British government in 1670, the Hudson's Bay Company controlled the North American fur trade for nearly 200 years. In the late 1820s, George Simpson, acting governor of the Company, toured Oregon Country (or, as the British called it, the Columbia District). Simpson had been given orders from London to select Indian boys to send to an Anglican mission school at the Red River settlement in Rupert's Land. The settlement is in what is now downtown Winnipeg in Manitoba, Canada.

Simpson persuaded Kootenai and Spokane chiefs to let him take two twelve-year-old boys to the Red River school. The boys were named Kootenai Pelly and Spokane Garry. They remained at Red River for four years, learning to read and write English, and were taught Euro-American history and geography. They learned to plant and tend crops and were instructed in the Anglican faith. The boys were baptized at the school on June 24, 1827, the first American Indians from west of the Rockies to be baptized by a Protestant minister.[1]

After Spokane Garry returned to his tribe, he evangelized about the supernatural powers of this Great White Father the soyapuu called "God" at tribal gatherings and trading posts. It was at these gatherings that the Nimiipuu would hear Spokane Garry preach.

The chief trader at Fort Colville (about 100 miles northeast of present-day Spokane), Francis Heron, wrote in his journal for April 14, 1830, "Last evening all the Indian Chiefs about the place were admitted into the Gentlemen's Mess Hall and a speech was made to them, repeated [translated] by Spokane Garry in a satisfactory manner."[2] Heron lists the tribes in attendance, which included the Nez Perce.

Many Nimiipuu were keen to partake of this supernatural power they were hearing so much about, although others were more skeptical about interacting with the Euro-Americans and of the spiritual power they claimed their Great Father gave them. But the lure of trade goods—and the economic power those goods represented—made interacting with the Euro-Americans necessary.

Many stories about what transpired next have come down through our tribal history. Nimiipuu historians Slickpoo and Walker say that four Nimiipuu men were enticed to journey to St. Louis, Missouri, to seek the "Book of Heaven" and accept the White man's teachings because of the gifts that would reward their people.[3] At the time, St. Louis was where trappers and settlers outfitted for the trip west.

Chief Lawyer's grandson, Corbett Lawyer, says his grandfather was present when Spokane Garry evangelized the religion of the one great God on that April evening in 1830 that Heron wrote about. Chief Lawyer also heard Spokane Garry talk at a rendezvous.

That late spring or early summer, Chief Lawyer returned to his village and discussed the possibility of going back east with an American Fur Company pack train, but by then the traders had already departed for St. Louis. Over the summer months they met with the Flatheads of western Montana and discussed sending some tribal members east to ask for teachers and the "Book of Heaven." In the late summer of 1831, the two tribes agreed to send a delegation to St. Louis. They would meet the American Fur Company at the following spring rendezvous and travel with them to St. Louis, where they would seek out their old friend, William Clark, now based in St. Louis as the Commissioner of Indian Affairs.[4]

The delegation consisted of four men, according to Josephy, one of whom was Ut-sin-malikan's brother, Kipkip Pahlekin. "He seems to have come from the village of the powerful Kamiah leader whom Lewis and Clark had met and called Tunnachemootoolt," Josephy writes. Another man from the Kamiah Valley was Tupyahlanah, whose name means Eagle. Three other Nimiipuu went east. Two men of about 20 years of age, named Hi-yuts-to-henin (Rabbit Skin Leggings) and Tawis Geejumnin (No Horns on His Head, or Horns Worn Down Like Those on an Old Buffalo), were accompanied by an older warrior living with the Flathead "named Ka-ou-pu (Man of the Morning, or Of the Dawn Light) the son of a Nez Perce buffalo hunter and a Flathead woman."[5] Two other men from the Flathead were members of the delegation.

No one knows for certain which tribal chief sent these men, but the results of this trip changed my people's way of life forever. It took me a long time to accept that Christianity was the cutting edge of colonialism. And perhaps I never have fully accepted the losses my people suffered, as I feel disillusioned and angry to this day.

Of the three Flathead and four Nimiipuu who embarked on the journey to St. Louis, only four returned. Two of the Flatheads turned back early; of the third Flathead, nothing is known. The four Nimiipuu delegates who did arrive in St. Louis found William Clark. The four were able to tell Clark of their peoples' interest in the White man's religion. They informed Clark they would welcome a missionary who could teach them about the Book of Heaven.[6]

While in St. Louis, two of the Nimiipuu delegation, Kipkip Pahlekin and Ka-ou-pu, died and were buried in the Catholic cemetery there. The two surviving Nimiipuu boarded a steamship on March 26, 1832. While on board, they met the famous painter George Catlin, who then painted a portrait of Hi-yuts-to-henin. They sailed up the Missouri River to the mouth of the Yellowstone River. Tawis Geejumnin died near the mouth of Yellowstone River, leaving Hi-yuts-to-henin the sole survivor. But Hi-yuts-to-henin never made it back to his homeland, either. He joined a group of buffalo hunters from his band and told them the story of his adventures to St. Louis. He was killed in a battle with the Blackfeet in 1833.[7]

While the Nimiipuu delegation was staying with Clark, a half-Wyandot man named William Walker seems to have paid a visit—the record on this isn't perfectly clear, but what happens next is. Walker was impressed that the Nimiipuu wanted to know more about the "Book of Heaven" and were asking for a teacher. He drew an exaggerated picture of Ka-ou-pu with a pointed head. (He may have been merely copying a sketch made by Clark of Clatsop Indians, as Nimiipuu did not shape their heads this way.) Walker sent the sketch along with a letter to his friend Gabriel P. Disosway, a Methodist merchant and a supporter of the Methodist missionary work. The sketch and Walker's letter, a plea for missionaries to help these "savages" who had travelled over 2,000 miles to seek the White man's truth, were published in the March 1, 1833, edition of New York's *Christian Advocate and Journal and Zion's Herald*.[8]

This single notice set off a race among the different denominations to be the first to answer the call to bring salvation to the Western "red man." The first to answer was Reverend Jason Lee from the Methodist Mission Board. His first encounter with the Nimiipuu was at the Green River Rendezvous at Hans Fork in Wyoming in June 1834. Here Reverend Lee obtained a first-hand look at the activities of fur traders and witnessed the Indians holding a service. Lee didn't stay with the Nimiipuu, settling instead in the Willamette Valley in Oregon, where he ultimately influenced the influx of White settlers to travel the Oregon Trail.[9]

The American Board of Missions sent Dr. Marcus Whitman, a Presbyterian, and Reverend Samuel Parker, a Congregationalist to meet the Native tribespeople. They arrived at the Rendezvous at Green River on August 12, 1835. Whitman wrote in his journal, "We had a talk with the chiefs of the Flathead and Napiersas [Nez Perce or Nimiipuu] tribes, in whom they expressed great pleasure in seeing us and strong desires to be taught." And Parker wrote in his journal:

> The first chief of the Nez Perces, Tai-quin-su-watish [Tack-en-sua-tis or Rotten Belly, from the present-day town of Stites] arose and said, "He had heard from white men a little about God, which had only gone into his ears; he wished to know enough to have it go down into his heart, to influence his life, and to teach his people." Others spoke to the same import, and they all made as many promises as we could desire.[10]

From the chief's interest, Parker and Whitman thought that the Nimiipuu were ready for missionaries to come and teach them. As a result, Whitman departed, leaving Parker to continue the job of visiting tribes in the region to find sites for possible missions before he arrived at Fort Vancouver in Washington Territory. Whitman returned east to recruit missionaries to come west and work with the tribes who were requesting teachers.

Whitman convinced the American Board to appoint another couple to travel west with him. He learned that a couple named Henry Harmon Spalding and Eliza Spalding were headed west to work with the Osage Tribe, who lived between the Missouri and Red rivers. He wrote to the Spaldings, convincing them to go west to Nimiipuu territory. William Gray, a single man, was appointed at the last minute by the American Board to also accompany the group. Thus, the party of five Presbyterians was ready to begin their journey west.[11]

While back east, Whitman married Narcissa Prentiss in February 1836. She travelled west with him and the others. The group of missionaries made history because they were traveling the Oregon Trail with White women, who were the first to cross the continental divide. The women traveled 1,300 miles, riding both side-saddle and in wagons. They may have been the first White women to travel that far west, but the Nimiipuu and the men and women of many other tribes had been crisscrossing

Turtle Island for thousands of years. In the coming decades, nearly half a million Euro-Americans would follow Whitman west on the Oregon Trail, setting the stage for troubling times for the Indians of the Pacific Northwest.

The group of missionaries arrived at Fort Vancouver in early September 1836. Leaving the women there, Whitman and Spalding returned inland to look for building sites for their missions. At the Walla Walla River, their Indian friends showed them a place called Waiilatpu, "Place of the Rye Grass."[12] There the Whitmans established their mission. They were met by a group of about 30 Nimiipuu led by Tackensuatis (Rotten Belly). Tackensuatis led them to Lapwai, "Place of the Butterflies." Spalding established his mission nearby. With the help of Tackensuatis and others, they built a log cabin for the Spaldings, and on December 23, 1836, the Spaldings moved in.[13]

The Nimiipuu might be construed as having bent to the ways of the Euro-Americans. Indeed, on the surface, it appears they asked to be christianized. But we have always practiced our own unique ways. Our songs, prayers, dances, and ceremonies have been passed down through millennia. When the early explorers, fur traders, and missionaries arrived in our lands, they observed many of these culture ways.[14]

The Nimiipuu neither spoke of nor justified religious freedom: we lived it. As the contributors to *Nez Perce Perspectives* write, "Because of our interest in acquiring new ways of thinking and new technology, our people were intrigued by the beliefs of others. Even so, our ancestors did not intend those different beliefs to ever replace our own."[15] The coming of the missionaries was seen as adding to what was already in place and not a complete change of culture. Slickpoo and Walker describe some of the results of forced change:

> The missionaries very much wanted the Nez Perce to take up farming and leave their old ways. But we were not very inclined to change our old way of life. For example, we preferred our mat houses to the log cabins that took so much time and work to build. Also, we felt that a man's status depended upon his ability as a hunter and fisherman, and it was woman's work to gather berries and such. It seemed to us that the white men were asking us to become like women when they wanted us to garden. Unfortunately, the missionaries interpreted this reluctance to change our way of life as laziness, a notion that could hardly have been further from the truth.[16]

Ut-sin-malikan was in his 40s when missionaries arrived in Nimiipuu territory. He and his band still lived in the Kamiah region. He observed and listened to those who went to Lapwai to hear what Reverend Spalding had to say. It is not known how often Ut-sin-malikan traveled to Lapwai, which was 65 very rough miles along the Clearwater river and 70 somewhat easier miles up and over the Camas Prairie (between Winchester and Grangeville, Idaho, separated from the Weippe Prairie by the Clearwater River). But he did visit, making sure he was present first-hand to witness, learn, and gain spiritual power.

The Spaldings took several Native children into their home, both as servants and as students.[17]

Spalding also baptized Nimiipuu children. In a letter, Spalding wrote, "Two of the eldest girls, called Mary and Martha, were taken ill during the summer of 1838 and both died. Mary died on the 25th of June and Martha on the 3rd of July." In another letter soon after, he added, "They both gave pleasing evidence of a change of heart—both were baptized a few days previous to their death."[18] These two girls were the first Nez Perce to be baptized by missionaries.

Ut-sin-malikan's children may have attended the Spaldings' school. A 1927 newspaper obituary for Ut-sin-malikan's daughter, Wa-le-won, stated that Spalding was her teacher for several years.[19] Wa-le-won's obituary also indicated that she was the first Nez Perce woman to accept the Christian religion at the hands of Reverend Spalding. Wa-le-won was two years old when Reverend Spalding arrived.[20]

If I dwell on how damaging Spalding and the missionaries were to the Nimiipuu, it is easy for me to become sad and upset. The missionaries worked in conjunction with the U.S. government's Indian agents to take our land, kill our people, and destroy our culture. When I write in such detail about the history of my people, it helps me acknowledge the wrongs we have experienced. By telling the story of our family's Nimiipuu history, we reclaim our heritage and practices as best as we can.

In the spring of 1839, Reverend Asa Smith wanted to move away from the Whitmans' mission at Waiilatpu and complete his original purpose: writing down the language of the Nimiipuu. Smith was a linguist who studied Nimipuutímt, our language, with great intensity, probably because he was bent on making good Christian servants of the people he supposedly served. It was suggested he spend a summer at the Kamiah area, the region where Ut-sin-malikan and many other Nimiipuu lived. After the summer was over, he decided to make Kamiah his permanent mission site to learn more of the language. His principal teacher was Chief Lawyer, whom he refers to in his diaries and letters as "My Teacher, The Lawyer."

Smith was a keen observer and recorded his observations in his diary. He described one of his first meetings in a Nimiipuu grass house, dated November 27, 1839:

> Met the people today in a grass meeting house, or rather lodge which they completed yesterday. A little more than 200 were present including all the young children. This will probably be the usual number during the winter.[21]

Another of Smith's observations was how the chiefs would pray throughout the day, as is noted in his diary, dated January 31, 1840:

> The Nez Perces have been in the habit of worshipping the sun and the earth. The manner is as follows. At sunrise they would take their pipe and light it, put it to their mouth and take three puffs, then direct the pipe stem towards the rising sun and emit the tobacco smoke in the same direction and say, "Thou Chief of the morning, smoke first and I will smoke afterwards." At noon they used to smoke in the same way and point up to the sun and breathe out the smoke in the same directions and say, "Thou Chief above, smoke first and I will smoke afterwards." The same also at sunset, "Thou Chief of the evening (or setting Chief) smoke first and I will afterward. In the same manner they would direct their pipe and smoke to the earth and say, "Thou Chief below, smoke first and I will smoke afterward." They would direct their prayer to these objects in this manner, "Bless us, Grant that we may not be sick, that we may not die, that we may travel prosperously. Give us plenty of food, &c."[22]

Both diary entries could be about Ut-sin-malikan, as Reverend Smith was living on land that belonged to Ut-sin-malikan. Smith went on to say that this manner of praying was only a "temporal blessing" and not a true prayer to Jehovah. The dogmatic Smith, like so many missionaries of the day, did not understand the Nimiipuu way of praying. Our people would give thanks to all living things, including sun, moon, earth, and all that surrounds us for our wellbeing. Smith and others thought this was "temporal" as opposed to asking for salvation and forgiveness.[23]

At this time, Ut-sin-malikan, along with other Nimiipuu, was still making a living according to the seasons. To the missionaries, our wandering was uncivilized. Living by the seasons did nothing, in their view, to "improve" the land. The missionaries wanted not only to bring the word of God and convert our people to the Christian faith, but they also wanted to encourage the Indians to become farmers, a "civilized" way of making a living. But sedentary agriculture was hard to accept for a people who for thousands of years had lived in balance with their resources, and who gave thanks for what was provided so that nature would in turn provide for them during this and every season.

At first, many converts were baptized, as the Nimiipuu were intrigued by the White man's religion. But soon the influx of more and more Whites into the region brought clashes between the two cultures. Disputes arose as to who had the authority to enforce rules about land ownership, killings, thefts, and more.

The Nimiipuu were hearing all the rules required to become a Christian, but they could see that not all Whites abided by those rules and, indeed, many who exhibited very un-Christian behavior. The missionaries began to introduce practices such as flogging, whipping Nimiipuu adults whom they thought were misbehaving in some way. The Whites, however, were not held to the same standards and did not receive the same treatment.

Laws from the Great White Father were drawn up by Dr. Elijah White, an Indian agent to the Nimiipuu in 1840, to help enforce the teachings of the missionaries:

> Whoever willfully takes a life shall be hung.
>
> Whoever burns a dwelling house shall be hung.
>
> Whoever burns an outbuilding shall be imprisoned six months, receive 50 lashes, and pay all damages.
>
> Whoever carelessly burns a house or any property shall pay damages.
>
> If anyone enters a dwelling, without permission of the occupant, the chiefs shall punish him as they think proper.
>
> If anyone steal, he shall pay back two fold, and if it be the value of a beaver skin or less, he shall receive 25 lashes, and if the value is over a beaver skin he shall pay back two fold and receive 50 lashes.
>
> If anyone take a horse, and ride it without permission, or take any article and use it without liberty, he shall pay for the use of it, and receive from 20 to 50 lashes as the chief shall direct.

> If anyone enter a field and injure the crops, or throw down the fence so that cattle and horses shall go in and do damage, he shall pay all the damages and receive 25 lashes for every offense.
>
> If an Indian raise a gun or other weapon against a white man, it shall be reported to the chiefs and they shall punish him. If a white person does the same to an Indian, it shall be reported to Dr. White and he shall redress it.
>
> If an Indian break these laws, he shall be punished by his chief. If a white man breaks them, he shall be reported to the agent and be punished at his instance.[24]

These rules created dissension among the Nimiipuu, between those who believed and accepted Christianity and those who still believed in the traditional ways. They could see there was not equal enforcement of the laws, that Indians and Whites were treated differently. Many Nimiipuu complained of injustices committed by White men. If a White man committed a crime, including murder, they were frequently not punished the way a Nimiipuu would be—if the White man were punished at all. No one knows if Ut-sin-malikan enforced any of these rules in his village. What is clear from later events, though, is that he closely observed the way the laws were implemented and saw that they were not applied being equally. Whites could literally get away with murder, and with theft of Native property, while the Nimiipuu were punished harshly for even minor infractions.

The term "heathen" was used by Spalding and the other Protestant missionaries to characterize Indians who resisted their instruction most, further contributing to the creation of a split within the tribe, a split that was political, social, and religious. Spalding added to the split by saying that non-Christian Indians were going to hell, a hot place where you would burn for eternity.

As time went on, the rupture among my people became sharper until it split the tribe into Christian and "heathen." Soon, the division would be characterized as being between treaty Christian and non-treaty "heathen" factions. This split is a wound that is not yet healed and is still felt among the descendants of Ut-sin-malikan to this day.[25]

A clear example of cultural misunderstanding that metastasized first into abuse, and then war, can be found in a letter from Asa. B. Smith to Walker, dated April 27, 1840. In the letter, Smith says he is discouraged and has the "blues" because the situation, he feels, has become untenable. He writes that:

It is doubtless true that the "Indians are the most promising race of the people in the world," not however because they are worse than other heathen, but because of their peculiar situation and the difficulty of doing them any permanent good.... I have but little hope of the adults. Their habits and prejudices are all fixed and it is difficult to bring the truth so to bear on their stupid degenerated minds as to produce any effect or even to warrant the hope that the Holy Spirit will make it effectual.[26]

The attitude of Smith, who lived on my great-great-grandfather's land, sheds light on an incident in which he complained that Ut-sin-malikan had threatened his life. By October 1840, missionary Smith had been living among my ancestors for about two years; Spalding had been there almost four years. Some of the other missionaries had been complaining of intrusions on their homes and of being threatened and being told they had to leave. Smith's issue with my great-great-grandfather seemed to have to do with payment for the land where Smith was living, the traditional lands of Ut-sin-malikan and his brother.

In his diary, Smith tracks the breakdown of his relationship with my great-great-grandfather. On October 13, he writes that Ut-sin-malikan and Yootim-malikin

demanded pay for the land. I refused to say anything about it, telling them that the land was given a year ago and they had promised to say no more about it, and now they had no business to say anything further about it. They pretended that when they gave me the land, they expected that I would give them goods and food, but I had not done it &c. ... They then ordered me in the most absolute terms to leave on the morrow.[27]

Within a couple days, Smith writes that "Mrs. S. is in great fear and is nearly sick in consequence of it. Jack, a White handyman who worked with the missionaries, slept in the kitchen last night and does tonight. Today he has been sharpening his knife and tonight laid it by his side ready for an attack if they should break into the house."[28] But, on October 19, Smith writes, Ut-sin-malikan "came this morning and tried to get initiated into my favor but I told him I had no confidence in his word & gave him back the tallow he brought me, but he would not take it, & went home."[29]

I think Ut-sin-malikan was frustrated and angry because he felt his land had been invaded by Smith. The Nimiipuu held that if you were given something, you were expected to pay back in like value and you continued to pay until the value was matched. That mostly unspoken cultural assumption has been the source of many clashes. There is no record of any payments for the land given by Ut-sin-malikan to Smith, or of any title having been given to Smith by Ut-sin-malikan. Smith and his wife left the community soon after this incident.

It's also possible that Ut-sin-malikan and his brother had been influenced by Atpashwakaiket (Flint Necklace), a Nimiipuu chief from the Asotin area and the father of Looking Glass. Atpashwakaiket was known to be anti-settler and advocated that his fellow Nimiipuu take a tough, uncompromising stance towards the Americans. Atpashwakaiket had told Ut-sin-malikan and Yootim-malikin that he and a group of Cayuse had tied up and held captive a Hudson Bay Co. trade officer, Pierre Pambrun, until he agreed to pay as much for beaver pelts as the Americans did.[30] Once he agreed, they released him, and ever since he had been "good."[31]

During the time that Smith was at Kamiah, he began to understand the Nimiipuu language and helped develop the first alphabet. He translated the beginnings of the gospel of Matthew. Together with Cornelius Rogers, Smith conducted a census of the Nimiipuu.[32] In this census I found a reference to Ut-sin-malikan. On November 11, 1839, Smith says there were 1,927 Indians, but this count did not include those gone to buffalo country or those from other bands not known to Smith at that time. Under Ut-sin-malikan, the census listed 18 men and 28 boys, 32 women and 32 girls, for a total of 110 in his band. This number also included his brother Yootim-malikin. It would also include his daughter, Wa-le-won, my great-grandmother, whom we believe was born in 1834. We know he had at least three other children, Obee Parsons, William Parsons, and a half-brother, Eugene Mallikin, Jr. Wa-le-hoo's mother was E-wa-wah-a-poo (the meaning of her name has also been lost). Ut-sin-malikan became a chief sometime before the missionaries came.

I was teaching a group of college students strategies for doing research at the Museum of Art and Culture in Spokane, when, at random, I pulled open a file drawer, pulled out a file, and discovered Wa-le-won's obituary. Under the headline "Aged Indian Woman Dies, Said to be first Nez Perce to accept the Christian Faith" the 1927 obituary continues:

> Mrs. Jane Condit, 93, said to be the first Nez Perce Indian woman to accept the Christian religion at the hands of the late Reverend Henry H. Spalding, and who was baptized by the Reverend Mr. Cowley, a Presbyterian missionary (he was at Kamiah for the years of 1871-1875) coming

from Spokane to assist Spalding in his work, this being in 1836 at the village of Spalding, when she was 2 years old.

Spalding was her teacher for several years after she had attained young girlhood. She was a member of the second Presbyterian Church in the old village of Kamiah for more than 50 years. Richard Paul Lapwai, grandson, is the only known surviving relative.[33]

The obituary is inaccurate, however, as it neglects to mention that Jane's daughter, Lydia, was also still alive, as were Lydia's sons, Titus J. Paul, my father, and Rueben Paul, who were both attending boarding schools. Jane's son, Homer, was also still alive at this time, although he never had children.

Wa-le-won (Jane Parsons) and her husband Tin-tin-nae-khom-kan (Jason Conditt), *taken around 1870. Paul Family Photo Collection.*

CHAPTER 6

Whitman Incident, Treaties, and Divisions

Tensions were building up between the Whites, the missionaries, and the Tribes of the Plateau. At Lapwai Mission, several Nez Perce were hostile toward the Spaldings. They believed Spalding's temper and dogma of the Christian faith was not of God, but of man. They did not like the harsh treatment of being whipped if they did not obey the Christian laws. Also, they resented the hypocrisy of the laws that were not the same for the Whites as for the Indians. For the same offense, the Whites were not punished while the Indians were punished. At Lapwai, the non-Christian Nez Perces were labeled "heathen" by the missionaries and were now growing in power and the number of Christian Nez Perce was declining. The beginning of division was happening.

I wondered where Ut-sin-malikan's loyalty lay, with Spalding, or the "heathen." Some of the history books I have read state that he was loyal to Spalding during this time period, but I still wonder what he thought of the hypocrisy of the laws and whippings. I would have had a hard time being loyal. How would he justify these whippings? Maybe he had prospered materially with land, livestock, and was beginning becoming a farmer. I don't believe he would totally give up cultural teachings or the honoring of living according to the seasons he was still Nez Perce.

Meanwhile there was also tension developing between the Cayuse and the Whitman's who were at the Waiilatpu Mission. These tensions would lead to the loss of life for the Whitman's and others. The story of the 1847 Whitman Incident is usually told from the missionaries' perspective, not from the Cayuse perspective. First, who gets to define what is or isn't a massacre as opposed to defending against an invasion or theft of land? For the Cayuse, a tangle of events and concerns for their lives led them to the attack at Waiilatpu Mission.

From the very beginning of creating the Mission at Waiilatpu, Whitman's mission was to convert the Cayuse 'savage" to Christianity and to "civilize" them to the ways of American society. Whitman and Samuel Parker were negotiating with the Cayuse for land for the Waiilatpu mission, Parker told the Cayuse that, in exchange for the use of the land, "a big ship, loaded with goods to be divided among the Indians" would come each year. Plows and hoes, and sundry goods would not be sold to the Cayuse but given to them.[1]

Whitman was not as successful in working with the Cayuse Indians and in fact had no converts among the Cayuse as Spalding had among the Nez Perce. Whitman never established a working relationship with the Indians of Walla Walla Valley. Whitman focused more on promoting the Oregon Trail and economic development for the Northwest. He founded the wagon trail over the Blue Mountains that became known as the Oregon trail. This was the trail that led to the Willamette Valley. Thousands from the east began to use this trail and stop at the Waiilatpu Mission.[2]

The Cayuse, in the 1840s, numbered perhaps 1,500 people.[3] They could see the never-ending stream of wagon trains bringing thousands more White settlers through their traditional hunting, gathering, and fishing grounds. In the first half of the decade, some 10,000 White settlers moved into the territory; there might have been 21,000 Indians living in the Oregon Territory at that time. [4] This influx was depleting the animals and hampering access to their traditional hunting grounds which, in any case, were often polluted with the litter of incoming settlers. The livestock the settlers brought were destroying pasture, which ruined the forage for the Cayuse's horses as well as the deer they hunted.[5]

A Cayuse chief, Young Chief accused Whitman and others of intentionally introducing diseases that killed with the arrival of Whites. Some Cayuse thought that Whitman might even be poisoning Indians. In fact, in 1841, attempting to deter what he considered theft from his garden, Whitman injected melons with tartar emetic, a poison that at minimum causes vomiting and can easily be fatal.[6] It is true the immigrants had indeed brought diseases, though not intentionally as Whitman's action was. When measles came to the Plateau peoples it was devasting.

> Measles is extraordinarily contagious, with 90 percent "attack rate" among the exposed, and while Old World peoples, having adapted over millennia, rarely died from it, New World populations were devasted. It's awful outward effects—hacking cough, raging fever, and an angry rash—were followed by pneumonia and encephalitis. A common native treatment of illness was to sit naked in a sweat lodge, enduring extreme heat as long as possible before plunging into a cold stream. However beneficial in other situations, the lodge's heat compounded the fever's effects while the icy water could send the body into shock.[7]

When the measles hit in the fall of October 1847, it seemed that all the White children survived and the Cayuse children died. At least two hundred died at the Waiilatpu mission under Whitmans' care, and many Cayuses suspected that Whitman's "care" was actually a death sentence. Cayuse perished from measles at nearly five times the rate than other groups.[8] Among the Cayuse it was held if a patient died while under the care of a healer, a "tewat," the healer's life was forfeit.[9]

To the Cayuse this was the last straw, on a cold afternoon of November 29, 1847, a Cayuse Chief, Tilokaikt, entered the Whitman home, asking the Doctor for medicine. Behind Whitman's back a second Indian named Tomahas struck the missionary on the head with a tomahawk. Then several Cayuse men came in killing. Soon Narcissa was slain and about a dozen men.[10] Forty-six Whites were taken as captives, among them Reverend Spalding's daughter Eliza. It is reported that most Cayuse did not participate in the killings and many even tried to help the survivors.[11]

Spalding had barely escaped the fate of the Whitman's. He had been there just a few days prior settling his daughter Eliza into Whitman's school. Father J.B.A. Brouillet, was also near the Whitman Mission when news came of the incident and knowing that the Cayuse were looking for Spalding as well, found him and warned him of the danger. Spalding avoided the Cayuse by not going to Fort Walla Walla but wanted to return to the Lapwai and his family. It took him three frigid nights to return, because he has lost his horse and had to travel at night so as not to be found by the Cayuse. When he did finally make it back to the mission he still had to hide because he saw that the mission had been destroyed. He was later reunited with his wife and family.[12]

In the meantime, a messenger who had witnessed the incident at Waiilatpu hurriedly rode to the Lapwai mission and warned Mrs. Spalding. Her husband was not there yet and she worried about the safety of her husband and family. There was also a young non-Christian Nez Perce warrior who had returned from Waiilatpu and brought with him other young warriors who went to the Lapwai mission wanting to kill the Spalding's. These Nez Perce were allied with the Cayuse thinking of driving the missionaries and settlers out of the country. Ut-sin-malikan and several other loyal Nez Perce to the Spalding's had surrounded the mission to protect Mrs. Spalding. This prevented the non-Christian Nez Perce from attacking because they did not want to kill their own tribesman. Wanting to help protect Mrs. Spalding, Ut-sin-malikan sent a message to William Craig, a White mountain man married to a Nez Perce woman. He had a farm a few miles from the mission and they would be safe at his home. Craig came and picked up Mrs. Spalding, her children, brother, and another woman named Mary Johnson and took them to his farm for safety. As soon as the party had left the mission the young warriors came and destroyed the mission. Reverend Spalding arrived after his family had left the mission and was escorted to William Craig's home by a loyal Nez Perce a few days later. About a month after this incident the Spalding's were escorted by several Nez Perce to Fort Walla Walla. When the news of the Whitman incident was received back east, the American Mission Board ordered all their missionaries to move out of the region for their safety, the Oregon missions were closed until 1871 when Spalding was allowed to return to the Nez Perce.[13]

Ut-sin-malikan, and Timothy, a devout Christian chief of a Nimiipuu band from the area of the Snake River now called Asotin, went to Waiilatpu to try to rescue the Spalding's little girl Eliza, who was taken captive along with 51 others from the Waiilatpu and Umatilla Missions.[14] They were not able to gain release of the captives. However, about a month later, Brouillet and Peter Skene Ogden, an employee of Hudson Bay Company, were able to ransom the survivors, among them Eliza Spalding for blankets, clothing, and thirty-seven pounds of tobacco.[15]

The Whitman Incident was seen as an act of war by the settlers who started to request American militia hunt the Cayuse men who had been at Waiilatpu. The Cayuse were harassed for three years as well as other bands of Indians. Hundreds of Cayuses were killed. After three years five Cayuse headmen surrender at a military outpost at The Dalles, Oregon. They were then taken to Oregon City for a trial. They argued that they were innocent as they were defending their people from Marcus Whitman's bad medicine. They were found guilty, then hanged on June 3, 1850, and buried in Oregon City.[16] The Cayuse five as they are now called, were Clokomas, Kiamasumkin, Isiaasheluckas, Tomahas, and Tilokaikt. (Tomahas was the grandfather of Red Moccasin Tops, who was one of the three Red Coat Warriors who was killed at the Big Hole battle during the Nez Perce Warr of 1877. The mother of Red Moccasin Tops was a Cayuse married to Yellow Bull, a Nez Perce war chief). These five surrendered to protect the Cayuse homeland and their people. As to why, Tilokaikt's own words provide a clue: "Did not your missionaries teach us that Christ died to save his people? So, die we to save our people."[17] There were Cayuse present at the trial, but they left and returned home before the five were hung and buried in Oregon City. The Cayuse must have discussed what happened to the bodies and why were they not returned to the Cayuse. The location of their burials was never recorded.[18] To the Cayuse the reasons for the hangings were political and for revenge, to prevent an all-out war.[19] Hoping to further the cause of repatriation, justice, and reconciliation, students from the University of Oregon have recently been working with the descendants of the Cayuse men, searching for their burial site. Members of the Confederated Tribes of the Umatilla Indian Reservation (among whom are the descendants of the Cayuse people) are hopeful that they will finally be able to honor their dead defenders.[20]

The Whitman incident was only the beginning of tensions and conflict between missionaries, settlers, and the Tribes of the Oregon Territory. The unrest between the settlers and the tribes in Oregon Territory continued after the trial, and the settlers were not satisfied with how the territorial government was addressing the needs of their protection. The Oregon Territory was too vast of an area for oversite by one governor for the territory. The area at the time consisted of what is now the states of Oregon, Washington, Idaho, and the western part of Montana. The settlers arriving north of the Columbia River wanted a territorial organization of their own. On March 2, 1853, the federal government established Washington Territory. The Boundaries would be from the Pacific Ocean, north of the Columbia River, and as far east as the Rocky Mountains. This would be what is today the states of Washington, Idaho, and part of western Montana. Oregon Territory would be what is now the state of Oregon.[21]

The United States Government wanted to begin having tribes sign treaties to address the unrest between the settlers and tribes. Ut-sin-ma-likan and fellow tribal leaders would be faced with making decisions for the safety of their people through this complicated process called Treaties. They would be at a disadvantage of understanding the language and laws of the U. S. Government and the men sent to explain the treaties.

Ut-sin-malikan would have a limited knowledge of the English language. He had been exposed to the language from late 1836, to November 1847, it was not an immersion of the English Language, but rather short language lessons that would have been offered by the missionaries Spalding and Smith. Ut-sin-malikan's friend, Chief Lawyer might have had more lessons because he worked closely with Reverend Smith in developing a Nez Perce book of the Bible, Matthew. He was Reverend Smith's teacher. Understanding the nuisances of each other's language takes longer than a few lessons.

For thousands of years, Indian people had made oral agreements with each other that were sanctified by tobacco and gift giving. The Europeans introduced their concept of agreements; they were written documents that would include the details of agreements between the tribes and the Europeans. However, most Native Americans could not speak or read English, which put them at a distinct disadvantage that was exploited by the non-Indians.[22] The leaders of the tribes would have to depend on translators who would have limited knowledge of the languages of the Sahaptin dialects. Each tribe had their own dialect of the Sahaptin language.

The leadership of the Plateau Tribes would be entering the treaty negotiations with limited understanding of agreements, but now would be introduced to the US Treaty making policy.

The goal of the U.S.'s treaty-making policy was "Not a grant of the rights to the Indians, but a grant of rights from them."[23] Whether that was ever an explicit policy of the US government might still be open for debate, but what is clear is that the combined desires to exploit the Pacific Northwest's resources, open the territory up to White settlers by relocating or removing its original inhabitants, and extending the railway to the West Coast were both unstoppable and genocidal.

The United States would send Isaac I. Stevens to the Pacific Northwest in 1853 with three official titles: he was the newly appointed Governor of Washington Territory; the Superintendent of Indian Affairs for the territory; and leader of the Pacific Railroad Survey group. The Euro-Americans looked to him to help "solve" the Native "problem." In 1854 he was appointed first to survey a route through the Northwest for a transcontinental railroad. He realized that tribes along the route would have to make concessions for the use of their lands. This led him to negotiate treaties with the tribes along a corridor extending from the Salish Sea near present-day Seattle, east across the Cascade Mountains and into the Columbia Plateau region, where the Yakama, Umatilla, Walla Walla, Cayuse, Palouse, Nez Perce, Spokane, Coeur d'Alene, Colville Tribes, Flathead and Blackfeet all lived.[24]

> Stevens' views on Indians had been shaped by the prevailing assumptions of his fellow Americans during the Jacksonian era. Their attitudes fell into two broad categories: one group believed that the natives were savages who, for their own protection as well as that of white society, needed to be isolated beyond a permanent Indian frontier. The other group argued that the Indians should be assimilated into white culture—taking the best from Indian and white civilizations. Common to both points of view was the assumption that all Indians were essentially the same—an assumption which lumped vastly diverse cultures under one label.[25]

Governor Stevens of Washington Territory and Joel Palmer, the Superintendent of Indian Affairs for Oregon Territory called for a treaty council with the Nimiipuu and other Plateau tribes and set a date of May 1855 at Mill Creek, near present day town of Walla Walla, Washington.[26] He wanted to meet with all the Plateau tribes at once. Now 62 years old, Ut-sin-malikan had been hearing from fur traders, missionaries, the military, and the now constant stream of White settlers that the time would come for a treaty that would take away their lands.

Ut-sin-malikan, along with the chiefs of other Nimiipuu bands, arrived at the treaty grounds on May 24. The gathered Nimiipuu warriors, numbering about 2,500, donned their regalia and rode their painted horses around the treaty grounds. Riding two abreast on their fine horses, the warriors circled the flagpole. Chief Lawyer, Joseph, Old James, Ut-sin-malikan, Metat Waptass, Red Wolf, and several others rode forward with mountain man and translator William Craig to be formally introduced to Isaac Stevens, the governor of Washington Territory. Their show of horsemanship and dancing was spectacular. While Stevens was impressed by the show, he failed to recognize the significance of the Nez Perce entrance. Our Nez Perce ancestors were not only honoring him as an important person, but they were also demonstrating that the Nez Perce are a strong and important people who expected to be treated as equals.[27]

Over the next several days, many representatives from other tribes of the Columbia Plateau and River joined the growing group, including Cayuse, Walla Wallas, Palouse, Yakama, and Umatillas. Spokane Garry of the

Spokane Tribe came to observe. Some 5,000 Indians came to the council—not all were friendly with the Whites.

The leadership of the tribe's present would be calling upon their understanding of law as described by Clifford Trafzer:

The Presence of *Tama'nwitt* at the Treaty Council of 1855

For Indian people attending the Walla Walla Council, the meeting provided an opportunity to articulate their view of the White settlements and the proposals put before them. Naturally, they emphasized the native view *tama'nwitt* (Columbia River Sahaptin) or *tama'wit* (Nez Perce), which is literally defined as "throw down," but which means Indian law, natural law, or divine law handed down by the Creator at the beginning of time. *Tama'wit* is essentially, the "rules to live by" that come out of the Indian religion and that are espoused in song and ritual. Through their translators the Indian leadership at the Walla Walla Council tried to convey to Stevens and Palmer their deep belief in *tama'wit,* so that the non-Indians might understand that the Indian leaders could not sell their land and resources. To do so would violate *tama'wit* Indian law. To sell the land, the leaders would have to break the spirit and the law, handed down to them for generations from the time of creation to 1855.[28]

The night before the council began, Ut-sin-malikan had been approached by a neighboring Cayuse who was anti-White and did not want anything to do with the treaties. Tension between the tribes was evident, and Ut-sin-malikan didn't want anything to do with the Cayuse. He spoke to a group of chiefs, including Lawyer and others, saying, "The Cayuses wish us to go to their camp and hold a council with them and Pee-o-pee-mox-a-mox. What have we to say to the Cayuses or Pee-o-pee-mox-a-mox? What are their hearts to us? Did we propose to hold a council with them or ask them for advice? Our hearts are Nez Perces hearts and we know them. We came here to hold a great council with the Great Chief of the Americans, and we know the straightforward truth to pursue and are alone responsible for our actions."[29] The interpretation given of Ut-sin-malikan's words could be close to what he was saying from his heart. The word for heart in Nez Perce is *tim'ine* which the interpreter would have some knowledge of this word, but the full meaning had varying nuisances. I believe Ut-sin-malikan was speaking from his heart and letting the governor and tribal leaders present know of how he and other Nez Perce had fought with the US Government in war battles already and knew the power of the

US government and were loyal to them. This loyalty is the opposite of the Cayuse leaders Pee-o-pee-mox-a-mox who opposed the Whites.

Lawyer then read from a book, apparently written in Nimipuutímt, where the advice of the great chief Ellis was recorded. Ellis was greatly admired and respected by the Nimiipuu, so his words had worth and weight. Ellis may have been Christianized at the same Red River settlement where Spokane Garry was baptized.[30] "Whenever the Great Cheif [sic] of the Americans shall come into your country to give you laws, accept them!" All the tribes have their own heart "but they have all received the white law."[31] Lines of conflict were being drawn, not only between White Americans and Natives, but between tribes and bands, as well.

General Palmer's rationale for establishing reservations was blunt, tragic, and traumatic:

> Three hundred and sixty years shows us that white man and the red man cannot live happily together; although we may live near together there should be a line of distinction drawn so that the Indians may know where his land is and the white man where his land is; you are able to judge for yourselves by the constant difficulties that are occurring here among you, between the whites and the Indians.[32]

The Nimiipuu Chief Looking Glass at first did not agree with the treaty process, foreshadowing the tragic future of conflict among the Nimiipuu. He and others also disagreed with the government officials for appointing Chief Lawyer as the head chief of the Nimiipuu. There were many Nimiipuu at the time who disagreed with this appointment. A Nez Perce at the time said, "The white man had no authority to tell us who should be our head chief, without consulting our hereditary chiefs or people who had their own appointed and recognized head men."[33] Throughout our history and to this day, there was never any one head chief who spoke for all the Nimiipuu bands.

On June 11 the Treaty of 1855 was signed by 56 band or village headmen. By the terms of the treaty—from the point of view of Stevens, who lumped all the bands together—the Nimiipuu accepted a reservation of approximately 25,000 square miles, roughly from the upper Grande Ronde in northeastern Oregon to the crest of the Bitterroot Range on the present Idaho-Montana border, and from the St. Joe and Palouse rivers in northern Idaho to the Wallowa Mountains in north eastern Oregon, and the neighborhood of Payette Lake, Idaho in the south.[34] We gave up nearly 60,000 square miles to the United States.

There were many terms and promises outlined in this treaty, among which were schools, flour mills, and lumber mills to be built. The government would provide farmers, blacksmiths, and teachers to train and teach the tribal people. The US government promised that its military would keep the White man from our lands and that in return we would not go onto White man's land once the boundary lines were established. There was also a promise of gold in payment for our lands and salaries for the head men for a period of twenty years.

Of all the promises made not a single treaty between the United States and Native peoples has been honored. The Treaty of 1855 is no exception.

Whites encroached onto tribal lands, especially after Stevens and Palmer, in June 1855, announced in the *Oregon Weekly Times* that all former Indian lands were open for settlement.[35] However, this was not true, because the treaties had not been approved by the Senate. In rushed hordes of land-hunters and prospectors. To the tribes in Washington and Oregon Territories it seemed the treaties were broken even before the ink was dry, intensifying already fraught relations.

Things were so bad that Stevens asked for another council of all the tribes. On September 11, 1856, Stevens lectured the tribes about the importance of keeping the laws of the treaty. Many of those who had opposed the treaties in the first place were not present, and those who did come did not want any more talking: they wanted their lands back.

Many of the Nimiipuu, though, wanted to support the United States and its laws. In 1858, Lieutenant Colonel Steptoe was leading about 150 troops, together with their Nimiipuu allies, to the gold fields on the Colville Reservation, well north of traditional Nimiipuu territory. The troops veered off course and encroached on the lands of the Spokane tribe.

On May 16, 1858, several hundred Spokanes, Coeur d'Alenes, Palouse, and Yakamas faced off against a force of some 150 White soldiers under Lieutenant Colonel Steptoe. Twenty-five soldiers were killed and several wounded. The Americans managed to escape with the help of Chief Timothy, Ut-sin-malikan and others.[36]

American soldiers began to attack any group of Spokanes, Palouse, Yakamas, and Coeur d'Alenes they encountered. There were killings, hangings, and tribes' storage caches were destroyed. Senior military officers met with a group of 21 Nimiipuu chiefs led by Chief Lawyer at Walla Walla. Among those chiefs were Spotted Eagle, Timothy, and Ut-sin-malikan.

Colonel Wright, seeking revenge for the defeat of Steptoe, formed a unit of thirty Nimiipuu scouts, which included Ut-sin-malikan. The unit was led by Spotted Eagle and the warriors donned the blue uniforms of the US Calvary. Under the command of Lieutenant John Mullan, this group of Nimiipuu was the first to be employed as a formal unit of the regular army.[37]

I have often asked myself why Ut-sin-malikan wanted to do this, to fight Indian against Indian. It is a question I am still pondering. Perhaps it was because of his loyalty to the United States government, or his encounter with the missionaries, fur traders, and the military, who strongly preached living by the law. He also must have recognized the power of the US military and would not want to do anything that would bring this powerful force to act against his band.

Newly armed with howitzers and long-range rifles that used Minié balls, the US forces were deadlier than ever. Lighter, more accurate, and with a longer range than with previous ammunition for muzzle-loading rifles, Minié balls greatly increased the lethality of long guns. On September 2, 1858, using Nimiipuu scouts, including my great-great-grandfather, a force of some 700 American soldiers led by a Colonel Wright battled Spokanes, Palouse, Yakamas, and Coeur d'Alene.[38]

In a report on the battle to his superiors, Wright noted Ut-sin-malikan for his bravery in fighting,[39] a story I found while researching early publications and government papers of this era. I was surprised to learn that Ut-sin-malikan was 65 years old during this encounter. He must have been in pretty good shape to be galloping at full speed "over the rocks and ravines," as Wright reported.[40]

A second battle between Americans and the Spokanes, Coeur d'Alenes, Palouse, and Yakamas occurred on September 5, 1858. Wright's troops won again and captured a herd of about 800 horses. Rather than take the horses back with them, Wright ordered the herd killed. It took two days to complete the task.[41] Wright described the herd as "the entire wealth of the Pelouse chief Til-co-as."[42] The killing of all those horses nauseated me. Horses were the lifeblood of Plateau Indian culture. Horses enabled us to travel great distances to hunt and gather, to provide for our people. Wright was heartless to kill so many horses, but he was also probably being strategic by knee-capping Native peoples, slowing down our ability to resist the encroachment of colonial-settlers. What did Ut-sin-malikan think of this action. Witnessing this slaughter must have colored his opinion of the soyapu, especially when it came time to sign the treaty of 1855.

There is another event that has disturbed me, and to which Ut-sin-ma-likan must have been a witness. Just after Wright forced a peace agreement between the Spokanes and the U.S., a Yakama who had been in the fighting, named Owhi, rode in seeking peace. He was immediately arrested. Wright sent out word to bring in Owhi's son, Qualchin. Unaware of what was happening, the next day Qualchin rode into the encampment. Because Owhi and Qualchin had dared to fight for their lands and had killed Americans, they were sentenced to death by hanging. Qualchin was hung immediately, and his father was later shot while trying to escape.

Soon after, Wright was back at Fort Walla Walla when a band of Palouse approached the camp. He excoriated them, saying that if they did not submit to his terms "I will make war on them; and if I come here again to war, I will hang them all, men, women, and children."[43]

What did Ut-sin-malikan take away with him from this? He heard, witnessed, and I am sure was never to forget how the United States Army treated Indians who had surrendered, yet were hung. "Don't break the law," is the first thought that comes to my mind—and yet, were the Americans' laws equitably enforced? Clearly not! Whatever Ut-sin-malikan may have thought, he remained staunchly on the side of the Whites. A member of Wright's staff, Lieutenant Kip, recorded in his journal the events of a peace council held later that September. Ut-sin-malikan said "I desire there shall be peace between us. It shall be as the Colonel says. I will never wage war against any of the friends of the White man."[44]

That, at least, was what was recorded by an interpreter. I'm not sure I trust the sources, as long before Lewis and Clark arrived in the Pacific Northwest, there were many Natives who had been driven west by the seemingly unstoppable colonial-settlers. Those Natives would have brought knowledge about the soyapuu and their ways. And not all Whites believed that taking from Indians was justifiable, including various mountain men who rejected the American culture of the east by escaping into the wilds of the west. It must have been very stressful for Ut-sin-malikan and neighboring bands, trying to see the truth: were the Americans bringing spiritual power and trade goods in the spirit in which the Nimiipuu were accustomed, where give and take was a form of mutual aid, or were they, in a sense, addicting the people to a way of life that would leave them with nothing? In hindsight, we know the answer but at the time, and especially in the early days of contact, it must have been confusing.

The treaties brought peace to Washington Territory for a while, but only staunched the flow of settlers for a short time. There were rumors that gold was found on the Nez Perce lands. The 1855 treaty was finally ratified in the spring of 1859 and was signed by President Buchanan on April 29, 1859.

Later in 1859, a White man called Captain Elias Pierce trespassed on the Nez Perce Reservation and discovered gold in Orofino Creek. Ut-sin-malikan must have had some knowledge of what gold does to a man, for he scolded the man who probably led Pierce to the gold. War Singer (Camille Williams), an important Nimiipuu tribal oral historian, related a story to L.V. McWhorter about this:

> A Medicine Man by the name of Kakachto Malweyat of Tawayewai, now Oro Fino, used to fish at headwater of Oro Fino Creek, now Pierce City. This old Indian used periwinkles for bait to catch brook trout. When breaking the cover of the winkles, he used to notice that cover was all yellow. This, he told a white man [probably Pierce]—about the yellow stuff in the fall of 1859. There was a big gathering at Lapwai or [now] Sweetwater from all directions of the reservation. Chief Ut-sin-malikin of Kamiah rebuked the old medicine man for telling the white man about the gold on Oro Fino Creek. He said that the old man will be blamed by the whole Nez Perce tribe for generations. So it all came as the chief predicted when Pierce and his friends arrived at headwaters of Oro Fino Creek and found gold. But they could not stake their mining claims as it was on Indian land. So these whites talked the situation over and found the way it could be done.[45]

Ut-sin-malikan must have known what would happen when gold was discovered. Natives had been murdered by the thousands in the California gold rush: bounties were awarded based on whether the Indian killed was a man, woman, or child. Information of this kind was traded back and forth at gathering places, like the ancient Celilo Falls location where people from hundreds of miles around gathered to fish, trade, party, find spouses, and swap stories.

News of gold travels fast. Keeping the Euro-Americans out of the gold fields was futile, mostly because there was not enough military available to enforce the treaty. In any case, the Indian Agent soon wrote, "I will most respectfully recommend that immediate steps be taken by the proper authorities to modify the treaty, with the Nez Perces, so as to give the government all this gold country. This is the only safe solution of this question by which the laws of the United States would be fully vindicated, and the rights and interests of the Indians protected, and the prosperity of the country ensured."[46]

Something had to be done. Tensions were mounting. Yet another council was held in April 1861 at Lapwai, now in Idaho but at that time part of Washington Territory. Chief Lawyer told those gathered that the Treaty of 1855 had not been lived up to and he wanted assurance from the American authorities that they would keep the promises they made. And yet another agreement was signed that opened the gold-bearing region to the Whites—on the condition that the Americans would provide a force sufficient to keep the Euro-American settlers off the rest of the Nimiipuu reservation. The first to sign this agreement was Lawyer, noted as Head Chief of the Nez Perce nation. The second to sign was Ut-sin-malikan, and third was Spotted Eagle. I believe Ut-sin-malikan signed this treaty in hopes that the United States would keep the gold seekers and settlers from taking over his homeland, to protect his village and family from being invaded.

While there was some effort to enforce the revised treaty, the opening of passage across the Nez Perce Reservation resulted in a flood of Americans rushing in. A tent city was erected overnight at the confluence of the Snake and Clearwater Rivers, which later became Lewiston, Idaho.[47]

Ut-sin-malikan was aware of the situation. If a payment was made, it was never the full amount due. Other provisions of the treaty, such as hiring teachers and doctors, were not honored. Alcohol was being sold on the reservation, another violation of the treaty. Many Indians were reportedly selling their prized horses for whiskey.

There was likely corruption and blame-laying within the US Indian Affairs bureaucracy. The position of local Indian agent turned over frequently and, as they made their reports, each blamed the previous person in charge for misusing funds. The agents complained of the inability of the military to keep Whites off the reservation, and preventing stealing, killing, and the selling of liquor.[48] The problem was compounded by the United States civil war, which sucked away funds slated for the Nimiipuu. The war also soaked up the regular army, leaving only volunteers and a small number of enlisted men in the West.

Within the tribe, fractures deepened. Anti-treaty, anti-White, and anti-Lawyer Nimiipuu taunted those who sided with the Americans, saying the US government was never going to carry out their promises. The divide between treaty and anti-treaty Nimiipuu tore at the fabric of our culture. There were many marriages between the various bands, and the bands tended to fall into either the pro-treaty or anti-treaty group. Perhaps as occurred during the American Civil War, close relationships were ripped apart by the soyapus' insistence on our giving up land and resources under the guise of treaties. There was further conflict because the Whites had decided that Lawyer was the Head Chief, a move the various band chiefs disagreed with, and which ran counter to our traditional, less hierarchical ways of organizing ourselves. Then, too, we were dividing ourselves by some adopting Christianity and labeling those who didn't as "heathens." And even those who did sign the Treaty of 1855, including Ut-sin-ma-likan, disagreed with many of the provisions of the document.

Tension eased a bit in the spring of 1863, as the United States paid the Nimiipuu some of what was owed. The payments were distributed among the people. A grist mill was built and, in the previous fall, a military post had been built at Lapwai. There were still concerns about White trespassers, and whether the ban on selling liquor on the reservation would be enforced.[49] Americans who understood that the injustices inflicted on the Nimiipuu wanted new negotiations. They knew that rising tensions could explode and result in a war.[50]

Another treaty council was initiated in May 1863 but was troubled from the start. The US government's reputation was soiled due to its failure to meet the provisions of the Treaty of 1855. No Nimiipuu showed up for the council, and only two commissioners and Superintendent Calvin Hale attended. The heavy presence of US army troops sent rumors flying that they were there to remove the Indians from the reservation.[51]

Chief Lawyer, Ut-sin-malikan, Spotted Eagle, and Captain John were induced to meet with the American government agent. The agent told the Nimiipuu, "As your friends, we propose to you to relinquish to the United States a part of your present reservation, and to take a new reservation, smaller than the one you now hold. We also propose that on this new reservation, each man or family shall have a piece of land in their own right (severalty), in their own name, just as the Americans do."[52] The "logic" of this proposition was the assertion that the US government would be better able to protect our people by managing a smaller area. The reservation, the Americans complained, was currently too large, and our people too scattered to be able to protect them all. The Americans were also annoyed that there was so much empty land not being exploited. Superintendent Hale offered to buy the lands we would be relinquishing. The thing was, though, the land the Americans wanted was the traditional grounds of Old Chief Joseph, White Bird, Toohhoolhoolzote, and other non-treaty band chiefs. They would never agree to give up their lands—and they never did. The lands of all the non-treaty bands were stolen, pure and simple.

Many other promises were made, such as building schools and bringing teachers, and putting up two churches and a hospital, but in the middle of the discussions, the council was made aware of Whites trying to take possession of reservation land. The trespassers had begun to build shacks on the reservation. Hearing the concerns of the chiefs, the commissioners asked Colonel Steinberger to send a detachment to remove the White trespassers. When news that the trespassers had been removed and the shacks torn down, the council reconvened.[53]

Chief Lawyer gave a long address recounting all the good relations the Nimiipuu had with the Whites, starting with Lewis and Clark. He reminded the Americans of how loyal the Nimiipuu had been, how they had fought with them and protected them. Lawyer concluded by saying, "I will now give you the great answer, dig the gold, and look at the country, but we cannot give you the country you ask for."[54]

Ut-sin-malikan emphasized this, saying, "You but trifle with us, we cannot give you the country, we cannot sell it to you."[55] It seems to me that Ut-sin-malikan is chiding the commissioners about breaking the promises made in the treaty of 1855. I also think Ut-sin-malikan was referring to *tama'wit* Indian law, which stipulates that they cannot sell the land because to do so would be breaking Indian Law.

The treaty council was at a stalemate and a break was called. A week or two later, the council reconvened, and the anti-treaty chiefs showed up. After much discussion among themselves, the Nimiipuu said they would not agree to reduce the size of their reservation but would be willing to relinquish those portions where gold had been discovered. They also agreed to relinquish the site of Lewiston and the country around it.[56]

In the end, the Treaty of 1863 was signed by Chief Lawyer, Ut-sin-ma-likan, Ha-haich-tuesta (Billy), and forty-nine others.[57] However, this treaty was not signed by several non-treaty Chiefs, including Old Joseph, Big Thunder, Eagle of the Light, Quil-quil-si-ne-na, and White Bird. This treaty became known as the "Steal Treaty," because the treaty chiefs had signed away the lands of the non-treaty chiefs and their traditional grounds.[58] I have pondered why Ut-sin-malikan agreed to sign this treaty that ran directly counter to the wishes of the non-treaty bands. He had relatives living in these villages. His sister was married to a man in Big Thunder's band, and they had children, Ut-sin-malikan's nephews and nieces.

There is one other story that sheds some light on this treaty. There had been a gathering of fifty-three chiefs, both treaty and non-treaty, held near the treaty grounds the night before the treaty signing. On this night there was debate between Big Thunder and other non-treaty chiefs and Chief Lawyer, Ut-sin-malikan, and other treaty chiefs about the proposed reduction of land. A witness to the proceedings was US Army Captain George B. Curry, who later wrote:

> The Debate ran with dignified firmness and warmth until near morning, when the Big Thunder party made a formal announcement of their determination to take no further part in the Treaty, and then was a warm, and in an emotional manner, declared the Nes Perce nation dissolved; whereupon the Big Thunder men shook hands with the Lawyer men, tell them with a kind but firm demeanor that they would be friends, but distinct people.[59]

This perhaps clarifies why Ut-sin-malikan agreed to sign the Treaty of 1863. They were now distinct people and no longer a tribe. Each would speak only for themselves. Still, the Treaty would force the non-treaty bands to move onto the reduced reservation within the year. This did not happen because the treaty had to first be ratified by the Senate and signed by the President before it could come into effect; President Johnson didn't sign until April 17, 1867.[60]

When news came that the Treaty of 1863 had been ratified and signed, Old Joseph tore up both the 1855 Treaty as well as his Bible.[61] The Wallowas were not immediately affected due to their remote location.

The 1863 Treaty tore the once vast territory of the Nimiipuu to pieces. The ecosystems the Nimiipuu had seasonally cycled through were now fractured by private property lines, threatening their ability to survive. They became ever more dependent on the government for supplies and farming equipment. The Treaty of 1855 had reserved 23,666 square miles for the Nimiipuu; the new reservation was now comprised of 1,188 square miles, a 14,386,000-acre reduction. While some traditions continued—trips to buffalo country, salmon fishing and drying, gathering of traditional roots and berries—many Nimiipuu now farmed, growing wheat and raising livestock.

And the new treaty was not honored, either. Miners, traders, and settlers continued to come onto the reservation and stake claims, and very few were removed. Ut-sin-malikan begged agents to stop selling liquor on the reservation.[62] Annuities were never paid. Little if any progress was made building mills, blacksmith shops, schools, or churches. In response to their complaints, the United States sent yet another agent, who told the people their reservation was still too large.

It was perhaps then that Ut-sin-malikan had a change of heart. During the council, Ut-sin-malikan is reported to have said that he had "spoke[n] to the people telling them that he thought more of the non-treaty side of the nation now than he did before."[63] Ut-sin-malikan again saw that the US government was not upholding this treaty of 1863, much like the 1855 treaty. I think he had empathy for those leaders who did not sign the treaty, because they too had witnessed the treaty of 1855 not being honored and suspected that more promises would not be honored with the new treaty of 1863. Ut-sin-malikan could be empathetic with the non-treaty because they were still trying to live by *tama'wit* Indian law, by selling their lands would be breaking their law and respect to the Creator. Ut-sin-malikan's land had been within the treaty boundaries for each treaty of 1855 and 1863 and did not break *tama'wit* Indian law.

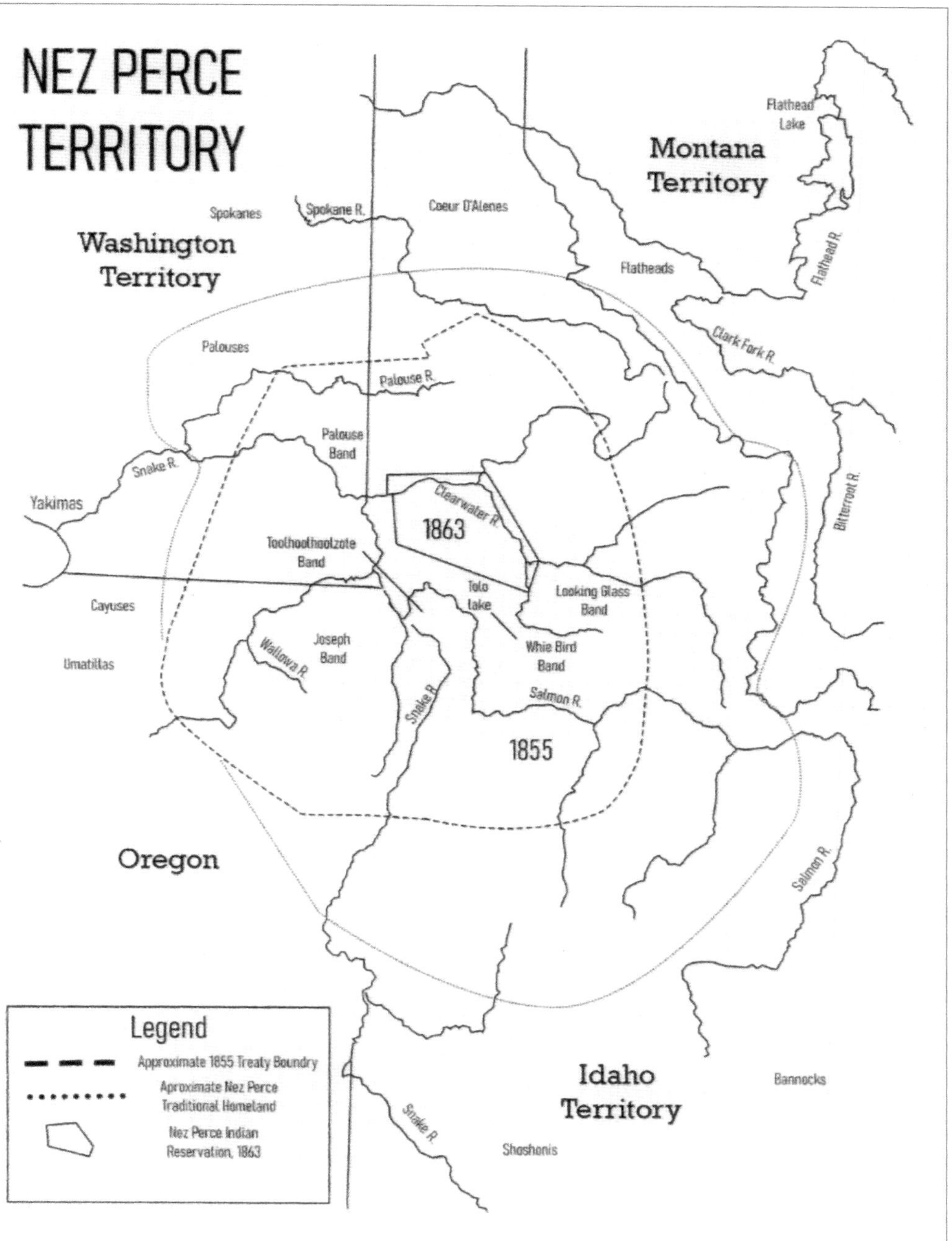

Map of the original Nez Perce territory (dotted line), within which is shown the area covered of the Treaty of 1855 (dashed line) and the final boundary defined in the Treaty of 1863 (solid line polygon at center). *Map created by Jerrod Arslanian.*

CHAPTER 7

Journey to Washington, DC

Chief Lawyer and his party, which included Ut-sin-malikan, were not pleased with how the treaty of 1863 was not being honored. He kept after the Indian agents to help him send a letter to President Johnson to ask for an expense-paid trip to Washington, DC, to talk about the Treaties and the unanswered grievances. Between 1855 and 1867, Indian agents and superintendents sent numerous letters to the Capitol, requesting the federal government to uphold the Treaty of 1855. Numerous newspaper editorials had used their bully pulpits to demand that the promised annuities be paid to the tribe. But Congress barely responded, if at all.[1]

By the latter half of the 1860s, with the Civil War out of the way of the affairs of his people, Chief Lawyer wanted to talk with the President directly. Finally, in 1868, funds for a trip to Washington, DC, were released.

The journey from Nimiipuu country to the home of the Great White Father took months. Chief Lawyer took with him Jason, Timothy, and 75-year-old Ut-sin-malikan, along with an Indian agent, O'Neill, and two interpreters, Robert Newell and Perrin Whitman (the son of Marcus). It is in Robert Newell's diary that I was able to find out what happened during the last months of Ut-sin-malikan's life.[2]

Chiefs Lawyer and Ut-sin-malikan, along with the rest of their party, departed Lewiston on horseback on March 27, 1868. After several days on horseback and in a stagecoach, they arrived at The Dalles on the Columbia River where, on March 31, they boarded a steamer bound for Portland, Oregon.[3] Wherever the chiefs went, they attracted attention and lots of stares.[4]

Ut-sin-malikan was soon literally at sea, traveling in ways foreign to him. He had probably heard of or seen the smaller steam ships that plied the waters of the Columbia as far inland as Celilo Falls, and knew of the big waters, but now he was experiencing it firsthand.

The party left Portland for San Francisco on April 11 on the steamer *John B. Stevens*—and almost immediately had to turn back to port, as they could not get past the notorious ship-killer, the Columbia Bar at the mouth of the river, due to rough weather.

They tried again the next day, and this time the *Stevens* made it out to sea. The weather was cloudy, and the 13th was another stormy day. Ut-sin-malikan became seasick, as did most everybody else. The weather cleared and they steamed into San Francisco on April 16. The party spent five days at the Cosmopolitan Hotel. The grand hotel, located at the busy intersection of Sansome and Bush streets, must have had an impact on Ut-sin-malikan and the others; surely, they ventured out to explore and see the wonders of the city.[5] Newell reports that he lunched at the famous Cliff House.

On April 22, the party departed San Francisco on the steamer *Montana*, bound for Panama. As the Panama Canal had not yet been constructed, they debarked from the steamer and traveled by railroad across the swampy isthmus to the Caribbean Sea on May 6, where they boarded another steamer, the *Morning Star*. Eight days later, on May 14, they arrived in New York. There, they stayed at the Metropolitan Hotel. Newell went on to Washington, DC, on May 15, while Perrin Whitman stayed for another day of sightseeing with Ut-sin-malikan, Lawyer, Jason, and Timothy.[6] The Nimiipuu men saw tall buildings, brick streets, cable cars, and *lots* of people. This experience could only reinforce what the treaty negotiators had said all along: the Whites were as numerous as stars in the sky.

On May 16, Ut-sin-malikan and the others arrived in Washington, DC., They boarded at Mrs. Beverage's Washington House, located on the corner of Pennsylvania Avenue and 3rd Street, close to the capital.

What happened over the next several days has been recorded differently by various historians. Before I tell you those histories, I want to describe a dream I had several years before my family and I began researching Ut-sin-malikan's life and times. In the dream, I saw a white-gloved hand pushing a Native man out a window. I had almost forgotten this dream completely but it came back to me as I learned more about our tribe. I believe the Native was Ut-sin-malikan, connecting with me, urging me to find the stories of my people so that his own story might not be lost. How many more of our ancestors are waiting to be remembered? We need to keep paying attention to our dreams—and exploring and digitizing our local archives.

In Newell's diary, Ut-sin-malikan is ill on May 17. Over the next few days, Newell reports that he visited the President, the Secretary of the Interior, and met with several generals. Presumably, the chiefs accompanied him on these visits. On his May 22 entry, Newell records that Ut-sin-malikan is very sick. On Monday, May 25, Newell records Ut-sin-malikan's death. Typhoid fever, Newell writes.

Family members and others disagree with Newell as to the cause of Ut-sin-malikan's death. An honored Nimiipuu historian, Wottolen, whose name means Hair Combed Over Eyes, offers a very different account of the events in DC. The blind old warrior gave this description of the journey of the Nimiipuu men going around the Cape, rather than across the Isthmus:

> Those chiefs were not sent to Washington to make any treaty. We had the Treaty of Walla Walla, 1855 on which all had agreed. Then came the blind treaty of 1863, signed by the Lower Nez Perces only. This treaty gave away the lands of the Upper Nez Perces but could not bind them lawfully. It was because trouble coming to all of the Nez Perces through miners and stock rustlers pouring into and overrunning our reservation, that these four delegates, all of them signers of the 1863 treaty, were sent to Washington. They were Lawyer, Timothy, Jason, and Utsinmalihkin, who traveled around Cape Horn by ship. I knew all those chiefs very well. Chief Utsinmalihkin was a good warrior.

> Nathaniel Taylor or his agent gave Lawyer, Timothy, and Jason whisky. Utsinmalihkin would not drink. A powerful speaker, he refused to sign the treaty. [He spoke] strongly against some of its wording and for this he was shoved from a high window and killed. This was told by Timothy when he returned home. Whites did this bad deed.[7]

Apparently, Ut-sin-malikan disagreed with the section of the 1863 treaty that stated, "Wherein the Indians then residing outside the reservation as defined in Article Two of the 1863 Treaty, shall be removed to and located on allotments within the reservation."[8] Oral history within my family argues that Ut-sin-malikan said it was wrong to sign away the Wallowas, the lands of Joseph, White Bird, and Toohoolhoolzote—and of the Paul family's great-grandfather, Seven Days Whipping.

Another oral history, recorded by Lucullus McWhorter from Camille Williams, has this to say about Ut-sin-malikan:

> All I know about Utsinmalihkin, he was seen lying near a gutter one morning dead. He laid there part of a day when a Women's club took care of the body and buried him. This is what a Miss Fletcher told when here allotting Indian lands, 1888-93. She was eight years old at the time and her mother belonged to the Women's Club. So, today no one knows

whether he was killed or probably fell from the window. I never heard that the three chiefs returned ever admitted how their partner died.[9]

My family's research turned up the death certificate which says that Ut-sin-malikan died of typhoid fever—but if that's the case, why was his body found on the sidewalk beneath the boarding house window? It's a weird coincidence, if that's what it is, that Fletcher was the child of one of the women's club members who cared for my ancestor's body. That same Fletcher, grown up, reappears in this story as a government worker assigned to break up collectively held Native lands into individual private properties called allotments.

And weird, too, that a distant cousin I came to meet through the process of reclaiming my Nimiipuu identity, had had the same dream as me. A white hand pushing Ut-sin-malikan out of a window. At the time I had this dream, I didn't know this cousin. It was only later, when we began to share what we knew, that we discovered we had the same dream.

There is one more piece of evidence from Chief Timothy, who was present at the time. One of Timothy's biographers said he believed "that Utes-sen-male-cun had been pushed from a window, and had not died from fever."[10]

The evidence all points to a murder and some sort of cover-up, all unsolved to this day.

Newell wrote in his diary on May 26, 1868, that

> Utes-sin-malikin buried at the Congressional Ground [cemetery] in Washington, DC. Four carriages attended by friends. Went to post office no letters, a warm day. The final vote on Impeachment [of President Andrew Johnson] taken and the result was acquittal. The [Senate] Court adjourned. Great excitement and many feel good and make merry.[11]

Ut-sin-malikan was buried with dignity far away from his home. He left behind on the Nimiipuu reservation a wife and four children, who were by this time adults, one of them being Wah-le-won (Jane Parsons Conditt), my great-grandmother. She was then age 32 and married to Tin-tin-nay-kol-un-kan (Jason Conditt).

Chiefs Lawyer, Timothy, and Jason (no relation to Jason Conditt) stayed in Washington to work on the treaty, and after several months, in August 1868, they signed an amendment which provided for the establishment of a fort at Lapwai, Idaho. This amendment also agreed that timber sales were to be controlled by the tribe, with the US military aiding in the protection of timber on the reservation. Soon after the signing, the chiefs returned to Idaho by train and stagecoach.[12] What did they think as they crossed the plains where the buffalo had once numbered in the hundreds of thousands and now were seeing hardly any. They were witnessing the change of landscape from open ranges to farms, towns, and cities.

When the three remaining chiefs arrived home in September, a feast was held to memorialize and honor Ut-sin-malikan. An old friend of Ut-sin-malikan, Chief Isk-utim, sang an ancient Nimiipuu religious song. Years later, these words were remembered and recorded by Charles "Sol" Webb. Webb was a Nimiipuu man who learned the song from his grandfather, Weptestma'na' (Eagle Feathers in a Row) who died in 1905. As mentioned earlier when I had discovered the song on the vinyl recordings I was elated. The song honors our ancestor, he was a respected chief, he is remembered, not forgotten. Chief Ut-sin-malikan is remembered for his leadership for our family and the Nimiipuu.

> A Ka-mi-kin-ikai Hiwi-hi-nata-tum
> Hiw ya ho lox pa win ti mas hi tse ma
> He ya he ya he ya ya he ya he ya-ya he ya
> He ya he ya he ya ya he ya ya he ya hey
> Ak'I ma ma sit e wes hiw tsi qi newew ku
> Nu ku ha lox pa win ti mes hiw ya tse
> Ma ya he ya he ya he ya he ya
> A he ya he ya Ya-Ya he ya heya
> He ya he ya heya-heya eya eya
> He ya ya heya eya eya he ya a
> He ya ya he ya ya
> Way above, a message travels
> Continually, the Sunday book reports.
> You hear yourself speaking this truth
> Forever, as foretold in the Sabbath Book.[13]

According to this song, Ut-sin-malikan was a truth teller, speaking from his heart. And although he also listened to those around him, he made his own choices.

In 2018, my family worked with the Congressional Cemetery and the United States Department of Veteran Affairs to replace Ut-sin-ma-likan's headstone. The National Cemetery Administration had been trying to contact descendants of Chief Ut-Sin-malikan to begin the process of replacing the crumbling headstone. Michael Brophy, the director of the Baltimore National Cemetery, helped guide us through the headstone design process: what type of stone we could use, and how many lines could be engraved on it. My brother Jesse and I conferred and decided on the words that would be engraved on the memorial:

Chief
Ut-sin-malikan
Nez Perce
1793-1868
Signed treaties
1855 and 1863
Respected leader
A visionary
Spoke truth
Sought justice
for all Nez Perce

My family was already headed to the East coast for the first Native American Boarding School Healing Coalition conference, at which I was giving a presentation. We were also going to commemorate the closing of the Carlisle Indian Industrial boarding school. Since we were in the area, we were able to schedule a ceremony to set the new headstone for Chief Ut-sin-malikan. The ceremony was held on October 9, 2018, Indigenous Peoples' Day, 150 years after our great-great-grandfather's death.

About 25 people were present for the ceremony. In addition to our family members, Facebook postings by both the Congressional Cemetery and *Indian Country Today* newspaper brought several members of the local Native community to the ceremony honoring our ancestor. A descendant of the Nimiipuu was there. He had once been to the Wallowas, the ages-old home of Chief Joseph's band. This man had brought soil from our ancient home, and he gave me a handful wrapped in a cloth bundle. At the base of the headstone, I dug a small hole where I placed this gift.

Michael Brophy gave an opening welcome, and my brother Jesse spoke about finding Newell's journal describing Ut-sin-malikan's last journey. In my remarks, I thanked everyone for coming, and described our struggle to rediscover our family history. We grew up in a time when we were forced to assimilate in order to survive. You didn't need to know your culture, because when you become Christian you are born anew. We were forced to bury our history and our culture. Fortunately, a few people did collect oral histories and stories which have been preserved.

Thus, my family helped rediscover the life of Ut-sin-malikan, who at the age of 12 greeted the first White men to enter Nimiipuu territory, followed by fur traders, missionaries, and US government officials. He was born, as all Nimiipuu had been, in a tepee attended to by his grandmother. He lived according to the seasons. He was taught the responsibilities of a chief and became a warrior. He accepted the friendship of the Whites and seemed to accept the laws given by Spalding, Dr. Elijah White, and Governor Stevens. He fought alongside Colonel George Wright and assisted the military as a scout, even into old age. He abided by the laws given him, but he began to question why the United States did not uphold those laws. He showed much patience during the years of treaty making, but that patience was running out by the time of 1867 council.

When he listened to the non-treaty chiefs in the 1867 council, he said he now respected them. The non-treaty chiefs believe the Ut-sin-malikan was killed because he spoke up for them.

To our family he was a warrior, chief, and beloved ancestor.

Ut-sin-malikan's old headstone with feather and abalone shell, July 2004. *Paul Family Photo Collection.*

The Paul Family at the resetting of Chief Ut-sin-malikan's new headstone at the Congressional Cemetery, on October 9, 2018. In front kneeling is Jesse Paul; standing left to right are Vonda Schuld, Jackie Paul Inglis, Roberta Paul, and Mike Foiles. *Paul Family Photo Collection.*

Ut-sin-malikan's new headstone with inscription, October 9, 2018. *Paul Family Photo Collection.*

Ut-sin-malikan's old and new headstones in the Congressional Cemetery, October 9, 2018. *Paul Family Photo Collection.*

CHAPTER 8

Finding Seven Days Whipping's Story

My great-grandfather was called Wa-tat-ooy-napt-lah-hayne but our family knows him as Seven Days Whipping. We don't know how he got his English-language name. In fact, we hardly know anything about him directly, although much can be inferred, as he lived through a tragic and well-documented period of Nimiipuu history.

My brother Jesse found a list of the names of Nimiipuu warriors who had served in the US Calvary in the Washington and Oregon wars of 1855-1856. Seven Days Whipping's name is on that list, and it's the only document we've found that names him. He would have been a young man, about 18 to 19 years of age during this time. In March 1861, the US Congress agreed to pay these men—but payment wasn't actually made until 1883. By then, my great-grandfather was dead, probably during or shortly after the War of 1877. Seven Days Whipping's name is fiftieth on the list of warriors and is accompanied by this note: "The only heir is a son who is attending school, either at Carlisle or Hampton by name 'Ka-kun-ne.'" Ka-kun-ne, Black Raven, is my grandfather, Jesse Paul, after whom my oldest brother was named. Black Raven, a boy at the time of the War, was at the Carlisle Indian Industrial School in Pennsylvania for eight years starting in 1880.

Seven Days Whipping was born in the Wallowa mountains, in northeastern Oregon, probably in 1836, into the band of Chief Tuekakas, known in English as Old Joseph. Old Joseph was the father of Hin-mah-too-yah-lat-kekht, whose name means Thunder Traveling to Loftier Mountain Heights, but known then simply as Young Joseph. To the world, he is known as Chief Joseph, the man who helped lead his band of Nimiipuu in the War of 1877 and then into exile after being taken prisoners by the Americans, even after they had ceased fighting and surrendered. The future chief was probably a few years younger than my great-grandfather.

Seven Days Whipping was raised to know the Sacred Circle of Life and he lived according to the seasons. Much of his life would have been like that of Young Joseph: they would have been living in the young men's lodge when they reached puberty and raised by the uncles and grandparents they had in common.

The Nimiipuu of the Wallowa mountains and valleys would come to be known as one of the non-treaty bands. However, at least some members of the band were curious and receptive to the messages of Christian missionaries, including Presbyterian missionary Henry Spalding. Spalding arrived at Lapwai, the Place of the Butterflies (near present-day Spalding, Idaho), near the end of November 1836. Old Joseph arrived soon after to spend many months with Spalding, joining hundreds of Nimiipuu who were camped near the Spalding Missions.[1] He was anxious to learn about the Euro-Americans' Great Father. In November 1839, after three years of study, Old Joseph was baptized into the Presbyterian Church by Spalding.[2]

Seven Days Whipping was a child during this time. His parents may have gone with Old Joseph to listen to Spalding, and they would have witnessed these events. In later years he would have heard the retelling of them.

Young Joseph was born in 1840 and was baptized by Spalding in Lapwai on April 12, 1840.[3] Family believes Seven Days Whipping was born around 1836 or 1837. Young Joseph and Seven Days Whipping listened to Spalding preach up until the time of the Whitman Mission Incident in 1847.

According to the census taken by the missionary Asa Smith, Old Joseph's band numbered 168.[4] This wasn't the real number, though, as some band members were not counted because they were on a buffalo hunt in Montana. Although based in the Wallowa mountains, during the winter months the band moved down to the mouth of the Grand Ronde River or the Imnaha River area. When spring came, they returned to higher elevations, to the beautiful Wallowa mountains, valley, and lake. The terrain was rugged but provided the needed foods for subsistence. They would also go to the camas fields (near present-day Weippe, Idaho) that brought all the Nimiipuu together. Here, stories were told of the events that had happened to others: meeting Lewis and Clark, as well as interactions with fur trappers at trading posts and rendezvous. These gatherings provided the time to court and marry a wife. It was perhaps at one of these gatherings that Seven Days Whipping met his wife, Um-al-wat. Later, after Seven Days Whipping died, Um-al-wat would remarry and change her name to Phoebe.

I wanted to find the story of Seven Days Whipping and, digging through my family's papers, I was able to piece together what he was doing during the Treaty time period of 1855. There isn't much to go on, but from the little bit we know, he was paid $33.29 to escort Governor Stevens. He was mustered into a mounted company in the military service of Washington Territory by Captain William Craig on December 15, 1855 and mustered out January 20, 1855.

In the early years of the eighteenth century, few settlers came to the Wallowas due to its remote location in the mountains. But Old Joseph's band ranged widely, and they had either met White trappers themselves or had heard stories at tribal meeting places about the influx of trappers, missionaries, miners, and other settlers. Old Joseph and his people were also anxious about the council that the White leaders called in the Walla Walla Valley, about 100 miles northwest of Wallowa Lake. This council would lead to the Treaty of 1855 and the establishment of the Nez Perce reservation. An 18-year-old Seven Days Whipping was probably one of the 2,500 warriors who paraded through the treaty council grounds that May.[5]

Soon after the Treaty of 1855 had been signed, Governor Stevens still had to finish making treaties with the Flathead and Blackfeet tribes of Montana. He set out, going through Nez Perce country, and several Nez Perce accompanied him. He left June 16, 1855, just five days after the treaty council was concluded, and he was able to negotiate the treaties with both tribes successfully.

On October 28, 1855, Stevens was just about to leave Fort Benton, Montana, when he received word that his life was being threatened by several tribal leaders from the Yakama and Cayuse tribes, after the encroachment of White squatters onto their lands. There had been several skirmishes between the US military and the Yakamas and Cayuse. This news reached the tribes of Coeur d'Alene, Spokanes, and Nimiipuu, who were all anxious about more settlers moving onto their lands. Stevens feared that the tribes would join forces with the Yakama and Cayuse. He decided to cross the Bitterroot Mountains, even though the mountain pass would be high with snow. He arrived at Coeur d'Alene Mission on November 24, 1855.[6]

Stevens wanted to meet with the Coeur d'Alenes, Spokanes, and Colville chiefs to discover whether they were inclined to join forces with the Yakamas and Cayuse. He called for a meeting to be held on the Spokane Tribe lands near Tshimakain Creek on December 3, 1855. The council lasted three days and Stevens listened to the tribes' concerns that the military was coming to remove them to the Nez Perce Reservation. Stevens reassured them that would not happen, because they had not signed the Treaty of 1855. But he wanted to try and make treaties with them now. Chief Spokane Garry told Stevens that there was not enough time to discuss a new treaty now and told him to come back later when he had time. Relieved that these tribes were not joining the Yakamas and Cayuses, Stevens then wanted to learn where the loyalties of the Nez Perce lay. He sent ahead Jim Craig, who was married to a Nez Perce woman, to request help from the Nez Perce.[7]

In the meantime, in early December Pee-o-pee-mox-a-mox of the Cayuse, who trusted neither the soyapuu nor their treaty, encouraged others to go on the war path with him. He wanted to staunch the rush of White settlers onto their lands, since nothing was being done by the US military to stop the encroachment.[8] Pee-o-pee-mox-a-mox's band of followers "captured and plundered" Fort Walla Walla.[9] The military caught up with Pee-o-pee-mox-a-mox and his people at the mouth of the nearby Touchet River, where they battled for four days. Pee-o-pee-mox-a-mox and several of his followers were killed. This incident put an end to the uprising of the Cayuse, Walla Wallas and Umatillas, at least for the moment.[10]

Governor Steven's party arrived at Lapwai on December 8, 1855 and received a warm welcome from Chief Lawyer. The chief had gathered about 2,000 tribal members as well as a force of 800 warriors.[11] Among them were Old Joseph, Ut-sin-malikan, and Seven Days Whipping. Even in late December, with the snow deep and still coming down, the pro-treaty Nimiipuu displayed strong support for the United States. Although Stevens knew that Pee-o-pee-mox-a-mox was dead, he still was nervous about traveling to Fort Walla Walla without an escort. Stevens decided to take 70 Nimiipuu warriors as an escort to Walla Walla, a force that included Seven Days Whipping and Old Joseph. This is the event that mustered Seven Day Whipping into service. Stevens said: "Tomorrow I wish to start for Walla Walla Valley. I want the Nez Perce's, who have horses and guns to go with me." Stevens also tells the Nez Perces about payment: "There will be payment made to you for this service, when the President can be written to, and we receive his answer. You will be paid like the White volunteers."[12]

On December 17, Stevens writes in his report: "This morning ammunition was issued to the Nez-Perce' auxiliaries. Sixty men had guns and 30 others acted as horse guard. Each warrior brought on an average three fine horses."[13] It is not known if Seven Days Whipping had a gun; given his age of 18, most likely not, but he would be one of the horse guards.

They left on a "clear night, bright, and frosty morning," December 15, 1855. The governor's son, Hazard (the first White man known to have climber Mt. Rainer) later recalled the journey:

> Here were the gentlemen of the party, with their black fur hats and heavy cloth overcoats; rough clad miners and packers; the mountain men with buckskin shirts and leggings and fur caps; the long-eared pack-mules, with their bulky loads; and the blanketed young braves, with painted visage, and hair adorned with eagle feathers, mounted on sleek and spirited mustangs, and dashing hither and thither in the greatest excitement and glee. Each of the warriors had three fine, spirited horses, which he rode in turn as the fancy moved him...The demeanor of the young braves on this march was in sharp contrast to the traditional gravity and stoicism of their race. They shouted, laughed, told stories, cracked jokes, and gave free vent to their native gayety and high spirits. Craig, [a mountain man] who accompanied the party, translated these good things as they occurred, to great amusement of the whites.[14]

According to records, the whole journey to Fort Walla Walla was bitterly cold, with one night the temperature plummeting to 27 degrees below zero. They reach Fort Walla Walla on December 24, 1885.[15] The warriors would have been "blanketed"; I also suspect Seven Days Whipping and the other warriors had buffalo robes to keep them warm. They were toughened and inured to the cold by the cultural practice of bathing in cold water even during the winter months.[16] (I have tried this a few times when I was younger, an experience that left me very chilled and I am in awe of the Nimiipuu warriors who endured this very cold journey.) On December 31, under the command of Captain William Craig, the Nez Perce volunteers leave Fort Walla Walla and return to Idaho. Soon after their arrival back home, they are mustered out of service on January 20, 1856.[17]

Like the discovery of gold in California, gold found within the boundaries of the Nez Perce Reservation brought an invasion of seekers—the usual panners, provisioners, and camp followers. The remote Wallowa area was not much affected, but the members of Joseph's band would have heard the many complaints of their neighbors. They too would begin to question the trustworthiness of the United States and doubt its ability to uphold the treaty promises, including the one to keep Whites off their lands. This is one of the reasons given for the reduction of the 1855 Treaty. When the 1863 Treaty was signed, Old Joseph was not one of the signatory chiefs nor were others whose land was to be included in the reduction. The Treaty was called the "Steal Treaty" by the non-treaty tribes, because their lands was signed away without their agreement or permission.

Old Joseph thought he was safe from the obligation of the 1863 Treaty because he had not signed the treaty. Several of the other non-treaty chief's also thought the same. Even though the Treaty of 1863 stated that all those living off the now reduced reservation would have to move within the new boundaries, the government could not enforce this because the treaty was not ratified until April 1867. Old Joseph and his village continued living as usual. However, soon after the Treaty of 1863 was ratified, government surveyors came to the Wallowas to lay out townships, which caused alarm among the Wallowa band. Old Joseph responded by setting out his own stakes marking the Wallowa band's territory. He was determined to show that Euro-Americans and Native peoples could live side by side. For a while, at least, this approach seemed to work.[18]

Seven Days Whipping would witness the death of Old Joseph in August 1871. He stood with Young Chief Joseph as his childhood friend took over the duties of leading the band and continued the struggle to keep the Wallowas for his people. But settlers and their livestock just kept pouring in and tensions were mounting over grazing issues and who had the right to what lands.[19]

Finally, in 1873, Young Joseph convinced Indian Agent Monteith that it was never the custom of the Nimiipuu to have a single head chief. Rather, they were divided into bands, each with its own chief. Each Nimiipuu band "claimed, occupied, and held the land within certain natural boundaries."[20] When the Whites had named Lawyer head chief, they had made a mistake because no single person had the right to sign away the Wallowas.[21] Monteith recommended setting aside the upper Wallowa Valley for Joseph and his band and that the lower Wallowa Valley be set aside for the small group of Euro-Americans settling there. (Today, the area is still sparsely populated.) The government acted quickly, and President Grant declared a portion of the Wallowas a reservation by executive order. But, due to a bureaucratic error, the lands that had been recommended for Joseph and the Whites were reversed. The lands in the "upper part of the river" were given to the Whites, instead of to Joseph's band.[22]

In 1873-74, White settlers rebelled against the executive order and used their political strength to have it rescinded. Because of the 1863 Treaty, they were under the assumption that the Wallowas were part of the lands ceded to the United States, and that these lands had been opened for settlement. This was the argument that Oregon governor Grover used, along with the congressmen from Oregon.

There were conflicts between Joseph's band and the White settlers. Joseph's older men helped avoid a full outbreak of war in the region. There were only 87 settlers in the Wallowas, but they proved to be powerful in motivating support to keep their "improved" lands. The protests of the settlers and the support of the Oregon Governor and congressmen led to President Grant rescinding the order on June 10, 1875.[23]

Monteith told Joseph the news. Almost immediately, Joseph's warriors, as well as warriors from the other bands affected by the 1863 treaty, held a council to discuss going to war against the Whites. These warriors included Eagle from the Light, White Bird, Looking Glass, and Toohoolhoolzote. Cooler heads prevailed, however, with White Bird, Looking Glass, Ollokot, and Joseph saying it would be foolhardy to go to war. The tribal shamans, too, urged them to be cautious.[24]

For years, murders of Nimiipuu people went unsolved or unpunished, and tensions mounted between settlers and Nimiipuu. Joseph continued to try to convince the government that the Wallowas belonged to him and his band, having been passed onto him by his father, Old Joseph. In late 1876, General Howard agreed to form a commission to settle the land disputes. But the commissioners' minds were already made up to move the non-treaty bands onto the Nez Perce Reservation.[25]

In November 1876, Chief Joseph met with the government commissioners, who demanded that Joseph and his band give up the Wallowas. They had a long list of justifications for moving and offered Joseph funds for the adjustment of present difficulties as well as help with moving. Joseph said no, replying:

> The creative Power, when he made the earth, made no marks, no lines of division or separation on it. The earth is my mother. I am made of the earth and grew up on its bosom. The earth, as my mother and nurse, is

sacred to my affections, too sacred to be valued by or sold for silver or gold. I cannot consent to sever my affections from the land that bore me. I ask nothing of the President. I am able to take care of myself.[26]

The Council ended with no progress. Joseph and his band were labeled malcontents for refusing to bow to the authority of the United States. In Joseph's thinking, the problem was with the Euro-Americans taking land that did not belong to them while at the same time calling themselves a just people. Joseph used this analogy to describe the Americans' way of making a deal:

> Suppose a white man should come to me and say, "Joseph, I like your horses, and I want to buy them," he said. I say to him, "No, my horses suit me, I will not sell them." Then he goes to my neighbor, and says to him: "Joseph has some good horses. I want to buy them, but he refuses to sell." My neighbor answers, "Pay me the money, and I will sell you Joseph's horses." The white man returns to me and says, "Joseph, I have bought your horses, and you must let me have them." If we sold our lands to the Government, this is the way they were bought.[27]

The commissioners did take note of a longstanding grievance, that the United States had failed to live up to its treaty obligations. The money promised for their service in the war of 1855-1856 was still unpaid, as was the debt for horses the Nimiipuu had supplied to the Calvary. Chief Joseph's father and others, including Seven Days Whipping, were among those not yet paid.

Chief Joseph again left the meeting thinking his people's land had not been sold to the Whites and that they maintained their sovereignty. However, the commission continued to meet after Joseph's band and others left. The commission decided that Joseph and all the other non-treaty bands would be moved to the reservation as soon as possible. Indian Agent Monteith was so instructed on January 6, 1877, and General O. O. Howard was ordered to enforce the move.[28]

Monteith conveyed the news to Joseph's band by way of four treaty Nimiipuu: Joseph's brother-in-law James Reuben, father-in-law Whisk-tasket, a nephew, and Old Captain John. They tried to persuade Joseph to come onto the reservation, but Joseph replied:

> I have been talking to the whites many years about the land questions, and it is strange they cannot understand me. The country they claim

belonged to my father, and when he died it was given to me and my people, and I will not leave it until I am compelled to.[29]

Seven Days Whipping, too, had fathers, grandfathers, and mothers buried in the Wallowas. This was another stab in the heart. The Nimiipuu, for whom the notions of treaties, reservations, and the myth of "improvement" were absurd and unsustainable, were betrayed once again by the pro-treaty Nimiipuu, who sided with the US government.

A meeting on May 3, 1877, was set to determine when the move to the reservation would take place. Monteith, Howard, Joseph, Ollokot, and the other non-treaty chiefs converged on Lapwai, Idaho. Others who came included White Bird, Looking Glass, and Toohoolhoolzote. They made one more plea for the other non-treaty Natives to be allowed to remain on their ancestral lands.[30]

The first to arrive were Joseph, Ollokot, and their friend, Young Chief of the Cayuse, and fifty members of the Wallowa Nimiipuu. They approached the fort in a column, the men in the lead, followed by women and children, all in their full regalia, and singing proudly." The men wore brightly colored blankets over beaded buckskins, their faces and the partings of their hair were painted red, and their hair was braided and tied with colorful cloth. Next came the women, also in bright blankets and shawls."[31] Seven Days Whipping was among this group. Most of the women and children had stayed behind near the mouth of the Grand Ronde River, so his wife and children were likely there, too. Others at the fort were the pro-treaty Nimiipuu, many of whom were wearing American-style clothing, creating a visible contrast between the two groups.[32]

Agent Monteith told Joseph and the others that they must move onto the reservation. General Howard, the enforcer, would stay until matters were settled. Toohoolhoolzote again emphasized the fact that they had not sold their lands and that the earth was in fact their mother:

> The Great Spirit Chief made the world as it is and as he wanted it, and he made a part of it for us to live upon. I do not see where you get authority to say that we shall not live where he placed us.[33]

Neither side could understand the reasoning of the other, and it appeared that no amount of talking would bring the matter to a peaceful resolution. Whatever General Howard and Monteith really thought, they were now in the position of having to be obedient to the Secretary of the Interior and to their country.

The next day, Toohoolhoolzote continued to insist that the earth was their mother and that they could not leave her. Howard finally had enough of this resistance and ordered Toohoolhoolzote arrested. Howard spoke to the remaining non-treaty tribes people, saying, "Will you go with me to look for reservation land?"[34] Given Howard's heavy hand, what choice did Joseph, White Bird, and Looking Glass have?

Joseph and the other non-treaty chiefs agreed to go with Howard and Monteith to select sites for their bands. Over the next few days, they rode over the reservation looking for desirable places for their bands. After all had made their choices, they returned to Lapwai on May 12, only to find that US troops were encroaching on Joseph's village on the Grand Ronde River and that more troops had arrived at Fort Walla Walla.[35]

On the morning of May 14, 1877, General Howard released Toohoolhoolzote and gave final instructions to the bands of Young Joseph, Looking Glass, and White Bird, telling them they had thirty days and no more to move to the reservation.[36] The rivers were full with the spring runoff and the bands asked why now: couldn't they wait until the fall when the rivers were low and they had time to gather their herds of horses and cattle? What was the hurry? It had already been nine years since the government had begun trying to move them onto the reservation. What would a few more months matter?

According to *Chief Joseph's Own Story*, Joseph thought Howard replied, "in a haughty spirit." Joseph recalled what Howard said to him and the other non-treaty chiefs:

> If you let the time run over one day the soldiers will be there to drive you on the reservation and all your cattle and horses outside of the reservation at that time will fall into the hands of the white men.[37]

Chief Joseph later recalled what he felt at the time:

> I knew I had never sold my country and that I had no land in Lapwai; but I did not want bloodshed. I did not want my people killed. I did not want anybody killed. Some of my people had been murdered by white men, and the white murderers were never punished for it… I said in my heart that, rather than have war I would give up my country, I would rather give up my father's grave. I would give up everything rather than have blood of white men upon the hands of my people.[38]

On May 15, 1877, the chiefs and their men set out with heavy hearts. They returned to their ancestral lands bearing the bad news. Seven Days Whipping was probably with this group. His wife, Um-al-wat, and their six children would be among those having to leave. The villagers must have been asking themselves, do we go in peace or do we stay and fight to the death? Their hearts had to have been heavy with grief, anger, and disbelief. Questioning themselves. Do we really have to leave the lands that have been ours since time immemorial? Knowing that troops were present in the country, they had no choice but to move peaceably or be moved by force.

Upon their return to the Wallowas, Chief Joseph held a council, which included all adult men and women of the village. They decided to move immediately to avoid bloodshed.[39] Young Joseph must have had a strong heart to stand up against the talk of war by the angry Toohoolhoolzote, who was inciting the young warriors of the Wallowa Band. Seven Days Whipping, being one of the older warriors, perhaps helped calm the waters.

Wa-tat-oyee-napt-la-hayne, (Seven Days Whipping) age 44 or 45 taken around 1870. *Paul Family Photo Collection.*

Um-al-wat (Phoebe Lowry), wife of Seven Days Whipping. Photo taken around 1890. *Paul Family Photo Collection.*

Wallowa Lake: Homelands of the Wallowa Nez Perce and Chief Joseph Band. *Paul Family Photo Collection.*

The War of 1877

We don't know which of Um-al-wat and Seven Days Whipping's six children were male or female, except for Black Raven, my grandfather. Black Raven was born about 1870, so was seven or eight when he and his family had to leave their ancestral home. The family would have packed their belongings, a familiar task to those who lived with the seasons, going from the winter campgrounds of the valleys to the spring camps around Wallowa Lake. But this time, the move would be permanent and would take them far from their beloved Wallowas, still one of the world's most beautiful places. How sad and heavy their hearts must have been as they packed. My great-grandparents and their children were leaving the lands of their ancestors, the lands where they had lived in harmony with the seasonal cycle of life. No more would they roam freely to live as they had for thousands of years. Never again would they see the sunset over the Wallowas or feel the fresh winds flowing over the mountains.

Seven Days Whipping would have been out with the other men gathering in the horses and cattle. They had several thousand head of cattle and horses spread across the rugged hills of the Wallowa mountains, valleys, canyons, and prairies. They did the best they could, but many, and probably most, were left behind.[1]

Finally, they set out for the Snake River and the crossing at Dug Bar, located a few miles east of where the Imnaha River runs into the Snake on what is now the Idaho-Oregon state line. The men made rafts and bullboats from buffalo hides. They piled children and old people on top of luggage and three or four ponies with riders towed each raft across the high, icy cold, swift-running water. On the other side, their possessions were spread out for thousands of yards along the river. They drove their cattle and horses across the river, but many were swept away. Hundreds of animals were lost to the high water and swift currents.

The crossing took two days. They rested for a few days before moving on to the agreed-upon area to meet the other non-treaty bands at Tepahlewam (Split Rocks or Deep Cuts) on the Camas Prairie beside Tolo Lake near present-day Grangeville, Idaho.² Most of the people managed to arrive at this area by June 2, 1877, just twelve days before they had to be on the reservation.

At Tepahlewam, the women gathered camas while the young men raced on their horses and played stick games. Chief Joseph's band numbered about 55–60 men, with another 100 or so women and children. The bands of White Bird, Toohoolhoolzote, and Looking Glass were a little smaller. Even though Looking Glass did not have to relocate, as his people were already living within the boundaries of the reservation, he was considered non-treaty because he had not signed the treaty of 1863 and he always sided with the other non-treaty bands. Also present were two small bands from the Palouse: they were Hahtalekin and Husishusis Kute, who lived at the confluence of the Palouse and Snake rivers. They had not signed any treaties and had aligned themselves with the non-treaty Nimiipuu. The gathering at Tepahlewam numbered about 600 to 650, with a total of 190 male warriors.³

Seven Days Whipping and his family were now camped, and the women dug camas to be prepared and preserved for winter use. Um-al-wat and children would be digging along with the other women of the camp. Some of the boys and young men would gamble on horse races.⁴ Those at the camp felt the tensions of the young warriors who were still angry at having to give up their ancestral lands and who did not always agree with the elders about moving on in peace.

The War of 1877 and its aftermath affected my family at a very deep level. I include here some of the events that led to the war of 1877, as understanding helps begin the process of healing. Seeking healing and reconciliation, my family and I have visited Big Hole and Bear Paw several times.

Many of the young warriors felt that the Nimiipuu should fight—not only for their ancestral homes, but to right the injustices against Nimiipuu whose murders had gone unpunished. One young warrior, Wahlitits, meaning Shore Crossing, was especially outraged by the unpunished murder of his father, Eagle Robe. Shore Crossing's father had shared his land with a White man called Larry Ott, but Ott fenced in Eagle Robe's garden, claiming it for himself. When Eagle Robe protested, Ott took out his pistol and shot him, mortally wounding him.⁵

Shore Crossing was also angry about the insult to his leader, Chief Toohoolhoolzote, who had been thrown into a guard house merely for speaking his heart. Shore Crossing enlisted his cousins Sarpsis Ilppilp (Red Moccasin Tops) and Wetyetmas Wyakaikt (Swan Necklace). The three set out to seek revenge on Ott, even though Eagle Robe had warned his son not to seek revenge but "to let the cruel white man live."[6]

The cousins did not find Ott but they did find another White man, Richard Devine, known to have set his dogs on any Natives he crossed paths with, and who had murdered a disabled Nimiipuu man.[7] The three warriors killed Devine. Filled with rage, they killed another White man, Henry Elfers, who was also "hostile to Indians."[8] Shore Crossing and Red Moccasin Tops continued down the Salmon River, bent on revenge, and not wanting to return to the Wallowa band's camp for fear Joseph's people would be implicated by their actions. Instead, they sent Swan Necklace back to the camp at Tepahlewam to tell the people what had transpired. Swan Necklace rode through the camp on a roan stallion stolen from Elfers, calling out the news. This report alarmed the Indians gathered there, as they were concerned that this would start a war. Almost immediately, the women began taking down the tepees and packing. Some of the other young warriors mounted their horses and went to join Shore Crossing on the Salmon River.[9]

All this took place while Chief Joseph and his brother Ollokot had gone back across the Salmon River to continue bringing the cattle herd, and butchering some for provisions. Seven Days Whipping and his family would have been at the Tepahlewam camp. Joseph and his brother were almost back at Tepahlewam when they heard the news of the killings. At the camp, they encouraged the others to stay and meet the soldiers to make peace.[10] The Wallowa Band stayed the night, but the other bands left and went to Sapachesap (Drive-In[11]), a cave on Cottonwood Creek.

During the night, a small group of Whites rode to Tepahlewam and surrounded the Wallowa band. The Whites had gotten close enough to be heard when suddenly a shot was fired. The bullet went through a tepee. Yellow Wolf responded by returning fire, but missed. The next morning, Chief Joseph and others decided to go to Sapachesap for the safety of all.

In the following days, there were more attacks by both the Nimiipuu and the settlers, which resulted in the bands of Toohoolhoolzote, White Bird, Paloos, and Chief Joseph all moving on to Lahmotta or White Bird Canyon, a place of safety.[12] Chief Looking Glass and KoolKool returned to their homes on the Clearwater River on June 10, both not wanting war. All these events occurred between June 2 and June 16, 1877.

The families of the bands were safe, but they were beginning to wonder what would happen next. The bands of Chief Joseph, White Bird, Toohoolhoolzote, and Husishusis Kute, a Palouse leader, were still hoping to avoid war. They knew the US military soldiers were on their way and would soon arrive at Lahmotta (now known as White Bird Canyon), a winter home of the White Bird band.[13] The soldiers arrived sooner than they feared.

On the morning of June 17, the first full battle between the Nimiipuu and the United States took place. The evening before, the chiefs and older men decided to send out a peace team of six warriors carrying a white flag when the soldiers appeared. At the same time, the old men, women, and children were directed to drive the stock to a safe area, and the warriors were told to prepare to defend the people.

The soldiers appeared at the top of White Bird Hill and slowly began their descent. The Nimiipuu were all in place, hidden and ready. The truce team rode out with the white flag, but when the soldiers came upon them suddenly, they either did not notice the white flag, or chose to ignore it, and fired.[14] We don't know if Seven Days Whipping was among the warriors. There were reports that many of the men were drunk and unable to fight, and there were those who chose not to fight, and others who were otherwise unable to fight. Seven Days Whipping's wife, Um-al-wat and their six children were safe in camp, out of sight of the fighting but able to hear the shooting.

Despite the cavalry's superior arms, the day ended in victory for the Nimiipuu. According to Yellow Wolf, many of the warriors were armed only with bows and arrows, with a few owning muzzle-loaders, fur trade muskets, and old shot guns. There were only about 65 warriors fighting that day.[15] The US force totaled about 110 soldiers and volunteers.[16]

What the chiefs and elders had tried to avoid—war—exploded into a conflict that would force them to retreat over 1,170 miles across four states, a journey lasting more than five months. Once they surrendered, the Nimiipuu were taken prisoner and held in exile for many years. Some, including Chief Joseph, were never allowed to return home. The Nez Perce War of 1877 has been well documented by numerous historians; I do not wish to retell all that happened. Rather, my intent is to share the events that affected my family, events about which we are still trying to find the truth and the wounds from which we are trying to heal.

Having found Yellow Wolf's story about the Nez Perce War of 1877, I had a clearer understanding of why and how my great-grandparents and grandfather both lived and survived this horrific time. Even as I try and tell the chronological order of the different battles that affected my family, I still cry and weep in the retelling.

I have visited most of the sites that affected our family. At each site I have varying reactions. At White Bird, I feel the tensions of the warriors arguing: "Do we go to war or not?" I feel my great-grandmother Um-al-wat worrying, "Will I be able to keep my children safe?"

But most of all I marvel at the strength she had to gather her children and move all their possessions on horses and travois. At each place where they stopped for more than a night's rest, she had the ability to prepare food from the preserved foods she had brought with her. It was the women who put up and took down the tepees. They had the dried foods packed away in baskets ready to be transported. They had the practice of moving all their possessions from summer camp to winter camp and wherever they needed to gather foods.

🐦 🐦 🐦

What I do not know is how she could spiritually, emotionally, and physically go on living after the loss of five of her children and her husband Seven Days Whipping. My grandfather was her only surviving son. As a parent, you fight to protect your children and keep living so they can live. You will do whatever it takes to protect your family.

The sequence of events that followed the White Bird Battle included several smaller encounters which added to the tensions, fear, and misunderstandings on both sides. At first, Chief Looking Glass's band was not aligned with those of Joseph, White Bird, and Toohoolhoolzote. But then his village on the middle fork of the Clearwater River, near present-day Kooskia, Idaho, was attacked. When one of his men came out to meet the soldiers with a white flag, a soldier shot into the village. On July 1, 1877, a skirmish ensued, and Looking Glass's band fled. The soldiers destroyed tepees and gardens and scattered the cattle and horses.[17] Looking Glass and his band joined the others who had set up camp at Peeta Auuwa (Peeta at Mouth of Canyon) near present-day Stites, Idaho.[18] Upon hearing of the attack on Looking Glass, Chief Halaklekin of the Paloos would join the Nimiipuu in the coming battles.[19]

General Howard was ordered to use his entire force to pursue the Nimiipuu and keep them within the Craig Mountain region. And pursue he did. The next battle occurred at the camp site of Peeta Auuwa on July 11 and 12. Four were killed and six wounded,[20] which is remarkable considering that Howard's forces numbered 560, and the Nimiipuu less than 100. On the afternoon of the second day, a small group of Nimiipuu warriors was able to hold the Americans at bay, while the main body of the Nimiipuu began their retreat to Kamiah, crossing the Clearwater and heading for the Weippe Prairie.

The Weippe Prairie was the site where Lewis and Clark happened upon the Nimiipuu 72 years earlier. The Nimiipuu had welcomed these strange White men, and Lewis and Clark had said they came in peace, and those that followed them would also come in peace. This statement was both tragic and ironic, for now the Nimiipuu were fleeing from White soldiers because the Whites could not live in peace in the same country with the Nimiipuu.

A council was held to decide what should be done: to stay and fight or to leave the area and try to find peace. During the council, it was decided that Chief Looking Glass would become the war leader. He encouraged the Nimiipuu to go to Crow country, away from the Whites of Idaho. It would be different in Montana: the White settlers there did not have a quarrel with the Nimiipuu. If they could not find peace with the Crow, then they should go on up to Canada to Chief Sitting Bull's camp. There they could stay until the bad feelings had died down and they could return. Not all agreed, but all knew that if they did not go, they would be left behind and they would be captured and possibly hanged.[21]

On the morning of July 16, the bands of Looking Glass, Joseph, White Bird, Toohoolhoolzote, and the Paloos bands of Husishusis Kute and

Hahtalekin gathered their supplies. All told, they were a group of 200 men and nearly 550 women and children, with 2,000 horses and pack animals. They began their trek toward the foothills of the Bitterroot Mountains, over which they would cross on the Lolo Trail. Seven Days Whipping, Um-al-wat, and their six children were depending on Looking Glass, who had crossed this trail many times to hunt buffalo in Montana. Looking Glass had also fought with the Crow against the Sioux.[22] At the same time, to pour salt in the wound and deepen the divisions within the Nimiipuu, Christian treaty Nimiipuu served as scouts for General Howard, some of whom could have been from Ut-sin-malikan's band.

I marvel at the mastery of the Nimiipuu ability to manage the rugged terrain of the trail and to maneuver through overgrown brush, narrow trails, and slippery rocks. They managed to cross the Bitterroots into Montana in nine days, arriving on July 25, five days ahead of General Howard. However, the general had wired ahead to a new post at Missoula with a small detachment of men under the command of Captain Charles C. Rawn. (The telegraph arrived in Montana in 1866.) There was also alarm among the settlers in the Bitterroot Valley, and they had mustered about 35 volunteers to go with Rawn to meet the Nimiipuu to ask them to surrender. This proposal was turned down by the chiefs. Then Looking Glass proposed a truce or armistice with the settlers, telling them the war was behind them and that they wanted to pass peaceably to buffalo country. The settlers agreed without telling Rawn.[23]

While they were traveling leisurely through the Bitterroot Valley, several Nimiipuu had dreams of impending danger. There was also an uneasiness felt among them. A member of the tribe called Wahlitits had a prophetic dream that has been preserved:

> My brothers, my sisters, I am telling you! In a dream last night I saw myself killed. I will be killed soon! I do not care. I am willing to die. But first, I will kill some soldiers. I shall not turn back from the death We are all going to die![24]

Another tribe member, Lone Bird, was uneasy with their slow movement through the valley. He rode through camp saying:

> My shaking heart tells me trouble and death will overtake us if we make no hurry through this land! I can not smother; I can not hide that which I see. I must speak what is revealed to me. Let us be gone to the buffalo country.[25]

Even with these warnings and the uneasiness felt by many, the bands moved slowly through the valley, buying supplies from the settlers. After several days, the bands reached Izhkumzizlakik, Big Hole, a camp long used while hunting in buffalo country, on August 7. Located on the Big Hole River at the confluence of Trail and Ruby creeks, the surrounding area was flat prairie with plenty of grazing land for the horses.[26]

At Big Hole, the bands expected they would be able to stay long enough to season tepee poles that could be dragged to Crow country. The women set about cutting poles, gathering camas bulbs, and cooking to replenish supplies.[27] Eighty-nine tepees were set up. Great-grandmother Um-al-wat would have been among the women doing this work. The children played games, the men went hunting, and life seemed almost normal. They must have felt the human instinct of wanting their usual routines, but still there was an uneasiness about what the warrior had dreamt.

Several warriors approached Looking Glass to request a scouting trip, but he declined. Many among the group thought the war was behind them, and as they had just passed through the Bitterroot Valley peacefully, there was no need to conduct further scouting trips.[28]

On August 4, Colonel John Gibbon set out in pursuit of the Nimiipuu with a force of 146 men commanded by 15 officers and bolstered by 34 citizen volunteers. Gibbon sent out scouts who soon located the Nimiipuu. Traveling through the night, he and his men got to Big Hole on August 8, where they took cover in a small stand of trees. There they waited for a signal to launch a surprise attack on the sleeping camp in the early morning of August 9.[29] Gibbon had not come to ask the Nimiipuu to surrender—he was there to kill, and when the volunteers asked if they should take prisoners, it became clear that Gibbon wanted no prisoners.[30]

> The Pre-dawn hours of August 9, the Palouse leader, Hahtalekin, went out to check on the horse herd, he was shot after a brief exchange with the soldiers. Before he fell, Hahtalekin sounded a warning.[31]

More gunfire lit up the dark as soldiers fired into the camp, into tepees, and at anyone who came out of the tepees. Most Nimiipuu were sound asleep and at first thought they were dreaming. Yellow Wolf described his first awareness of being under attack:

It must have been about three o'clock in the morning, just before daylight, when I heard it—a gun—two guns! I knew not what was the trouble. The sound was like a small gun, not close. I was half sleeping. I lay with eyes closed. Maybe I was dreaming? I did not think what to do! Then I was awake.... I grabbed my moccasins and with others ran out of the tepee. I only had a war club.... Men and women were lying flat on the ground, listening.... I heard one woman call out, "Why not all men get ready and fight? Not run away!"[32]

There was confusion all around. The men were caught off guard, and many did not have their guns nearby or had no guns at all. Where were Seven Days Whipping and Um-al-wat? Did gun shots come whizzing through their tepee? Did they run, or did they try to stay inside hoping the shooting would not last long? Maybe they acted as described by the oral history given by Young White Bird, who was about nine years old at the time:

Right away the troops began shooting. Bullets were like hail on the camp; on the tepees. The noise was like Gatling guns, as I have since heard them. The sound awoke me. I heard bullets ripping the tepee walls, pattering like raindrops. I did as my mother told me. Horses hitched overnight, ready to go for the other horses, were all killed. I ran only a little ways when I came to a low place in the ground. I stopped and lay down. Several women were there, and mother came fast after me. I heard the voice of a man speaking very loud. He came where we were lying and called, "Soldiers right on us. Are now in our camp. Get away somewhere. You will be killed or captured."

Mother picked me up, saying, "Come, son, let us get away somewhere." She took my right hand in her left and we ran. A bullet took off her middle finger, end of her thumb, and shot off my thumb as you see. The same bullet did it all. Mother pointed to the creek and said, "Get down to the water! Then we may escape."[33]

Somehow, some of the people, including many of the women and children, knew to run to the creek for safety. Those who remained behind were murdered while sleeping in their tepees. Another survivor, Eelahweeman, who was twelve years old at the time, hid in a shallow of the river with his younger brother and five women, including his mother. He later reported, "When the soldiers saw us they began shooting at us. I saw one woman killed. It was my mother.... I looked around and saw all four of the other women had been killed."[34] Still another account tells of a woman who had given birth just the night before. She was killed in her tepee, her baby at her breast with its head smashed in.[35] Many deaths, much confusion….yet the warriors were able to rally and fight back.

Yellow Wolf described how the warriors responded:

> These soldiers came rapidly…. I now saw tepees on fire. I grew hot with anger. Women, children, and old men who could not fight were in those tepees. Up there above that old pole bridge crossing the creek—about one hundred steps from the blazing tepees—I heard an Indian voice loudly announcing: "My brothers! Our tepees are on fire! Get ready your arms! Make Resistance! You are here for that purpose!" He was answered with war whoops by those who had guns.[36]

Yellow Wolf explained that it was just a few warriors who drove the soldiers back. He said, "If whipped, better to die than go in bondage with freedom gone."[37] The fighting abated for a while, after someone hollered an order, "All the brave warriors have been killed, with Sarpsis Ilppilp our last best man. We must stop now until later on. We will then fight again."[38] With this mid-morning order, the Nimiipuu warriors returned to camp to view a most awful sight.

Many of the warriors found their wives, children, and horses dead and their tepees destroyed. There is no accurate record of how many died. Many were buried secretly so they would not be found. Still others died along the trail as they were retreating. The estimate varies from 60 to 100. All families were affected.[39] Did Seven Day Whipping find his children among the dead? Where was his wife Um-al-wat? How did she escape? When they found each other, was Um-al-wat crying and holding onto her only surviving child? "HOW?" is the question that I keep asking. Where did my great-grandparents muster the strength to bury their children and move on?

The survivors asked each other how anyone could kill women, children, and the old, none of whom could defend themselves. Even over the painfully loud sounds of guns firing, could they not have heard the cries of grief? Gibbon's response, recorded after the war, was cold comfort:

> In his report he stated that it was not yet light when the soldiers charged the camp and they were unable to distinguish the warriors from the non-combatants. Second, women fired on the soldiers from the tepees and had to be fired on in return.[40]

Gibbon's statement conflicts with what he'd told the volunteers, who stated that they understood they were not to take prisoners. The murder of the elderly, women, and children was a horrific wound not only to our family but for the Nimiipuu who lost their loved ones. It is a wound that is still being healed to this day. The excuses that Gibbon gave for the killings were that some women were fighting back, which, according to a 98-year old woman survivor named Penahwenonmi (Helping Another), there was only one woman who fought; she was Wahlitits's (Shore Crossing) pregnant wife who shot the trooper who had murdered her husband.[41] Gibbon blamed the deaths on the early morning darkness; the women and children were fired on because they were running away from their tepees. This suggests that if they had stayed in their burning tepees, they would not have been shot. He was deaf to the screams of children burning alive in the tepees and he did not mention the one lodge in which five children sheltering there were murdered.[42]

A Nimiipuu warrior did not kill women and children in battle. Chief Joseph said: "never make war on women and children; we could have killed a great many women and children while the war lasted, but we would feel ashamed to do so cowardly an act."[43]

By the afternoon of August 9, the Nimiipuu had control of their camp again. Nimiipuu warriors dismantled the Gatling gun and make off with a load of ammunition. They were able to save most of their possessions and supplies. The women stanched the bleeding wounds with cold mud packs. Those who were able dug shallow graves to bury their loved ones. The warriors gathered up firearms and ammunition from the dead soldiers. Thanks to Joseph and Teminisiki (No Heart), they were able to get most of their herd of two thousand horses and keep them away from the soldiers. That evening of August 9, a council was held to plan their retreat. Everyone was to pack and make ready for travel, and the families were to go. They began to pack up the camp and leave while still dark, on the morning of August 10. Several warriors stayed behind trying to locate injured people before the Indian scouts could kill them. They put their wounded on travois or tied them to saddles. Many of the wounded died and were buried along the trail. The Nimiipuu dead and wounded were hidden or carried away to confuse the military's efforts to count how many have been killed.[44] Gibbon reported finding eighty-three dead, mostly women and children. The Nez Perce estimates of fatalities ranged from forty-three to a hundred. [45]

General Howard showed up to Big Hole on August 11, two days after the Big Hole battle. Upon his arrival, his troops helped bury the dead soldiers. Howard's Bannock Indian scouts (known enemies of the Nimiipuu) found the graves of the Nimiipuu and dug them up, mutilated and scalped them, and left the remains on the field. It was reported by Howard that wolves and grizzlies later fed on the bodies.[46]

Not all the bodies were found. A few years ago at the Big Hole National Battlefield, an archelogy team unearthed a human female skeleton whose chest had been split open.[47] It was also reported that there are most likely other bodies and the Nimiipuu descendants did not want to disturb them.

I do not know what happened to my great-grandfather and great-grandmother and their six children. The only clue I have found is my grandfather Black Raven's testimony regarding the estate of his mother, Um-al-wat (by then known as Phoebe Lowry). Black Raven said, "I am the only one living."

I have had dreams of this battle many times and I am almost certain this is where Black Raven's siblings lost their lives. To me and my family, a surprise attack on a sleeping camp is murder. Along with the dreams comes a deep ache in my heart. I don't know if Seven Days Whipping died that day or later, in exile. Family oral history says he did survive the battles and made it to exile and died somewhere in one of the camps. I have searched the lists of Nimiipuu in exile and have not found either of his names. Since many Nimiipuu had several names over the course of a lifetime, it's possible that's why I can't find him: he simply went by a different name in later years. Or he could be one of the unidentified Nimiipuu warriors who died in battle. What is known is that great-grandmother Um-al-wat was widowed sometime after the battle at Big Hole and remarried while in exile.

Big Hole Battlefield, near Wisdom, Montana. *Paul Family Photo Collection.*

The tepee poles at the Big Hole Battlefield campsite. *Paul Family Photo Collection*

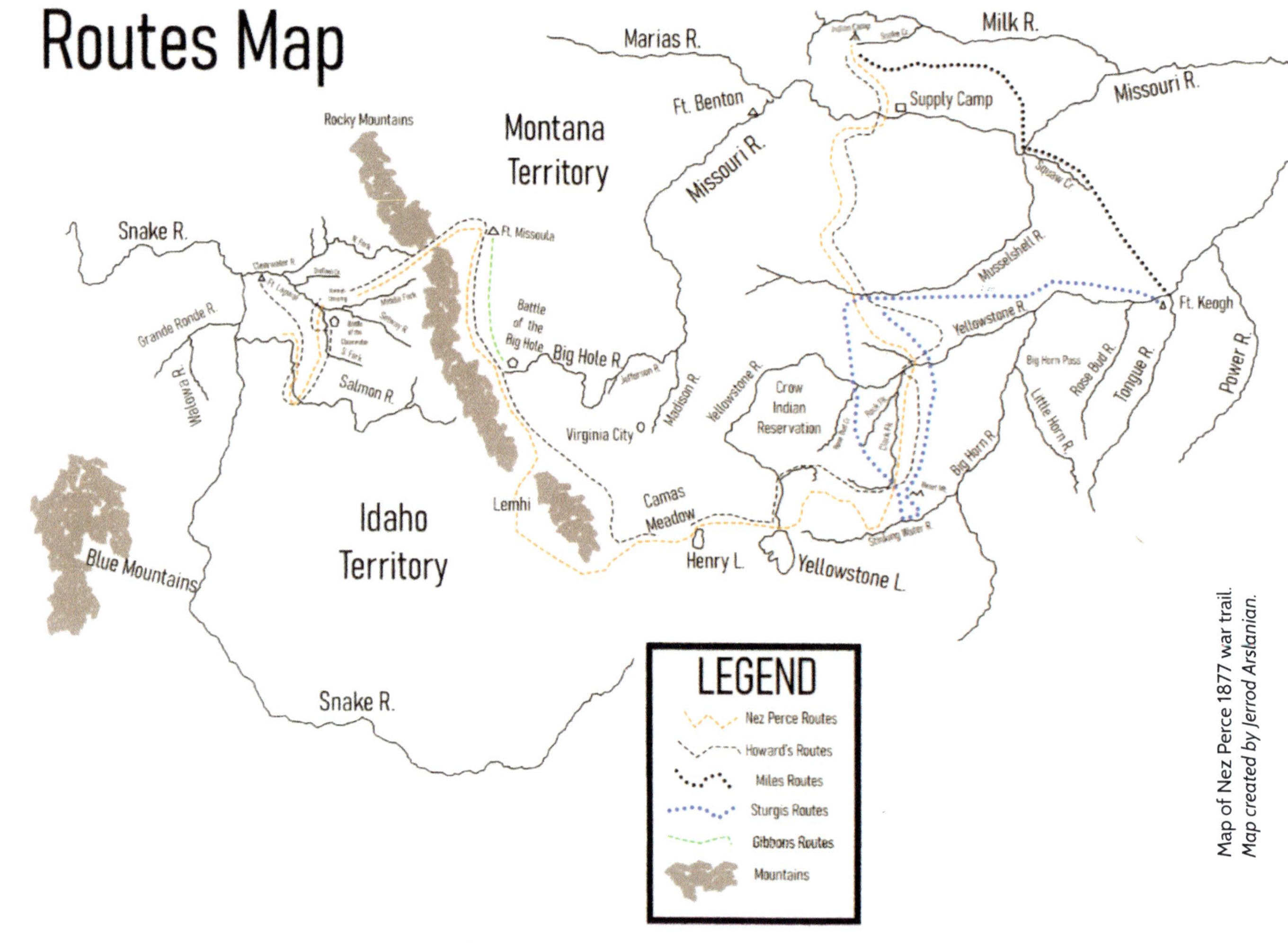

Map of Nez Perce 1877 war trail.
Map created by Jerrod Arslanian.

CHAPTER 10

The Final Battle and Exile

The Nimiipuu bands pushed on, searching for safety. There was no time to fully grieve the loss of loved ones. The survival of the remaining families, including Seven Days Whipping, Um-al-wat, and their son, Black Raven, meant they had to keep moving.

The Nimiipuu continue towards Camas Meadows, Idaho, where another skirmish occurred, and then on through Yellowstone Park and up to Canyon Creek (near Billings, Montana). They then followed the trail north through the Judith Gap, hoping to get to Canada.[1] They headed for Bear Paw, which the Nimiipuu call Tsanim Alikos Pah (Place of Manure Fire): while there was not much firewood, there were plenty of buffalo chips to burn.[2] It is also called Snake Creek. Hunters had been sent ahead to kill buffalo for food for the people. The hunters were successful, and camp was made early on September 29.

In the meantime, though, General Howard had ordered Colonel Nelson Miles to intercept the Nimiipuu with 383 soldiers from Fort Keogh (now known as Miles City), Montana. Colonel Miles left on September 18 and arrived at Bear Paw on September 30.[3]

The Nimiipuu families were tired and ready for rest. But there was an air of uneasiness from some, who said that they should not stop so soon, that they should move on—they were only 40 miles from safety in Canada! Scouts had been sent out, but they did not see Howard's soldiers; in fact, Looking Glass thought Howard's troops were two days behind them, meaning the families could relax. What they could not have known was that Miles was advancing from the east.[4] They stayed the night and were planning to leave midday. Some of the families had their packs ready to go early in the morning, but others did not.

When Miles realized the Nimiipuu had stopped, he rushed his soldiers into formation and mounted a surprise attack on the morning of September 30, 1877. While Looking Glass was urging people to eat, saying there was "plenty, plenty time,"[5] two of their scouts shouted a warning: "Stampeding buffaloes! Soldiers! Soldiers!"[6] Some of the families who had their packs ready rode out of camp, heading north for Canada. Joseph's band was not ready: this included Seven Days Whipping, Um-al-wat, and Black Raven. They were caught in the attack, as were the bands of Looking Glass and Toohoolhoolzote. White Bird II, a young child of 10 and the son of Chief White Bird, told how it was for him:

> It was morning and we children were playing. We had hardwood sticks, throwing mud balls. I looked up and saw a spotted horse, a Cheyenne warrior, wearing a war bonnet, come to the bluff above me. He was closely followed by the troops. Some of the children ran back to the camps, some hurried to the gulch. I was with these last. Bullets were flying. We had to get away. I had no moccasins. I jumped in the creek and swam across… When I got away I had only a shirt as clothing. Cold, wet, I was freezing. Some were on horses, and one woman showed pity for me. She took me up behind her…[7]

My seven-year-old grandfather, Black Raven, could have been playing, too, and in the confusion of the attack, must have run someplace for safety. Some of the women tried to catch horses and ride out of the camp; others sought shelter wherever they could. On the evening of September 30, under cover of darkness the Nimiipuu began to make their defensive preparations to protect the non-combatants. Deep shelter pits were dug into the creek bottom, to protect from the gunfire of the troops.[8]

From another account I found what Um-al-wat might have done. Here is an excerpt from an oral history by an unidentified woman:

> We digged the trenches with camas hooks and butcher knives. With pans we threw out the dirt. We could not do much cooking. Dried meat and some other grub would be handed around. If not enough for all, it would be given the children first. I was three days without food. Children cried with hunger and cold. Old people suffering in silence. Misery everywhere. Cold and dampness all around. In the small creek there was water, but we could get it only at night. In traveling, we had buffalo horns for purpose of water. With strings we could let them down while crossing streams horseback. We carried them with us all the time. They came handy here.[9]

The Nimiipuu warriors jumped to the defense quickly and the American troops soon learned they were battling skilled fighters. The first day's battle resulted in heavy casualties for the soldiers: twenty percent of Miles' 383 soldiers were unable to continue fighting.[10] Twenty-three Nimiipuu died that day and many were wounded; a third of their horses were captured by

Miles' men. The Nimiipuu warriors were able to keep the camp site intact, and all the while the women were digging trenches for protection.

Not all were caught in the confusion of the attack. Many tried to escape. It is not known for sure how many men, women, and children escaped that day to attempt a run for Canada. Many died trying; their bodies were found later. Others were never found.[11]

Under cover of night, warriors who had been cut off were able to make it back to camp. In addition to being unable to light fires for warmth or to cook, the weather now turned cold and snow began to fall. Yellow Wolf was one who was able to steal back to camp at night; he describes what he found: "you have seen hail, sometime, leveling the grass. Indians were so leveled by the bullet hail…children crying with cold. No fire. There could be no light. Everywhere was crying, the death wail."[12] Not all had blankets but, somehow, everyone made it through the night. Other warriors stayed on the bluff overlooking the Nimiipuu camp. During the night they used knives to dig rifle pits: "some had board-bladed knives taken from soldiers at Big Hole."[13]

Chief Ollokot's wife describes the hardships of the non-combatants during the five-day battle: "we slept only by naps; sitting in our pits; leaning forward or back against the dirt wall. Many warriors stayed in their rifle pits all the time."[14] Um-al-wat and Black Raven would have been in these pits; the pits ultimately saved the lives of many Nimiipuu.

The next day, October 1, the fighting resumed, but now both sides had dug themselves in and were left with fighting via sharp shooting. Miles tried to cut off the supply of water to the Nimiipuu camp but was unsuccessful. It soon became evident that Miles needed reinforcements. Late morning on October 1, Miles sent emissaries to attempt talks of surrender. The messages went back and forth before Chief Joseph agreed to go into the soldiers' camp. He was detained there, but then an army officer was caught and held captive in the Nimiipuu camp. Both Joseph and the officer were held for more than a day before an agreement to exchange the prisoners was finally reached.[15] The exchange happened on October 2.

The fighting continued for two more days, with Howard arriving on the evening of October 4. With the arrival of more soldiers, the possibility of escaping to Canada now seemed untenable for the Nimiipuu. Howard brought two pro-treaty Nimiipuu with him, whose daughters had married into the Joseph band. The two were Jokais (Worthless or Lazy), known to Whites as Captain John, and Meopkowit (Baby or Know Nothing), known as Captain George.[16] These two came to Chief Joseph's camp on the morning of October 5, with a message from General Miles: "We will have no more war!"[17]

The besieged Nimiipuu held a council, which Yellow Wolf later recalled:

> This seemed to relieve Joseph, who had apparently been accused by the others of having offered, four days before, to surrender the Nez Perces to Miles. "You see, it is true," he said to the council members. "I did not say, 'Let's quit.' General Miles said, 'Let's quit.' And now General Howard says, 'Let's quit.' You see it is true enough! I did not say, 'Let's quit!'"
>
> "When the warriors heard those words from Chief Joseph," said Yellow Wolf, "They answered, 'Yes we believe you now.'"[18]

What this signified to Joseph and others was that the siege was a draw and *not* a defeat. General Miles assured Joseph, saying, "I will take you to a place for this winter; then you can go to your old home."[19] With this promise, Joseph returned to his camp and told his people that the war had ended. He only spoke for his people, and not for Chief White Bird or the others.

The formal surrender is described as follows:

> On the afternoon of October 5, Joseph rode slowly up a steep rise at the west end of the bluff. Walking beside him were five other men, their hands on his horse's flanks or on his leg. The six spoke softly among themselves. Joseph's chin was on his chest and his hands crossed across the saddle's pommel. His Winchester carbine lay across his lap. A gray shawl was around his shoulders, and his hair was in two braids and tied up with otter skin. It was obvious, that if not the band's war leader, he had put his life repeatedly on the line. He had grazing wounds on his forehead, shirt peppered with bullet holes.[20]

Chief Joseph arrived at the spot between the creek and where the Seventh Cavalry's first charge had occurred. Howard and Miles were waiting. When Joseph got to the spot, he slid off his horse and walked toward them. He offered his gun first to Howard, but Howard waved his hand to Miles. Handing over his rifle, Joseph said:

> Tell General Howard I know his heart. What he told me before, I have it in my heart. I am tired of fighting. Our chiefs are killed. Looking Glass is dead. Toohoolhoolzote is dead. The old men are all dead. It is the young men who say, "Yes" or "No." He [Ollokot] who led the young men is dead. It is cold, and we have no blankets. The little children are freezing

to death. My people, some of them, have run away to the hills, and have no blankets, no food. No one knows where they are—perhaps freezing to death. I want to have time to look for my children, and see how many of them I can find. Maybe I shall find them among the dead. Hear me, my chief! I am tired. My heart is sick and sad. From where the sun now stands I will fight no more forever.[21]

According to Yellow Wolf, the chiefs and officers crossed themselves and shook hands all around. The Indians lifted their hands toward the sky, where the sun was then standing. They said: "No more battles! No more war!"[22] The men surrendered their guns, ammunition, and the army seized their horses. On that day, surrendering together with Joseph, were 87 men, 184 women, and 147 children, a total of 418. Relief was felt throughout the camp, including Seven Days Whipping, Um-al-wat, and Black Raven. Soon, soldiers and Nimiipuu joined together to build fires and prepare hot food, and blankets were given to those who were cold. The people could now stop running.[23]

Not all surrendered with Joseph. White Bird and members of his band, along with some members of Toohoolhoolzote and Chief of the Palouse Husishusis Kute, slipped away by night with 233 people, headed for Sitting Bull's camp in Canada. This group was separate from those that slipped away on the first night of battle. The journey took them several more days. Sitting Bull's Sioux welcomed them, as historian Alvin Josephy writes, "as fellow-victims of the Americans."[24]

The weather was still cold, and it took two days before Miles could get everything ready to move the Nimiipuu, who are now federal prisoners. The army physicians treated the wounded—both Nimiipuu and the soldiers—and both sides buried the dead. As a family, we have often wondered if Seven Days Whipping was wounded at Bear Paw, and was among the wounded being treated; if so, how hurt was he? On the morning of October 7, 1877, the Nimiipuu loaded the elderly, women, and children into wagons, loaded 40 wounded warriors onto brush-filled wagons, and transported another fifty or sixty wounded Nimiipuu by travois. Joseph and able-bodied warriors rode and others walked. They were accompanied by three companies of the Seventh Cavalry and five companies of the Fifth Infantry artillery. They were headed for Fort Keogh or Tongue River cantonment, where the Tongue River flows into the Yellowstone River, eastern Montana. They arrived October 23.[25]

As I read the first-hand accounts of the war, I felt the terror of those battles, and I found that I was suffering from secondary post-traumatic stress. I felt the horror of women and children being killed for no reason other than they were Indian. These accounts were telling me what it must have been like for Um-al-wat, Seven Days Whipping, and Black Raven. I became numb and overwhelmingly sad. As I wrote my own account of the war, I kept stopping and crying. The story of the deaths of children is not written in history books; there, they are merely statistics. But the loss was real, and it hurts. My heart was hurting, a deep ache permeated my entire body. The murder by American soldiers of Um-al-wat's five children, I realized, was the source of an unspoken, almost forgotten grief that had nevertheless been passed down through the generations. And, I realized, because I knew it, because I now felt it, I could now help heal that intergenerational soul wound—for myself, my family, and perhaps for others as well.

The Nimiipuu thought they had reached their temporary winter camp at Fort Keogh and would be allowed to go back home when warmer weather arrived. However, the Nimiipuu would be betrayed yet again by another broken promise. Authorities senior to Miles and Howard disagreed with and overruled the terms of the surrender.[26]

General Sherman, Commander of the Armies, had a policy of "no leniency or charity towards Indians." He also viewed "war as hell" and believed "the only way to treat an enemy was to crush him totally, to destroy his ability and desire to ever make war again."[27] With his "March to the Sea" and burning Savannah to the ground, he had brutally executed this policy during the Civil War, and he argued Native Americans should receive the same treatment. In 1867, Sherman said, "The more we can kill this year, the less have to be killed the next year, for the more I see of these Indians, the more convinced I am that they all have to be killed or be maintained as a species of paupers."[28]

Sherman's brutal policy was widely shared by other army commanders. Under Sherman was General Sheridan, who was of the same thinking, and he ordered Miles to rescind the terms of surrender. To Miles' credit, he did respond by saying the "Nez Perce trouble was caused by the rascality of their [Indian] Agent, and the encroachment of the whites."[29] This protest had no effect. Miles was given orders to send the Nimiipuu first to Fort Lincoln at Bismarck, North Dakota, and from there it would be decided where they were to go in Indian Territory.[30] Sherman said the Nimiipuu "must never be allowed to return to Oregon."[31]

Indian Territory was a place designated by the US government for Native American Tribes, an area thought to be undesirable by White people. This concept of Indian Country was proposed in 1825 by Secretary of War John C. Calhoun. It was supposed to be a permanent Indian reserve on western lands that the Whites had no use for. At first most of the eastern Tribes were forced to relocate to Indian Territory, which was west of the Mississippi River. The territory included the present-day states of Nebraska, Kansas, and Oklahoma. The reserve was supposed to be for Native Americans only, but Whites wanted the fertile lands in Nebraska and Kansas, so in 1854 the Kansas-Nebraska Act was passed by Congress to reduce the size of Indian Territory to most of the state of Oklahoma.[32] This would be the Indian Territory that the Nimiipuu would eventually be moved to. The Nimiipuu were aware of Indian Territory because a neighboring tribe, the Modoc Tribe of Oregon, had been sent there in 1872 after the end of the Modoc War.

On the morning of October 31, 1877, the Nimiipuu left Fort Keogh after spending eight days there. Those who were well enough to ride on horseback or in wagons were sent overland. Those who were ill or wounded, along with the elderly, the women, and young children, were sent by water in fourteen mackinaw flat boats. Mackinaw flatboats were used for bringing supplies to forts and inland towns along the Missouri and Yellowstone Rivers. There were 18 to 32 feet long, tapered slightly at each end and flat-bottomed so they could be hauled up onto beaches and pebbled shorelines. They were made of whipsawed lumber, caulked with pitch and tar, and had four long oars. Each boat could hold twenty to twenty-four people and each had a cooking and serving outfit on board.[33]

Seven Days Whipping, Um-al-wat, and their son, who was about seven years old, were most likely on one of the flat boats. They were given army rations of dried pork, green coffee, sugar, hard tack, rice, navy beans, and flour. The women would sleep on shore at night and in the early morning they would build a fire to prepare the coffee and food for breakfast. Did great-grandmother Um-al-wat prepare these strange foods? How would the food taste to her son and the others? Would it make them sick? Or did she tend to her wounded husband? I imagine she did all these tasks and more. Sometimes along the river when they stopped for lunch or evening, they would be able to gather bullberries, which were tart but added to their meager diet. They floated down the Yellowstone River to the Missouri River and Fort Buford. Just before they arrived at the fort, a wounded warrior died, and they buried him on the south side of the Missouri River.[34] Could this warrior have been Seven Days Whipping?

They arrive at Fort Buford in the Dakota Territories after nine days, arriving on November 8; this stop was only a short overnight stay to reload supplies and get more blankets.[35] The fourteen flotilla flat boats continued down the Missouri River to Fort Lincoln, near Bismarck. The weather was cold and ice was forming in the rivers. One boatman noticed how frightened and helpless some of the Nimiipuu were, and another said, "They set up a moaning, no doubt their death chant."[36] Another boatman was puzzled as to why the Nimiipuu had blank faces and deepening depression, why they did not express joy or emotion. Today this lack of emotion would be considered as post-traumatic stress syndrome related to warfare.[37]

The Nimiipuu in the mackinaws arrived at Fort Lincoln on November 16, a couple of days before the overland group. To their surprise, the town of Bismarck sent out a large welcome. When Miles rode into town with Chief Joseph by his side, a band began playing "Hail to the Chief."[38] The city wanted to host a special banquet for Chief Joseph and an invitation was published in the Bismarck *Tri-Weekly Tribune*:

To Joseph, Head Chief of the Nez Perces,

Sir:

Desiring to show you our kind feelings and the admiration we have for your bravery and humanity, as exhibited in your recent conflict with the forces of the United States, we most cordially invite you to dine with us at the Sheridan House in this city. The dinner to be given at 1 ½ p.m. today.[39]

The people of the city surrounded the travelers, and seeing how tattered they looked, gave them food. Not all could go to the banquet, but the citizens of Bismarck took those who could not attend to dine elsewhere in town. The townspeople's actions showed the Nimiipuu that not all Whites hated them. But despite the invitation to dine, many of the Nimiipuu were too depressed to eat.[40]

The welcome in Bismarck was short-lived. Joseph met with Miles twice while in Bismarck and Miles reiterated the surrender agreement that the Nimiipuu could return to Idaho in the spring. However, federal army authorities above him told him that the Nimiipuu had to be sent to Fort Leavenworth, Kansas. Miles could not bring himself to tell Joseph, so he sent Ad Chapman, interpreter for the Nimiipuu, to share the change in plans. On the evening of November 22, Chapman went to Joseph's tepee, and he broke the unwelcome news that they would have to move onto Fort Leavenworth. Joseph resisted at first, and conferred with his leaders about what to do with this news. After much discussion, they realized they had no horses, or supplies, and were left with no choice but to go on in peace.[41]

The Nimiipuu would spend the winter at Fort Leavenworth, Kansas. They were taken to a place they would come to call Eeikish Pah, "the hot place."[42] Preparations began for transportation by rail. Eleven passenger cars and two baggage cars were delivered to Bismarck. Companies B and G of the First Infantry, commanded by Captain Robert E. Johnston, were assigned to deliver the Nimiipuu to Fort Leavenworth. The cars provided by the Great Northern Railroad were run-down passenger cars. The Nimiipuu would be sitting on seats facing each other, with no sleeping facilities for them. Each car was provided with minimal drinking containers and one open lavatory that emptied onto the tracks below as they traveled. Most of the Nimiipuu would not use the lavatory because of the flashing tracks beneath them. They would wait until the train stopped, so the engines could take on water, then the Nimiipuu would use this time to go and relieve themselves.[43] This train ride would have been a first for the Nimiipuu as well as for my great-grandmother Um-al-wat and grandfather Black Raven. What did they think of the rumbling wheels of the train on the tracks, and seeing through the windows how fast the scenery passed by? Would they be afraid or dazed? Certainly, it was a new experience. The food provided was rations of beef, hardtack, canned beans, and coffee. Again, the women cooked the beef before boarding the train.

On the morning of November 23, Chief Joseph and the Nimiipuu prisoners boarded the train bound for Fort Leavenworth. The train traveled east through Jamestown, Dakota Territory, and Moorehead and Brainerd, Minnesota, and on to the Northern Pacific junction west of Duluth and south to St. Paul.[44]

At Jamestown, Captain Johnston, Lieutenant Reed, and Dr. Reed took Chief Joseph and several other captives out to supper. Because the officers had to provide their own meals, they opted to dine at a café about a hundred yards from the train. The officers returned to the train without Joseph.

The train started moving down the tracks, and from the back of the train folks yelled "Joseph, Joseph! stop the train!" The train crew looked back and saw Joseph running toward the train, with loaves of bread dropping from his blanket. He said he was walking by a bakery window and saw the bread; he went inside and bought the loaves to give to his wife and others who did not get supper.[45]

The train arrived at St. Paul, Minnesota, on November 24, 1877. The army took the first census of the Nimiipuu and Palouse. They record 431 Nimiipuu and Palouse prisoners: 79 men, 178 women, and 174 children; this total would have included Um-al-wat and Black Raven. It was here at St. Paul that the Nimiipuu baggage cars were transferred to another train, and the Nimiipuu transferred from the five coaches to the five Milwaukee and St. Paul cars. The train left for Fort Leavenworth.[46]

The trip's next leg would take them south, and the train changed track lines three times before they finally arrive at Fort Leavenworth on November 27, 1877. The Nimiipuu had tried to stay clean on this train journey, but no bathing or laundry facilities were provided. They arrived haggard and soiled. Even if they had extra clothes to change into, the baggage cars that had traveled with them most of the way got lost and did not catch up to them until four days later

Having arrived at Fort Leavenworth, they were loaded onto wagons and taken to where their new camp was set up, which became known as the tent village. By late evening of their first night, they had been fed army rations and settled on hay-and -ticking bed sacks in army tents. They were told this was a temporary home until the Indian Bureau could find a new place for them to live in the spring.[47] I will describe more of the exile camp life in the next chapter about Black Raven.

Another census of the Nimiipuu was taken on December 4, 1877: it indicated there were 418 prisoners: 87 men, 184 women, and 147 children. This was a more accurate census when adjusted for age and gender. Thirteen children had died between November 23 and December 4 while three babies had been born on the train journey.[48]

Reports from the time state that 21 people died while at Fort Leavenworth.[49] Seven Days Whipping may well have been one of the fatalities, but we may never know for sure. As I mentioned earlier, none of the lists of warriors reveals either of the two names by which we know him. He would have been about 40 or 41 years old. He might have been wounded in one of the battles; if so, the conditions at Fort Leavenworth might have contributed to his death. Within our family, we speculate that he might have died from wounds sustained at one of the battles, or he might have died somewhere on the exile trail, which would have been at Fort Buford, Fort Leavenworth, or Quapaw Reservation, or at the final stop at Ponca Reservation, Indian Territory, Oklahoma. This left Um-al-wat without a husband and Black Raven without a father—but it left me the beneficiary of a miracle, as they survived war, disease, incredible hardship, and broken hearts. It is their spirits that inspire me and my family to find and tell our stories of healing and reconciliation.

Bear Paw Battlefield near Chinook, Montana, 40 miles south of the Canadian border, October 1993. *Paul Family Photo Collection.*

Titus Paul and Roberta Paul looking at the marker for Chief Joseph's campsite at Bear Paw, October 1993. Seven Days Whipping would have his campsite nearby. *Paul Family Photo Collection*.

Titus and Roberta Paul walking across a bridge at the Bear Paw Battlefield, October 1993. *Paul Family Photo Collection*.

Drawing of Bear Paw Battlefield by the author, 2003.

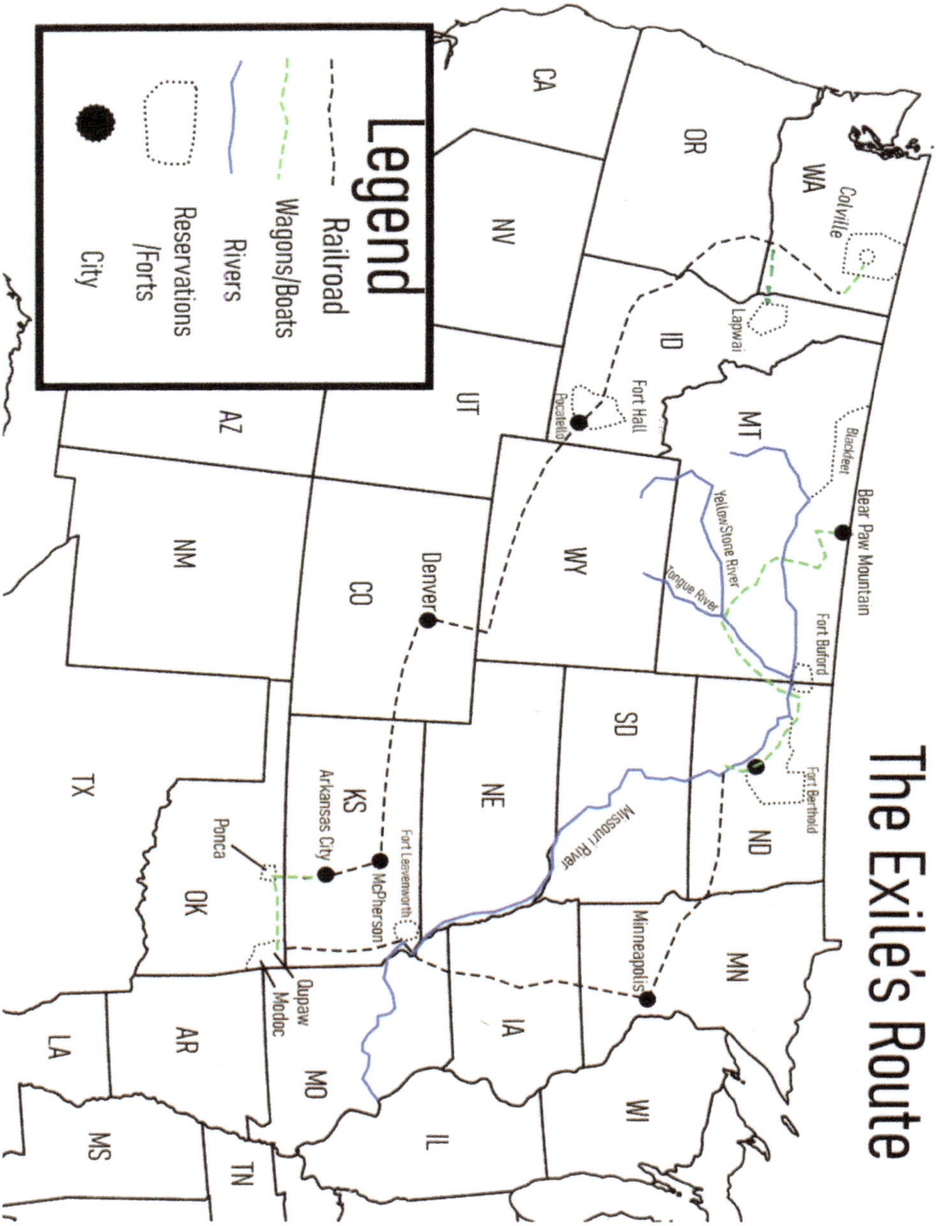

Map of the Nimiipuu Exile Route, 1877: from Bear Paw surrender site to Fort Leavenworth, Kansas; on to Baxter Springs/Quapaw Reservation; to Ponca Reservation. In 1855, 119 Nimiipuu returned to Lapwai, Idaho, and 150 Nimiipuu in Chief Joseph's Band were sent to the Colville Reservation in Washington. *Map created by Jerrod Arslanian.*

CHAPTER 11

A Healing Path

In 1993, my father, mother, and I attended a pipe ceremony at the site of Bear Paw battle. The sacred pipe ceremony signified that we were coming together for peace and healing. My parents were elderly and a bit fragile; my father was 86, my mother 80. Two weeks earlier, I had slipped on a rug, twisting and spraining my ankle. I bought my first pair of Birkenstocks. They were the only sandals that fit my swollen foot.

As I was walking down to the site of the ceremony, I fell and twisted my ankle again. I was mad at myself for being clumsy, and in pain. I knew my parents couldn't pick me up and walk me down to the site. A man stopped and asked if he could assist me. Relieved, I said yes. I leaned on his arm and continued limping down to the site. I asked this man who he was.

"I am a descendant of a cavalry soldier," he said. I could hardly believe my ears. I found myself stiffening and becoming angry. Then, as he was helping me, I tried to be friendly and asked him, "Why are you here?"

"I am here to make amends," he replied.

"Amends?" I muttered to myself. I became even angrier. I didn't want this man touching me. But then I asked myself, "Robbie, why are you here?" I reminded myself that I was here to forgive. But that day, I was not able to forgive that man. Trying to be polite, I coolly thanked the man for helping me to the site.

About 200 people were present for the ceremony. It was a big day: all the sites of the War of 1877 were being inducted into the National Park system. The ceremony was deeply moving. We honored our ancestors, both those who had died here at Bear Paw as well as those who had been forced into exile. (I'll tell the story of exile in a moment.) Those present included descendants of the non-treaty Nimiipuu who, after exile, had been returned to Nespelem, and descendants of those who were allowed to return to Lapwai. Descendants of survivors who had escaped to Canada were there, too. As I had already learned, there were descendants of US cavalry soldiers here also. Descendants of members of the Royal Canadian Mounted Police were here, as it was they who greeted the Nimiipuu who fled to Canada.

My father and I spent part of the day walking the battleground, contemplating the areas where our ancestors had dug in to defend themselves. We wondered where Seven Days Whipping had dug in and what his fate had been. And what, we wondered, of Um-al-wat and young Black Raven—where had they been and how had they survived?

The pipe ceremony organizers invited male descendants of Nimiipuu warriors and all veterans—White and Indian—to take a place in the circle. I gently suggested that my father take a place in the pipe circle, and he agreed.

As far as I know, no one in my family had participated in a pipe ceremony for many decades—probably not since the time of the 1877 War. We had been raised as strict Presbyterians and were told not to participate in any Indian ceremony. I wanted our family to reconnect and saw this as an opportunity to do so. I stood behind my father, along with other Nimiipuu women and friends. As the peace pipe was passed around the circle of men, each said who he was and which band he was from. But when the pipe came to my father, he just passed it along. I was horrified, thinking to myself, "What have I done? Have I pushed him so far he doesn't want to participate?"

At the end of the day, I felt sad. I knew I would need to return. The wound is deep. But I also could not let go of the ceremony where Father did not smoke the peace pipe.

When we returned to the hotel for the evening, my mother asked my father, "Dad, how come you didn't smoke that peace pipe?" Father sat in silence for a moment, and then he said, "Oh, I might have gotten some germs." I laughed and breathed a sigh of relief.

I've returned to Bear Paw three more times. The first two times that I returned, I was with my second husband, Phil. On our first visit to the site together, we walked the path of the battleground, then he let me be by myself. I wanted to try to sing a song, but no words would come—I was too choked up.

The second time we returned, I walked the grounds alone, letting myself feel the grieving spirits of the ancestors. I stood near the campsite of Joseph. Black Raven and his family would have been here at the time. Again, I tried to sing a healing song, but all I could do was cry. What did come out of my mouth was mournful and inarticulate. The words were not yet ready to come out. As I stood and cried, I raised my arms to the Creator, asking for healing. Soon will come the time when I bring my adult children and granddaughters to this place for more healing. My children and their children want to come and be part of this healing journey; we all pray for that time to come.

The third time I returned to Bear Paw was in 2016, to participate in the Chief Joseph Trail Ride. My sister and I had joined the Nez Perce Appaloosa Horse Club, a group that retraces the trail of the Nez Perce War of 1877. We wanted to ride the trail of our ancestors together. Each year, the group rides about 100 miles of the trail. It takes 13 years to complete the entire trail.

I convinced my husband I could drive the pickup with a camper by myself. I reminded him that I knew how to drive big rigs. I learned to drive on a grain truck and stick shift when I was a teenager. Phil sent me off with love and told me to call when I had cell service.

The ride began about one hundred miles south of Bear Paw with 180 riders plus support teams. My sister and I were part of the support teams, so we did not ride a horse. Each day the riders would ride about 20 miles to the next stop. The support teams would drive the campers, horse trailers, and food wagons to the next stop. Each night there were 300 or more people gathered at the camp site. There was much camaraderie, storytelling, and laughter as we gathered each night. Others would walk by our campsite of Nez Perce ladies and say, "You're having too much fun over there!"

One night a sudden storm pelted us with rain and hail as thunder boomed so loudly it scared me, my sister, and the horses. My sister and I were safe inside our camper, but the hail pounding on the roof of the camper was deafening. I was on the upper bunk but quickly jumped down to climb in bed with my sister, seeking protection. Several young Nimiipuu got wet as their tents were blown over. We wondered what our ancestors must have experienced, fleeing US soldiers with little gear. Unlike them, no one was the worse for wear, and everyone took shelter in cars and trucks and trailers.

The closer we got to Bear Paw, the more I could sense and feel my ancestors. My sister and I speculated what it would have been like to walk this trail, cold, hungry, and with horses exhausted, probably too tired to be ridden.

On the final day of the ride, I was emotional: not quite in tears, but with a gnawing disturbance in my stomach. The Nez Perce riders rode into the Bear Paw National Battlefield park and made three rounds around the flagpole, leading a saddled but riderless horse. The riderless horse represented fallen warriors whose lives were lost during battles.

Later that afternoon there was a ceremony commemorating this final battle. Young Nimiipuu girls rode in, dressed in regalia; when they arrived at the ceremonial circle they dismounted and performed a welcome dance for the gathered crowd of hundreds. The Nez Perce drum group played the Grand Entry Flag War song, with everyone standing in respect.

My sister and I wore our regalia and were seated in the front row. There was quite a commotion when we arrived. A great nephew of General Howard was there, dressed in a military uniform of that era. He posed for pictures with my sister and me. Lots of pictures were taken, and to our surprise one of the photos appeared in the November/December 2016 issue of *Cowboys and Indians* magazine. At the conclusion of the ceremony, the drummers played a friendship round dance. All were invited to participate. My heart was still heavy, but I was glad to have been a part of this healing commemoration.

My family has returned to Big Hole as well, now a site maintained by the National Park Service. In August 1994, four years after the first Bear Paw visit that launched us on our healing journey, 20 members of my family attended another commemorative event at Big Hole. There was a pipe ceremony on the battlefield, and a circle of the Nimiipuu and US cavalry descendants—male and female this time, as well as Indian and White—were asked to join the circle. A chair was set out for my elderly father, and he readily took his place. The ceremony began and the pipe was passed along. When the pipe reached my father, he took it and smoked, and said, "I wish everyone here peace, prosperity, and good will." I asked myself, "Has he come to reconciliation with his parents' and grandparents' wounds?"

On this occasion, the leader of the pipe ceremony asked if anyone else wanted to speak. My mother nudged me—I felt my great-grandmother nudging as well. With this encouragement, I said, "I am Tawlikitsanmay', Woman of the Forest, the daughter of Titus J. Paul, granddaughter of Ka-khun-ne Black

Raven Jesse Paul and great-granddaughter of Wa-tat-ooy-napt-lah-hayne Seven Days Whipping and Um-al-wat Phoebe Lowry. My great-grandparents lost five children here. Grandfather and Great-grandmother are the only ones who survived the war. I am here to heal. It does my heart good to see the young boys carrying the sage around the circle to cleanse the ground and honor our ancestors. I thank you for allowing me to speak."

It was a good day that ended with a dinner and friendship round dance. On this, one of our first healing journeys, I was embraced by multiple generations of my family.

Two Nimiipuu elder women thanked me for speaking at the pipe ceremony circle. These women always thanked me for speaking "from the heart," as they were often at these events.

I didn't know what happened to my people after they surrendered. It's not a story that is well documented nor had it been spoken of within our family. We have pieced together bits and pieces, and I am trying to find more of the story of what happened. We knew that we were sent into exile and had traveled through Fort Lincoln, North Dakota before putting onto a train taking them to Fort Leavenworth, Kansas. We also knew they had been to Baxter Springs and then Ponca Reservation, Oklahoma, before they were allowed to return. What we didn't know were the details of how they traveled and what the conditions were for each part of the journey. In July 2008, my husband Phil needed to travel from our home in Washington State to Duluth, Minnesota, for a business conference. We decided to travel together and retrace part of the exiles' trail.

I knew that the wounded as well as captured warriors, women, and children were taken by wagon to Fort Keogh, which is now Miles City. Those who could ride their horses were accompanied by General Miles to Fort Keogh. We stopped at the old fort, at the confluence of the Tongue and Yellowstone rivers, that had been built by General Miles. The army's intended use for its garrison was to reduce warfare by Indians in the region and to persuade them to resettle on reservations. They used the Yellowstone River to bring supplies by boat or mackinaws from the eastern United States via the Missouri River.

The only buildings left standing were the officers' quarters, which had a small museum, and a stone building used to store ammunition. I asked the person working at the fort if they knew anything of the Nez Perce War, that the Nez Perce had been sent here after their surrender. The person I spoke to knew nothing of this history, which puzzled me: why not know the history of the fort?

I wondered if Seven Days Whipping had been among the wounded, and if Um-al-wat and Ka-khun-ne were hungry and afraid when they arrived at Fort Keogh.

General Miles had wanted to return the Nez Perce to Idaho but was overruled by Generals Sherman and Sheridan, both merciless Indian killers. Instead of going home in peace, the survivors of the war were punished with exile. From Fort Keogh, the Nimiipuu were sent to Fort Leavenworth, in Kansas. On the way, they passed through Fort Buford and Fort Lincoln. The wounded, along with women and children, were put on mackinaw boats and floated down the Yellowstone to Fort Buford. It must have been very cold on the Yellowstone, which often froze by late fall. We have no record of how Um-al-wat and Ka-khun-ne kept warm, or if Seven Days Whipping was with them. As far as I know, from Fort Buford they were floated down the Missouri, a much wider river, to Fort Lincoln. Joseph and his warriors rode their horses, accompanied by a battalion of the First Infantry. They arrived in Fort Lincoln in early November 1877.[1]

On our trip, Phil and I stopped at Fort Buford, located near Williston, North Dakota. When we arrived, we went to the visitor center where a gentleman was sitting behind a desk. I was startled by how fast he jumped up to greet us, as if thinking, "At last! People to talk to!"

The guide gave us a first-class tour of the fort, telling us the history. The fort was built at the confluence of the Yellowstone and Missouri rivers. Established in 1868 and able to house six companies of soldiers, it was one of the largest forts west of the Mississippi River. The buildings still-- standing were originally the officers' quarters and a stone powder magazine. They have rebuilt the mess hall where the soldiers would eat and entertain themselves with music and dancing.

The guide took us through the officers' quarters, which had many artifacts. He told us Chief Sitting Bull had surrendered in this building in 1881. I asked the guide if he knew of the Nez Perce War and about the Nimiipuu being here in November 1877 on their way to Fort Lincoln. They had stayed the night, taking on more supplies to float onto Fort Lincoln. I believed that Chief Joseph would have meet with the Post Commander while there and would have meet the commander in this officer's quarters. The guide had not heard of this history and thanked me for the history lesson.

There was a cemetery on the grounds of the fort. When I stood nearby, I felt a stirring, a feeling that told me there was a Nez Perce buried here. The feeling stuck with me for a while.

In Bismarck, North Dakota, we stopped again so I could visit the archives there. I was able to view and print off several newspaper articles about the Nez Perce War. At the time I quickly glanced through the articles. We left Bismarck and continued onto Jamestown, North Dakota. Back on the road, I read some of the articles. We had a room at an older hotel in downtown Jamestown, near the railroad tracks. As I was reading, I found something interesting:

"Joseph Left at Jamestown," a headline read. The article continued:

At Jamestown Conductor Law invited Joseph to supper with him. Joseph accepted and after he was through strolled away from the eating house into the village in search of bread and some good things for his family. He has a good heart and means that Mrs. Joseph and little Joseph shall have something to eat as well as himself. While he was making his purchases the train pulled out and Joseph was "left." A mile or two from the station a passenger discovered the important loss and went pell mell through the cars crying, "Joseph's left." The conductor immediately started the train back and soon met Joseph. He was running for dear life and was far more scared than when Miles took him in. There was a golden opportunity to escape but he dreaded it more than anything in his experience since his capture. He was not a Cole Younger [a member of the Jesse James gang]. When he got on board he was panting like a dog and sweating like a wood chopper in July, but he still had that bread for Mrs. Joe and tiny little Joe. He said the faster he ran the faster the train got away from him. The conductor suggested that it was a harder chase that Howard had when after Joseph. Joseph laughed heartily at the remark and apparently thought it a good joke. When he was seated, he threw aside all his clothing including his shirt, down to his breeching. He wanted to get cool. Meantime little Joe went for that bread."[2]

The next morning, I took a photo of the tracks and felt a connection of spirit to Joseph and my great-grandmother Um-al-wat and Black Raven, and the other Nez Perce who had been on the train. I pinched myself, I was standing where my ancestors had been so long ago. Another article in the Bismarck *Tribune* reported that a young woman had been dared to kiss Joseph. She did so, giving him a kiss on the lips, then giving him her wedding ring.[3] There was another article a few days later by someone called Susannah, who chided the young lady for kissing Joseph. She wrote:

> "Everyone to her taste," as the old woman said when she kissed the cow, and if folks want to kiss Indians or ugly White men either, nobody cares if they do. Only it isn't right to hold the whole town responsible for so exceptional a breach of individual taste. It may be true that "half a loaf is better than no bread," but it seems to me that such tasteless crumbs as these would prove starvation diet to any one possessing a just appreciation of these little offerings of friendship. Just think of it! Kissing an Indian with three squaws and no mustache! Ugh![4]

These articles I had collected gave me a sense of how the Nimiipuu were accepted in Bismark, and more info about Joseph, he was already becoming famous. At the time of the 1877 Nez Perce war, the press followed the battles and it seemed the war was the front page news story to read.

I recently returned to this cache of newspaper clippings and found one about "Joseph's Arrival at Buford" which confirmed a feeling about Seven Days Whipping that I had back in 2008. "Many of the Nez Perce Prisoners are suffering from wounds received in General Miles battle, and one of the numbers died just before reaching Buford. I learn that they are singularly uncomplaining with regard to wounds, and do not always acknowledge that they have received them to get along without showing them."[5]

Could it have been Seven Days Whipping who died in Buford? I suspect that he and several more Nez Perce are buried near there. As I write this, the spirits of my ancestors are stirring within me, as if to confirm that indeed it is Great-grandfather Seven Days Whipping who passed away at Fort Buford—which would explain why we couldn't find his name on the lists of exile survivors. A journey to honor and recognize Seven Days Whipping will be planned in the near future to go to Fort Burford and do an honoring for him, he is not forgotten.

CHAPTER 12

Finding Black Raven's Story

My grandfather—my father's father—was Ka-khun-ne, which my family translates as Black Raven. At boarding school, he ended up with or was given the name Jesse Paul. He was the son of Seven Days Whipping and Um-al-wat. Of the couple's six children, he was the only one to survive the 1877 Nez Perce War. Family oral tradition says he was born in the Wallowa Valley of northeast Oregon and brought into the world in a tepee with the help of his grandmothers and aunties. Some of the records say he was born in 1870, while others say 1871; my guess is he was born in 1870, because he was listed as age 10 when he entered the Carlisle Indian Industrial School in 1880.

Black Raven spent his early years in the Wallowas with his parents and siblings. He lived seven snows before he and the rest of his family were caught up in the Nez Perce War of 1877. Having survived the war, Black Raven and Um-al-wat were forced by the US government to live in exile, first at Fort Leavenworth, from December 1877 to mid-July 1878; then the Quapaw Reservation, Indian Territory, Oklahoma, from July 1878–June 1879; and then to Ponca Reservation, Indian Territory, Oklahoma, June 1879–May 1885, when they were finally released to return to Idaho. We as a family view the exile as an extension of the Nez Perce War: we are prisoners of war according to government records and are treated as such.

The first mention of Black Raven that we found in our research was on a US government list of the Nez Perce warriors that were mustered into service on December 15, 1855, and mustered out January 20, 1856. The list names Black Raven's father, Seven Days Whipping, as one of the Indians owed money for their service to the US government. Even though payment for their services was approved by Congress in March 2, 1861, the warriors on this list had not yet been paid in 1883. Black Raven is listed as the son and heir of Seven Days Whipping who had ridden with the US Cavalry. On the list, his name is spelled "Ka-kun-nee." My family and I have made notes on our copies of the document, trying to work out what that might be in Nimipuutímt. One family member made a note saying that "kun-nee" means "black" or "blanketed" or "with blanket." There are other notes with an alternate spelling, ko-koh-tseets kuneen, which means "Black Raven" in Nimipuutímt.

Drawing of Black Raven by the author.

A search of the records from the Carlisle Indian Industrial School turned up correspondence from the school's superintendent, Richard H. Pratt relating to Black Raven. In a letter to the Commissioner of Indian Affairs, dated January 11, 1883, Pratt wrote:

> I have to inform you that we have a boy named Jesse Paul, who is invoiced to us as Kuam-ol-not, but who claims the name of Ka-kun-nee that his father (now dead) was named, "Seven Days Whipping" and his statement is corroborated by our oldest Nez Perce boy.

> Very respectfully
> R.H. Pratt
> Lt. Supt.

As a family we believe that Black Raven's mother Uma-al-wat became a widow before entering the exile journey to Fort Leavenworth, Kansas. We know that she remarried while in exile, but do not know when that occurred. She married Eugene Lowry and adopted the English name Phoebe. I will talk more about him later.

Um-al-wat and Black Raven, experienced exile together as a widow with her surviving child. The conditions at Fort Leavenworth were deplorable. After a few days in the temporary tent village, they were moved to a permanent camp site on the inside of an oval racetrack located on the Missouri river bottomlands of the military prison. Chief Joseph was disgusted that they had to draw water from the dirty Missouri River. Their human waste was deposited into thirty-foot-long latrines, riddled with feces, flies, and terrible odors. The old fort had a honeycomb of latrines covered with ash and dirt, but which did little to prevent dysentery, typhoid, and injuries. In addition, most of the Nimiipuu and Palouse had arrived with little warm clothing, and it took a month for the army to issue them surplus Civil War garments.[1] Were Um-al-wat and Black Raven among those who had little clothing? How were they handling the miserable living conditions? They would have had to adjust to a new environment, unfamiliar scenery, and new foods. These conditions no doubt made them miss the fresh mountain air of their home territory, as well as the smell of pine trees, clean water, and being able to eat their traditional roots and meats.

After two weeks, the Nimiipuu and Palouse had replaced the tents with tepees. Some were made of buffalo hides, but most of the hides had been lost during the war and now they were being issued canvas for their tepees. The furnishing of the tepees depended on what they had been able to save and bring with them. Some had buffalo hides for bedding, but most did not and were given straw to sleep on. The women complained that the canvas was not suitable for tepees and leaked water when it rained. After living there for five months, the Nimiipuu had forty-eight leaking lodges, which offered very little protection from the heavy spring rains. They were given cast iron stoves to warm their homes. Wood was supplied and they piled the wood around the exterior of their tepees to provide insulation.[2]

The Nimiipuu were given army rations of butchered beef, salt pork, hardtack, beans, flour, coffee, sugar, salt, and tobacco. "Each person received an average of eleven pounds of uncooked bone-in-beef and about seven pounds of flour per week. Salt pork and hardtack were limited to about one pound per person per month. Moderate portions of soap and salt were issued, and green coffee was restricted to about half a pound per person per week. Women dried or smoked the beef on outdoor racks or in special lodges and prepared the beans and flour, although baking powder and soda were not available. No fresh vegetable was provided."[3]

A hospital tent had been set up on their arrival at Fort Leavenworth. Dr. Comfort was assigned to care for the Nimiipuu. During the first three months, he treated war wounds as well as recent injuries, childhood illnesses, coughs, colds, bronchitis, tuberculosis, digestive and bacterial disorders, bronchial infections, pneumonia, and arthritis. In the spring, when malaria became prevalent, he treated the Nimiipuu with small doses of quinine. Just prior to the transfer of the Nimiipuu to Quapaw Reservation in Indian Territory, Oklahoma, the malaria epidemic was full-blown, and Dr. Comfort did not have enough supplies to treat the more than four hundred Nimiipuu.[4]

Um-al-wat and Black Raven lived through these deplorable conditions and malaria. I am sure they lost cousins and friends during this time. They would have had to rely on their spiritual, emotional, and physical strengths and lean on each other to get through this time. The Nimiipuu tried to hold onto their religion. That first winter at Fort Leavenworth, they held winter ceremonies. These activities attracted many tourists, who were very curious about these Indians from the west. They were so curious that they began invading the Nimiipuu camp every day, and the army had to limit the tourist visits to two days a week. Grandmother, how did you handle the tourists who often would just come to your lodge and peek in? I suppose you endured, but I would have been irritated. The women became entrepreneurs, making baskets and beaded items to sell to the tourists. I can imagine my grandmother working on a basket or beading items to sell to help buy needed supplies and food for herself and son as well as to share what she had with others.

While at Fort Leavenworth, the Nimiipuu experienced various atrocities, including sexual assaults on the women. In addition to serving as a home for the Nimiipuu, Fort Leavenworth was a prison for felons, who often escaped. Some of these prisoners would go to the Nimiipuu camp, rob them, and commit rapes. The soldiers assigned to oversee the Nimiipuu would also commit rapes. The women complained, but nothing was done about the assaults. The rapes were not acknowledged until 1881, after Reverend Archie Lawyer had arrived when they were at the Ponca Reservation, Indian Territory, Oklahoma. He spoke of the robberies and sexual assaults in a memorandum presented to the President and Congress. These assaults caused physical harm, psychological injuries, unwanted pregnancies, and sexually transmitted diseases.[5] "Mothers, grandmothers, and *tewets* tended to physical and emotional injuries. Dr. Comfort treated the growing number of cases of venereal disease."[6] These physical and psychological wounds lasted a lifetime. My heart aches when I read this section of history.

The curious public would see that we were not as wild as everyone thought and would hear the story from Joseph of how the terms of the surrender had not been honored. He told those that would listen that the surrender was a mutual surrender and Colonel Miles had said that they would be allowed to return to the reservation in Idaho. Eventually Joseph had the opportunity to speak to local leaders. They were sympathetic and understood the dishonoring of the surrender. Thus began an allyship to help Joseph and the Nimiipuu petition the US government to allow them to return to their homelands. In the meantime, members of the US government, including the secretary of the interior, the secretary of war, and the commissioners of Indian affairs, along with Generals Howard, Sheridan, Sherman, and McDowell, and Nimiipuu school teacher James Reuben all recommended permanent expulsions of the Nimiipuu to Indian Territory. There was no consultation with Chief Joseph about this transfer. It was decided to send the Nimiipuu prisoners to the Quapaw Reservation, in Indian Territory, Oklahoma. Congress passed an appropriation bill of

$20,000 to move the Nimiipuu on May 9, 1878, and the funds became available on July 1, 1878.[7]

After eight months at Fort Leavenworth, Nimiipuu were being prepared to leave. While at Fort Leavenworth, they survived on the limited rations the Army spared them, all while dealing with homesickness, disease, and the death of their loved ones.[8] During their time at the fort, twenty-one of them had died, including Chief Joseph's baby daughter. A small graveyard had been prepared by the Nimiipuu. It was surrounded by six-foot-tall peeled saplings and held the bodies of their loved ones.[9]

The move did not take place until the heat of mid-July. On July 19, they were taken to the Fort Leavenworth rail depot for first leg of their trip: the 300-mile trip to Baxter Springs, Kansas. They were cramped into passenger cars, forty adults and twenty-five to thirty children in each car. There were not enough passenger cars, so a baggage car was employed to cram in the rest of the Nimiipuu. They also had six baggage cars loaded with their belongings, tents, and equipment. The trip took several hours.[10] Conditions during the trip were reported by Inspector McNeil, who oversaw the trip:

> We got them on the cars about 4 A.M. the 21st, when we pulled out of Fort Leavenworth without military guard or attendants, except the humane ministrations of Dr. Comfort who was detailed to accompany the Indians to Baxter. We made but few stops and those only for supplying drinking water. We arrived at Baxter between 6 and 7 in the P.M.... The heat of the day had been terrific. Two children died that day and one the night before died.... Agent Jones at once made arrangements for wagon transportation of persons and materials to the new camp, there being none fit to walk in this terribly hot weather.[11]

The Nimiipuu exiles were aided by some Modocs on the seven-mile trip from the rail station at Baxter Springs to their new home. The Modocs had been exiled to Indian Territory from Oregon after the Modoc War of 1872-73.[12] The Modocs welcomed the Nimiipuu by bringing them potatoes and green corn to supplement the government rations of flour and beef. They combined what foods they had to create a welcome feast.[13]

Located in northeastern Oklahoma, the Quapaw Reservation was made up of several tribes: Quapaw, Shawnee, Ottawa, Confederated Peoria, Miami, Wyandot, and Seneca. Each tribe had assigned lands within the reservation and was managed by the Quapaw Indian Agency. When the Nimiipuu arrived, they were placed onto the lands of the Modoc.

Having arrived too late in the year to plant gardens, the exiles had to depend on government rations. They had no shelter for the first ten nights, as squalls of rain drenched the camp, adding to the misery of the already sick and weak Nimiipuu. The supplies of quinine and other medicines was exhausted.[14]

The conditions at Quapaw were no better than they had been at Fort Leavenworth. An article in the *Arkansas City Traveler*, on September 25, 1878, states, "Of the four hundred Nez Perce Indians recently located at the Quapaw Agency, forty have died and a hundred and sixty [are] lying sick."[15] In fact, 47 died within the first two months at Fort Baxter. Members of the Board of Indian Commissioners visited the encampment and were appalled at the conditions. They immediately telegraphed St. Louis for a supply of quinine, at the time, the only anti-malarial treatment available.[16] It seems miraculous that more did not die due to the lack of quinine, and that my great-grandmother Um-al-wat and her son Black Raven survived the malaria epidemic.

The Indian Agent Jones was a corrupt agent. He had not ordered enough food to be set aside for the needs of the Nimiipuu. The agent scraped enough funds together to buy some cattle and supplies for them. The Nimiipuu proved themselves to be resourceful: the men hunted prairie chickens, quail, and deer, staying within the boundaries of the Quapaw reservation. They also fished, even in the winter, as they knew how to ice fish. The women made baskets from willow and would trade them for fresh food. I can imagine many women joining together with great-grandmother Um-al-wat to make baskets, using their basket-making skills and adapting to using the willow materials instead of hemp. The baskets were also used for storage and to cook in.[17]

The Nimiipuu tried to settle in, and they were able to erect sixty-three lodges in an oak forest on about twenty acres. The families were again given army rations, but the Indian Agent Jones did not always give them their rations and often they would not have food for two or three days at a time. By mid-winter of 1878-1879 the Nimiipuu were suffering from coughs, bronchitis, tuberculosis, arthritis or rheumatism, constipation, and psychological disorders. Joseph complained to Indian Agent Jones, stating the food was wretched, not enough medical attentions, and lack of housing. So many Nimiipuu were sick and dejected after so many deaths the camp was often silent except for the sounds of mourning marking another death.[18] This complaint brought no relief or action to address the problems.

While the Nimiipuu were doing their utmost to survive at Quapaw Reservation, three Nimiipuu Christian ministers from the treaty Nimiipuu band were sent to Indian Territory. Their aim was to accelerate the interdictions of Christianity and other federal programs. The three were Reverends Archie Lawyer, Mark Williams, and James Reuben. They left Lapwai, Idaho, on November 8, 1878, and arrived at Quapaw Reservation on December 6, 1878. Lawyer was able to bring with him his mother's double buffalo hide tepee. It was to be used to hold church services and council meetings.

However, the reception for these three, especially James Reuben, was mixed. Reuben had fought against the non-treaty Nimiipuu during the Nez Perce war and many considered him arrogant.[19]

While in exile the Nimiipuu still practiced the old ways of *we' set* or seven drum. With the coming of the three Nimiipuu Presbyterian ministers, many of the Nimiipuu chose to practice Christian faith. Chief Joseph did not become Christian, but attended the church services alongside his followers. It was thought that only the non-Christian were in the Nez Perce war of 1877.

> Otis Halfmoon, whose Catholic relative was incarcerated at Fort Vancouver, agrees that Catholic and Presbyterian Nimiipuu fought and went into exile alongside with their non-Christian relations, because family was more important than politics or theology.... Otis Halfmoon also concurs that Christian detainees used a wall of silence to hide from federal officials in the prison camps.[20]

This mostly occurred at Fort Leavenworth, Kansas. With the arrival of Lawyer, Reuben, and Williams in December 1878 to the exile camps, first at Qupawa, and later at Ponca, Oklahoma, many were able to come forward then to express their Christian faith.

With Joseph having complained about their living conditions, a council was held to decide on a better place on the Quapaw Reservation to put the Nimiipuu. But Chief Joseph and his headmen declined to cooperate in the selection of lands, referring to the "hot land" as, "like a poor man; it amounts to nothing."[21]

At last, the Commissioner of Indian Affairs, E. A. Hayt, agreed to let Joseph and his headmen choose a more suitable place in Indian Territory. In the fall of 1878, Hayt, Joseph, and Husishusis Kute traveled west through Indian Territory and found a place within the Ponca Reservation.

Commissioner Hayt agreed to the new location and promised the Nimii-puu they could move the following summer.[22] The Ponca Reservation was located in north-central Oklahoma, near the border with Kansas. There were several tribes located on this reservation and it was managed by the Ponca Indian Agency. The other tribes on this reservation were the Ponca, Pawnee, and Otoe, each with their assigned lands.

In January 1879, Joseph and Yellow Bull were allowed to go to Washington, DC, for a personal hearing with President Hayes. On January 14, 1879, Joseph gave an impassioned speech to a large group of cabinet members, congressmen, and diplomats, saying:

> My friends, I have been asked to show you, my heart. I am glad to have a chance to do so. I want the white people to understand my people. Some of you think an Indian is like a wild animal. This is a great mistake…
>
> I cannot understand why so many chiefs are allowed to talk so many different ways and promise so many different things…. I do not understand why nothing is done for my people. I have heard talk and talk, but nothing is done…. If the white man wants to live in peace with the Indian he can live in peace…. Treat all men alike. Give them all the same law. Give them all an even chance to live and grow. All men were made by the same Great Spirit Chief. They are all brothers. The earth is the mother of all people, and all people should have equal rights upon it. You might as well expect the rivers to run backward as that any man who was born a free man should be contented penned up and denied liberty to go where he pleases…. I know that my race must change. We cannot hold our own with the white men as we are. We only ask an even chance to live as other men live…. Let me be a free man—free to travel, free to stop, free to work, free to trade, where I choose, free to choose my own teachers, free to follow the religion of my fathers, free to think and talk and act for myself—and I will obey every law, or submit to the penalty.[23]

Joseph's speech stirred many emotions and inspired supporters to take up the Nimiipuu cause to be allowed to return to Idaho. But there were more obstacles to overcome. The process of getting help to lobby for them to return took a few more years. One major obstacle was the White settlers in Idaho and Oregon: they did not want Joseph to return, while the pro-US Christian Nimiipuu did not want the non-treaty Indians to come back and cause problems. A group of White Christians in Kansas City, Kansas, came forward saying they would help. That gave Joseph hope—hope that he and Yellow Bull passed on to their people.

In mid-June 1879, the exiled Nimiipuu moved to the lands that Joseph and Yellow Bull had chosen within the Ponca Reservation. Yet again the Nimiipuu packed up and traveled to another hot place unknown to them. They traveled by wagon; all told, there were 65 wagons with teams of horses. The wagon train averaged about 20 miles per day and would start at 4:00 or 5:00 in the morning and stop by noon for lunch. This schedule was to avoid the heat and humidity of the hottest part of the day. They traveled 177 miles in nine days, arriving at the Ponca Reservation on June 15, 1879. The Nimiipuu settled at the mouth of the Chikaskia River,[25] about 30 miles south of Arkansas City, Kansas.

They experienced another outbreak of malaria, and not enough quinine had been ordered. Many more Nimiipuu died due to the lack of quinine. It was reported that between April 1879 and August 1879, twenty had died. The census taken at this time listed 370 Nimiipuu in August 1879.[24] I don't know what state their bodies and souls must have been in, but it's hard to imagine Um-al-wat and Black Raven witnessing malaria that sicken half of their number and not wanting to just curl up and die.

Compounding the stress and trauma of exile and relocation, Indian Agent William Whiteman had no provisions for the tribe when they arrived at Ponca Reservation. He had to seek help in securing supplies to support the Nimiipuu through their first winter in their new home.

Gradually, though, conditions improved. The three Christian Nez Perce ministers, hired by the US government to teach and preach to the exiles, continued their work. Williams became ill and had to return home. Lawyer and Reuben stayed on and began a day school for anyone who was interested in learning. Several Nimiipuu children attended and Ka-khun-ne, being a curious nine-year-old, most likely attended the school.

The Euro-American philosophy at that time was that farming would civilize the Indians. If they plowed and planted the land, they would become self-sufficient. But some of the Nimiipuu could not or would not do this kind of work—it went against their religious beliefs: plowing Mother Earth was a violent act, the same as cutting Her. Agent Whiteman thought that hard work would distract the exiles from their misfortunes. But after learning of their attitude towards farming, he wrote in his annual report that "the men he found to be indolent, hard work had nothing to fear from them, they will handle it very gently."[26] However, the Nimiipuu had more freedom here at Ponca. They were able to obtain cows, horses, pigs, chickens, and ducks. The Nimiipuu were familiar with managing large herds of livestock. They had kept large herds of horses and cows prior to the war in the Wallowas. The men tended to the cows and horses and the women managed the chickens and ducks. The fowl gave them fresh eggs and the livestock provided the meat.[27]

Most of the group were able to start farming and till the land and plant crops. The weather was detrimental to their success, however. Some summers were so hot that the crops dried up before they could harvest; there were successful summers, too, where they were able to plant and harvest potatoes, corn, carrots, turnips, green beans, pumpkins, watermelons, and muskmelons.[28] Some winters the temperatures were below freezing, and most Nimiipuu did not have wooden houses. The three winters from 1882-1885 had temperatures from -6 to -20 degrees. Most of the Nimiipuu and Palouse did not have log homes until fall of 1884; even these provided little shelter because they were unheated.[29]

A researcher found that the Nimiipuu men did take on jobs to help their families. The men became teamsters and drove wagons of supplies from Arkansas City to the Ponca Agency. The women used their skills of beadwork, basket-making, and sewing gloves, moccasins, and other arts. They sold these items to the border towns of Arkansas City and Winfield. Their skill at making leather gloves made their products in high demand and they sold more than 1000 pair of gloves in Arkansas City. The women added beadwork to some of the gloves, which were purchased by cowboys and ranchers and brought in more money. The gloves sold for $0.75 a pair. Over a couple of years, they sold 3,600 pairs of gloves for a total of $2,455. The men brought their wives to town to sell their items, but some of the widows did not own horses, so they had to walk to town or ride with their friends who had horses. Sometimes they were in town but the cowboys and ranchers were not, so they were not able to sell their items.[30] It is not known if great-grandmother Um-al-wat was among those able to sell her items. What I do know is she taught her granddaughters the art of making gloves when she returned to the reservation. The family has two beautiful pairs of gloves that we treasure.

During this time, a split became further defined among the Nimiipuu prisoners. The new Christian Nimiipuu adopted the western style of dress. The men cut their hair and wore western style clothing. Even though Chief Joseph did not become Christian, when he spoke with government officials and attend Presbyterian functions, he wore western suits. Joseph wore tall Stetson hats adorned with feathers and beadwork. Many of his followers still choose to wear their hair long, either braided or hung loose. The non-Christian men wore shell ornaments and wore Stetson hats with feathers, while the Christian men wore more conservative hats without feathers or adornment. The Christian women wore western style dresses made from calico and made clothing from the government-issued checkered cloth and wool cloth. They gave up their large shell earrings and learned to crochet collars for their dresses. The non-Christian women still wore their shell earrings and beaded jewelry and bright-colored head scarves. Both Christian and non-Christian women wore long shawls and favored the color red. All were able to buy trade cloth shirts for their husbands and children.[31]

Even though the conditions improved, sickness and death were still rampant. The cycle of hot summers and the mosquitoes brought malaria. Every Nimiipuu was treated for malaria at least three times between 1879 and 1885.[32] "Malaria accelerates population decline, degrade population regenerations, and is particularly harmful to women and children. The disease also causes miscarriages, reductions in fecundity and potency, and anemia. More Nimiipuu women and children than men died in captivity."[33] A government physician who came to look after the Nimiipuu reported that "[h]e found in many cases the Indians were sick in soul even more than in body. Deaths came from broken hearts as well as from malaria; nor should it be overlooked that most of the band were either old people or children, a fact that accounted in some measure for the high mortality."[34]

Ka-khun-ne was seven years old when he went into exile. At age nine or ten, he and his mother had survived two camps and were now settling into the third. As I learned more of his story, I struggled to understand how some could go on, despite great odds and in the face of such suffering. I looked for understanding in the experiences of other cultures and researched the Jewish holocaust. A book by Viktor Frankl, *Man's Search for Meaning*, helped me understand. I gleaned from the book this important thought: "He who has a *why* to live can bear with almost any *how*."[35] What was the "why" for Ka-khun-ne and his mother? What hope did they cling to? Perhaps each other and to the others of their tribe? Perhaps, too, the messages they might have heard from Joseph and Yellow Bull, as well as the help being provided by the church in Arkansas City, Kansas. In his preface to Frankl's book, psychologist Gordon Allport writes that, for Frankl, in the end all that remains is "the last of human freedoms—the ability to choose one's attitude in a given set of circumstances."[36]

While in exile, Joseph, Yellow Bull, and others never gave up hope of returning to Idaho. They consistently maintained that the US government had not honored the terms of surrender that had been agreed to with General Miles. Along with the rest of their people, they hoped to someday return to their ancestral homes. As a direct result of Joseph's speech in Washington, DC, social groups petitioned the government for the Nimiipuu return. The entire speech and additional information were later published in the *North American Review* in April 1879.

In addition to the day school he started, Reverend James Reuben also held Sabbath school and preached "the Word" in Nimipuutímt. He sought aid from the local Presbyterian Church in Arkansas City, Kansas, and requested help with ministering and preaching. A Reverend Fleming agreed to preside and offer communion monthly and to help with baptizing and receiving Nimiipuu into the membership of the Presbyterian Church.[37] The Presbyterian Church of Arkansas City was a member of the Emporia Presbytery and helped them to adopt a resolution in support of the Nimiipuu. The resolution states, in part, that the "Presbytery has heard… of a Presbyterian church of ninety-eight members among the Nez Perce Indians upon our border, as one of the most remarkable and encouraging works of grace with which it has been our happy privilege to be connected" and further, that the "Presbytery affirm[s] to the board of Home Missions its most profound interest in these Indian people, and invoke[s] in their behalf, the tenderest interest and care of this board in the future."[38]

Together with the Emporia Presbytery and the work of the Nimiipuu lay ministers James Reuben and Archie Lawyer, 150 Nimiipuu were brought into membership during this time. The Emporia Presbytery also influenced the Synod of the Presbyterian Church of Kansas to draw up a memorial on behalf of the exiled Nimiipuu, which was sent to the President Ulysses S. Grant, asking for the restoration of the Nez Perce Indians to their home in Idaho Territory on April 20, 1882.[39] I am not sure if Great-grandmother Um-al-wat joined while in exile; my guess would be that she did, along with her second husband Eugene. When she returns to the Nez Perce Reservation, her home was next to the Spalding Presbyterian Indian church along with several other tribal members. It was a common practice for several Nez Perce Christian members to live next to the church they attended.

The momentum to allow the exiled Nimiipuu to return grew. In addition to the Presbyterian Church, help came from General Miles, the Indian Rights Association, and other American philanthropical organizations. All this stirred public opinion in favor of a Nimiipuu return. Also, the United States was going through a reform on Indian policy which aided the process.[40]

James Reuben petitioned the government to bring home the widows and their children. The Commissioner of Indian Affairs recommended allowing 33 widows and their children to return to Idaho. Congress agreed and granted permission in 1883 but without funding for travel. But their desire to return was so great that the Nimiipuu raised the funds through the sale of their beaded items and other handicrafts.[41] In May 1883, Reuben expressed their feelings of those who were allowed to return:

> Language cannot express our joy when we remember that our feet will soon tread again our native land, and our eyes behold the scenes of our childhood. The underlying love for home, which we have cherished in our hearts so long, has caused our tears to flow for years, but now we are but one step from that home.[42]

Congress's act set in motion a period of intense petitioning, urging the return of the remaining tribal members. In an act passed in 1884, the Secretary of the Interior Henry Teller was given the power to decide the fate of Joseph's band. There were several problems to overcome. One was that many of Joseph's men were still wanted on charges of murder—but why, I'd like to know, was this "murder" when Joseph's people were defending themselves? That is one-sided thinking, in my view, the United States was supposed to be based on "justice for all," but this is clearly a case where that did not apply to the Nimiipuu. As my father pointed out when we visited Big Hole, the US Calvary's slaughter of women, children, and the defenseless was clearly a case of murder.

However, back in Idaho the sentiment of the White settlers who had suffered from the war were in no mood to forgive and were not ready to allow the Nimiipuu warriors to return to Idaho or the Wallowas.[43] The impasse was resolved by dividing the tribe into two groups. On September 16, 1884, Commissioner Price sent a telegram to Indian Agent Scott, stating that he planned to split the Nimiipuu exiles and relocate them. Christians would be sent to Lapwai, while those that remained loyal to Joseph would be sent to a reservation at Colville, Washington Territory.

When Joseph and his leaders received this word, they called for a council meeting for September 18. Many of the Nimiipuu would accept going to Lapwai, but they did not consent to being separated. Joseph spoke at the council, saying he did not want to go to Lapwai, but he wanted them to return to the Wallowas. He did not want to go to this strange land at Coville. He also insisted they would not move without a firm commitment from the federal government to their destination and statement of their rights. They all rejected Price's offer of being split. In November 1884, Price denied their immediate release.[44]

The Nimiipuu did not give up hope, however: a new president, secretary of the Interior, and commissioner of Indian Affairs would be taking office in March 1885. In the meantime, even though Commissioner Price had denied the Nimiipuu their release, he was still under orders from the Secretary of the Interior to provide funding for their release. He included $10,000 for their relocation in the Indian Appropriation budget, but there would need to be other funds to cover the costs. Price stated:

> It was dangerous for the prisoners to be returned to Idaho because of outstanding criminal indictment and anti-Nimiipuu sentiment. Despite their earlier refusal to be separated, the captives were now considering the Colville split. Those who were not subject to indictment or punishment could be returned to Lapwai, and the rest of the prisoners would be relocated outside of Idaho.[45]

By April 8, 1885, Joseph seemed somewhat resigned to accepting the separation of the bands. When asked what he thought about this separation, he stated that "it would have been preferable to consult the prisoners before making any decisions concerning them. He also held that they had been cheated out of the Wallowa Valley, Oregon."[46] On May 12, Joseph and others agreed to be sent to the Northwest regardless of the Coville spilt and the risk of possible indictments or revenge. The new Commissioner of Indian Affairs, John D.C. Atkins, let the Secretary of the Interior know that the Christian Nimiipuu would return to Lapwai and the rest of the group would be sent to Colville because of outstanding indictments.[47] Not all the Nimiipuu who followed Joseph to Colville had indictments. Many of these were women and children.

Acting on the tribe's behalf, Joseph, Yellow Bull, Yellow Bear, and Hsuih-suih Kutte, a Palouse, surrendered the 90,000 acres of land that had been allocated for them in Indian Territory in return for the expense of removal.

There was to be financial aid to help with resettlement, as well.[48] Eventually these lands would be turned over to the Tonkawa Tribe. They were originally located in southeastern Texas and were forced to relocate to the Ponca Reservation in 1885, about the same time as the Nimiipuu were leaving.

The release of the Nimiipuu was finally approved and a Dr. Faulkner of Washington DC, was assigned to be the relocation supervisor. He arrives in Arkansas City, Kansas on May 6, 1885. He wires ahead to Agent Scott that he wants the Nimiipuu to be ready to leave Ponca Reservation by May 21. Supplies had been ordered for the long trip to Idaho that would be ready to load at the train station. The preparations begin in earnest. They sell their livestock, women and children begin to pack their belongings. Many are worried about leaving so many of their relatives buried in the cemetery. Earlier in March the men had started to cut lumber and build a fence around the 100 graves, now rush to finish the fence before leaving.[49]

I wonder what Great-grandmother Um-al-wat was preparing to pack. How many friends and relatives had she lost who are buried in the cemetery? Her heart must have been aching realizing that her son Ka-khun-nee (Black Raven) would not be making the trip with her. He had been sent off to Carlisle Industrial Indian School in February 1880, along with four other Nimiipuu youth. Plus, there were three other youth sent in 1883. They would not be making this journey home with them at this time. There would also be youth that had been attending Chilocco Indian Boarding school (it was only 20 miles from Ponca Reservation) being rushed to the train station to meet their families. I will talk more about how he and the others were selected to go to these boarding schools in the next chapter. How would she let him know that she was leaving Ponca Reservation and going to Lapwai? Was she happy and sad at the same time?

The Nimiipuu loaded their wagons on May 19 and finally May 20 the thirty-four wagons needed for the journey to Arkansas City to meet a train began. The weather was rainy and made the roads muddy. The wagons slowly trudged through the muddy roads, some were able to go faster than others, which caused many of the wagons to arrive early the next morning of May 21. It took most of the day for their belongings to dry out. On the morning of May 22, the Nimiipuu loaded their belongings into baggage cars. At 1:15 PM the train whistle blew and the train pulled out of the train station.

Dr. Faulkner, who accompanied the Nimiipuu on their return journey, described the day as both joyful and mournful:

The morning of the 22nd was a time of hectic activity and great excitement, beginning at daybreak, when the lagging members of the band reached the camp, and continuing for several hours while the baggage was loaded on the train. It was an occasion for grief as well as joy, which was marked by howling and crying as the Indians mourned their parting from the dead they were leaving behind. Just before the train pulled out, an instructor arrived bringing all the Nez Percé pupils from the Chilocco School. Finally, at 1:15 P.M. all were on board, and the expedition took its departure.[50]

These cars did not have seats, only backless wooden benches to sit on. They would sleep on the floors around the benches and when they stopped for the evening, they would build fires and cook their meals. The Nimiipuu again experience hot temperatures traveling on the train. They travel through Kansas, then to Denver, Colorado; Cheyenne, Wyoming; Utah, Pocatello, and Boise, Idaho. They finally arrived at Wallula Junction, Washington Territory, on May 27, 1885.[51]

The cross-country journey took seven days. At Wallula, the band was divided. How hard this must have been to have to say goodbye to relatives and friends. Brothers and sisters separated. Faulkner reported no deaths or accidents on the trip. Agent Monteith met the exiles with a detachment of soldiers from Fort Walla Walla. There were 118 Nimiipuu being sent to Lapwai, traveling with Agent Monteith and the soldiers as escort. There were 92 adults, twelve children and 14 infants.[52] Among this group would be Great-grandmother Um-al-wat and her new husband Eugene. Um-al-wat had changed her name to Phoebe now and would be known as this among my family to this day. This group continued by train to Riparia, via Grange City, Washington Territory. At Riparia they boarded a steam-boat and traveled on the Snake River to Lewison, Idaho. They arrive June 1, 1885. They are greeted by men from Lapwai with horses and wagons. Agent Monteith limited the number of Lapwai Nez Perce men, he did not want the people of Lewiston to misinterpret the presence of too many Nez Perce. The wagons were loaded and left for Lapwai, about 12 miles to the east.[53]

There were five hundred people waiting to greet the returning Nimiipuu. They formed a semicircle with eight to ten people deep around the returnees. There were ceremonies and speeches given to welcome them back. One of the returnees, Tom Hill responded for the refugees.

He spoke of the long confinement in a dreary land, a land of many sorrows; spoke feelingly of their constant longings for their mountain home, which they had given up all hopes of ever seeing again; humbly acknowledged the goodness and mercy of God in permitting some of them to stand once more on the banks of the Lapwai in the presence of so many old-time friends; referred gratefully to the interpositions of the Church and the law in their behalf, and closed with the announcement that their only desire now is to be henceforth law abiding people and believers in the God of Heaven.[54]

Another remembrance of this day shared how the hand shaking began after Tom Hill's speech:

Hand-shaking began, which lasted for over an hour…the long procession of our people filed past and took the hand of everyman, woman and child. Friend meet with friend, fathers and mothers with their long lost sons and daughters. It was very touching to watch the play of features…identifying the face of a relative or friend, and…to hear the glad expressions. "Is that you, ___!" "It is you, father!" or "Is that you, brother!" Only one who had a heart of stone could have stand by and not entered with spirit into the joys of the occasion.[55]

There had to be tears of sadness as the ones who were among the greeters looking for relatives, were not seen. Hugs for those who did return, tears by those who did not see their relatives return. How hard was it for Great-grandmother to have to tell that five of her six children did not return with her, who was hugging and crying tears with her at the loss of her children?

The weary travelers camp at the meeting camp grounds for the evening. Within weeks, many had joined the Presbyterian churches at Lapwai and Spalding. However, life was not ideal, the returnees lived in continued threats and punitive actions, and many of the returned Christians burned their feathers and drums and refused to speak to outsiders about the war.[56] Great-grandmother Phoebe joins the Spalding Presbyterian Church. We do not know how long her husband Eugene lives after they arrive back. We do know Pheobe lives until the age of 80, dies May 2, 1918. I have often wondered if she felt safe or threatened after her return. Could she find peace and security. Does she hold onto hope of seeing her son Black Raven return to the reservation and help our people? I believe she does and this gives her the strength to continue living the best that she can until she is able to see her son return.

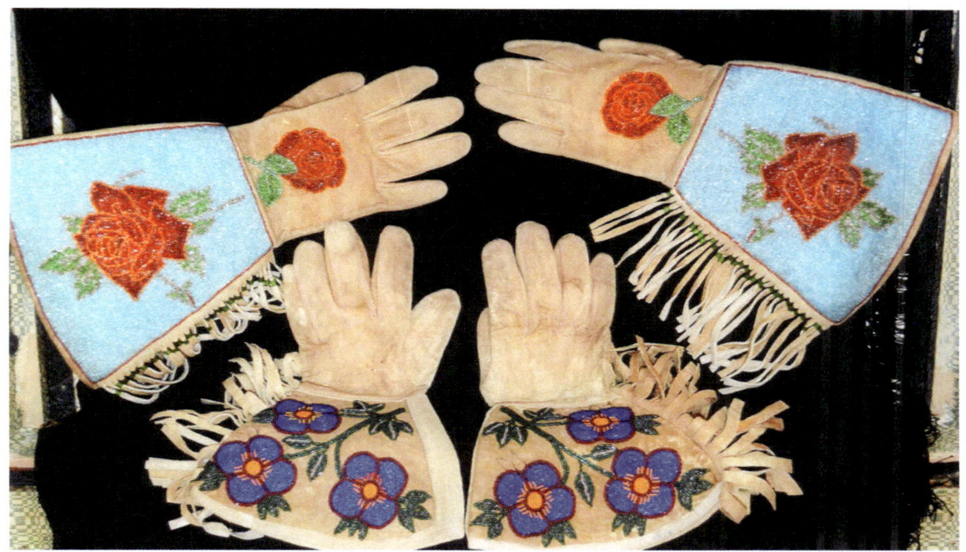

Beaded gloves made circa 1918 by Esther Paul, who was taught to bead by her grandmother Um-al-wat (Phoebe Lowry).

Back at Wallula, Chief Joseph's Nimiipuu group and Husishusis Kute Palouse group of 150 were loaded onto Northern Pacific railroad cars. The numbers given for the breakdown of adults and children vary from researcher to researcher. One states the group consisted of 103 adults, 34 school-aged children and 13 younger children. Another states there are 120 adults, 16 children, and 14 infants. They both total 150 going to Colville. They travel north through Pasco, Connell, and on to Spokane Falls, Washington Territory (present-day Spokane). From here they are loaded onto wagons and escorted by military soldiers to Fort Spokane, which is located at the confluence of the Columbia and Spokane rivers. Both groups stay at Fort Spokane until September 1885.[57] From here, they are escorted to the Colville Reservation. There is no reception for these returnees. The Colville Indian Agent is furious that the expatriated had been forced to this reservation. The other tribes who live there did not welcome them either. They refused to let the newcomers settle on their assigned lands. They shared no old customs and relationships and no languages or spiritual beliefs with the Nimiipuu. The reservation had never been their home territory. The Nimiipuu experienced a lot of hostility in the beginning years. But over time, the tribes did establish workable relationships.[58]

Chief Joseph and his followers fulfilled their agreement made at Bear Paw: they remained at peace with the United States. The returnees did face non-Native aggressions just as their friends and relatives in Lapwai did. Chief Joseph never gave up wanting to return to the homelands of the Wallowa, and when he traveled guards accompanied him. He was both admired and hated by the non-Natives all his life.[59] He dies of a broken heart on September 21, 1904, buried in a Catholic Cemetery in Nespelem, Washington.

These numbers of returning Nimiipuu and Palouse, both non-Christian and Christian, do not reflect the actual losses. From the first census taken of the Nimiipuu there were 147 children. When they leave Tonkawa, there are only 35. The infants listed would not have been counted in the census of the arrival of the Nimiipuu at Fort Leavenworth. The parents' loss of 112 children during their time in exile was felt for generations to come. This also does not count the number of children lost in the surprise attack at Big Hole, Montana. Great-grandmother Phoebe, who lost five of her children in the war and its aftermath, was far from alone in her grief.

After completing writing of this chapter, I was overcome with emotion. I was feeling sadness, anger, and whelmed. At first, I just walked around in a daze, not sure what to do with all this emotion. I then relied on what I had done when I began this healing journey, I go outside and sit on the ground. Let the air move around me and breathe. I sat for a long time, but the feelings had not abated. Later that evening our power went out, leaving us in the darkness of the evening. I soon discovered that we had no candles or lantern to offer light for us. My husband decided to go to bed, but I decided to stay in the living in room in the darkness. I was still feeling the emotions and I knew I needed to move through them. When I was outside, I was trying to just push them away. Now here in the darkness I could since my great-grandmother Um-al-wat with me. I began to recall each move she had made while in exile, felt her loss, but I also felt her strength to keep going, not to give up. It was as if I was moving through the storm of the exile with her. I acknowledged that she had moved through the storm and thanked her. I told her I have not forgotten her or her journey of survival. I am here because of her and the strength she gave to her son Black Raven.

I also have a photo of Um-al-wat, it was taken after her return from exile about 1890. When I look at her stature and face, I do not see a defeated woman. I see a woman who has a face of courage, strength, and spirit.

The Paul family has visited the cemetery of the Nimiipuu at Ponca Reservation which is now looked after by the Tonkawa Tribe. We have been there twice as a family with parents, brothers, sister, and nieces and nephews. I visited in 2023 with my husband. When we are there at the cemetery, we light sage to smudge and cleanse the area and light sweetgrass to bring good spirits. My family has stood and cried at the lone headstone that was provided as a remembrance of the Nimiipuu buried there while in exile. When I am by myself, I find that I am still shaken and saddened by this horrific loss of family members. But I also remember Great-Grandmother saying to me in dreams: "Tell our story so we are not forgotten."

Exile cemetery at Ponca Reservation, where the Nimiipuu who died in exile are buried. Now located on the Tonkawa Reservation and maintained by them. Pictured are members of the Paul family in June 1999, from left to right: Kim Enz, grandaughter of Titus; Titus Paul, Titus' daughter Roberta Paul, and her son Mike Foiles. *Paul Family Photo Collection.*

CHAPTER 13

Carlisle Indian Industrial School

The United States was entering a new stage of answering the question, "How do we civilize and Christianize the savage American Indians?" A question I take offense to. Many thought we could not be civilized because we were too "savage." Who is to say who is civilized and who is savage? How is an oppressor more civilized than the group of people they oppress? An oppressor that uses force to subdue and impose that there is only one way to be civilized, is savage and uncivil.

In the circumstance of two distinct and very different cultures trying to understand each other, the thinking was to separate using treaties and forming reservation boundaries. Then the missionaries were sent to the reservations to help civilize the savages through religion. They would bring a Christian God to show the Indian how to take on moral values of Christianity. Civilized meant becoming farmers who used the large land holdings of the Native Americans. To not use this land for farming was to not utilize it as God intended.[1]

When the missionaries came to the Northwest in 1829, the lands of the Plateau peoples were still pristine and untouched by Whites. As was shared earlier in this book, the missionaries Whitman, Spalding, and Smith thought the only way for us to become civilized was to become Christian. "In 1871, Congress officially confirmed the altered state of Indians: they were now deemed to be wards of the government, a colonized people."[2] Once White settlers began landing on the shores of Turtle Island (now the United States), the people who had escaped religious persecution in Europe were now beginning their own persecution of the Natives of Turtle Island by imposing their Christian God. Thus, colonization began.

The news of this new policy led to philanthropic observers decrying the cruel and brutal manner by which the Native Americans became wards of the government. Public opinion was passing judgment on the government's treatment of its Indian wards, saying it was unnecessarily shortsighted, harsh, and even cruel. But still the thinking was: "Indians not only need to be saved from the White man; they need to be saved from themselves."[3]

Several organizations had begun to address reforming interactions with Native populations. One organization was the Indian Rights Association, founded by Herbert Welsh and Henry Pancoast in 1883. They wanted to "secure the civilization of the two hundred and ninety thousand Indians of the United States (inclusive of the thirty thousand Natives of Alaska), and then prepare the way for their absorptions into the common life of our own people."[4] Most of the philanthropic reformer organizations were well educated and financially secure, and almost every member came from the upper echelons of eastern US society. "They were guided by the universal tenets of evangelical Protestantism, never doubting for a moment that their effort to uplift the Indians was a fulfillment of their Christian obligation to extend the blessings of Christianity to all the peoples of the world."[5] With all this effort from the philanthropic organizations, the Native Americans were never consulted. Not one of these organization had a Native American on their boards.

The reformers for Indian Rights were optimistic that the Indians could be saved and this could be accomplished in three areas: land, law, and education.

LAND

Regarding the land issue, the reformers deplored the reservation system for two reasons. First, it perpetuated the Indians' attachment to the tribal outlook and lifeways, as tribal values placed a high regard on communal property holding and gift-giving. Second, the reservation system was linked with the rationing system, which was well intentioned but consequently instilled an attitude of dependency.[6]

LAW

The law aspect of reform was going to be the Allotment of Lands. Allotment would smash the tribal connection, force Indians to work the land, and eventually bring an end to the rationing system. Congress passed the General Allotment Act, commonly known as the Dawes Act, named after Henry Dawes, the sponsor of the bill in 1887. The allotment process was defined as follows:

> The reservation would be surveyed and divided up among the Indians: 160 acres to each family head, 80 acres to single persons and orphans over eighteen years, and 40 acres to single persons under eighteen. Second, to protect the allottees from avaricious whites, the actual deed to the allotment remained in the hands of the government for twenty-five years,

during which time the land could not be sold or encumbered. Third, the citizenship status was conferred upon all allottees whereupon they would become subject to the criminal and civil laws of the state or territory where they resided. Finally, after all the tribal members had received an allotment, all surplus land might be sold to white settlers. The proceeds gained from these sales would be held by the government for the tribe's "education and civilization." Reformers viewed the Dawes Act as a major victor; in one bold stroke, it held out the possibility of smashing the tribal bond and setting Indians on the road to civilianization.[7]

EDUCATION

The reformers used education to teach the Indians the knowledge, values, mores, and habits of Christian civilization. Their strongest argument for education was that the members of the older generation were not able to be civilized; tamed, yes, but their hearts would remain attached to their old ways. The reformers' hope was to train the young, thinking this would quicken the cultural revolution. The White civilization had taken centuries to attain its present level, but if Indian children would enter school now, they would enter the struggle of life with roughly the same advantages as their more civilized White neighbors. "Indians could, in effect, be catapulted directly from savagism to civilization, skipping all the stages of social evolution in between."[8]

The reformers had four aims for Indian education:

First, teach the basics of reading, writing, and speaking the English language.

Second, individualize the members of the tribes. Tribal society had somehow gotten matters all wrong; rather than operating on the progressive principle that the whole of society stood to benefit when the individual's acquisitive instincts were given their full play, tribal life was rooted in the idea that the welfare of the community depended upon the individual curbing material desires. Whereas a Protestant American measured an individual's worth by his capacity to accumulate wealth, and the Indian did so by what they gave away.

Third, Christianization. "A really civilized people cannot be found in the world except where the Bible has been sent and the gospel taught; hence the reformers believed that the Indians must have, as an essential part of their education, Christian training."

The fourth aim was Citizenship. "As the commissioner of Indian Affairs said in 1890, 'the general purpose of the Government is the preparation of Indian youth for assimilation into the national life by such a course of training as will prepare them for the duties and privileges of American citizenship.'"[9]

The reformers thought three types of schools would help the education of the Indian youth. These were the reservation day school, the reservation boarding school, and the off-reservation boarding school. Prior to the reformers interceding, the missionaries often had schools for their converts and children. This was the early introduction to Christian education. With the signing of treaties, the reservations were formed and some schools were opened, but not on a consistent schedule.

From 1820 to 1870, the reservation day school used this method of daily instruction with the Indian children, in hopes that the youth would share their schooling with their parents. For the reformers, this approach was not an effective tool for achieving assimilation, as the Indian youth would return home in the evening and return to their traditional ways of camp life.[10]

The reservation boarding school was developed in the late 1870s. The school was located on the reservation, but the students lived at the school during the school year for eight to nine months. This model set up greater control over the children. They would be allowed to go home during Christmas vacation and the summer vacation period, but sustained confinement was key to the civilization process. However, when the students returned home during vacations, they would return to their traditional ways.[11]

The third model, the off-reservation boarding school, became one of the White Americans' preferred models of education for the Native Americans. Colonel Richard H. Pratt created the prototype of the off-reservation boarding schools based on his experience with the prisoners he took to Fort Marion, Florida, known as the St. Augustine Experiment.

In the spring of 1867, Pratt was assigned to Fort Gibson Indian Territory (now Oklahoma) as a second lieutenant in the US Cavalry, in a newly-formed unit enforcing governmental policy on the western frontier.[12] Under Pratt's command were African American soldiers—called Buffalo Soldiers by Native Americans on account of the texture of their hair—and Indian Scouts. He found them to be good and faithful men who were obedient and trustworthy.

While at Fort Gibson, Pratt gave serious consideration to the statement "all men are created equal."[13] Contrasting this with another statement, "all persons born or naturalized in the United States are citizens thereof," he questioned how these statements applied to his company of Buffalo Soldiers and Indian Scouts. If they were all equal, why were Black soldiers segregated into separate regiments, and why were Natives segregated by the various tribal reservations? Why weren't all men given equal opportunities and allowed to assume their rightful places in society? Could he help them attain their rightful places?[14] Pratt began to challenge the prevailing view among White Americans that Indians were simply too primitive to learn reading, writing, and arithmetic.

Pratt was placed in charge of a group of 72 Indian warriors who had been charged by the US Army with a host of crimes committed during the so-called Red River War of 1874. He was chosen to accompany them from Fort Sill in Indian Territory (Oklahoma) to Fort Marion, near St. Augustine, Florida.[15] Pratt realized his opportunity to put his educational philosophy to the test. He put the Natives into military uniforms and cut their hair.[16] He taught them to care for their uniforms and to take pride in their appearance, explaining that Whites would judge them on that basis. He encouraged them to create arts and crafts and allowed them to sell their creations to the tourists who came to see these transformed "savages," as well as keep their profits. He then brought in teachers to teach reading, writing, and math to the group of Comanches, Kiowas, Cheyenne, Arapahos, and one Caddo.[17]

Not all the prisoners were able—or willing—to assimilate. A Cheyenne warrior named Making Medicine, for instance, liked to speak in his own language when in chapel—"just one or two words"—but Pratt would stop him. The other prisoners, also forced to stop speaking their Native languages and not knowing how to say what they wanted in English, relied on Indian Sign Language. Another Cheyenne, Bear's Heart, would dream of buffalo hunting, then awaken, certain he had been on a hunt—something Pratt did not want to hear. Comanche chief Black Horse said, "They offered us farming and Christianity. I could accept neither." Wistfully, a Cheyenne man named Big Nose said of the boats they could see in the bay at St. Augustine, "They are our tepees in the distance." These men, and others, wanted badly to escape Fort Marion.[18]

The prisoners were held at the fort from 1875–1878. While Making Medicine—considered to be a founder of modern Native art—survived to become an Episcopal deacon,[19] several of the prisoners died at Fort Marion. Considering his success in turning "savages" into "civilized" men in this living laboratory at Fort Marion, Pratt thought the process could be reproduced on a larger scale.

In addressing the "Indian Problem," reformers believed that total assimilation was both practical and possible in a relatively short time-frame.[20] Pratt's educational philosophy of total assimilation was in lock step with the dominant culture. At a Baptist convention in 1883, Pratt said, "In Indian civilization I am a Baptist, because I believe in immersing the Indian in our civilization and when we get them under holding them there until they are thoroughly soaked."[21] Whether this "soaking" is a gentle bath or a kind of drowning, it could not be accomplished on reservations, where the Native people continued many of their traditional practices. Thus, a system of boarding schools was needed to remove Native children from their families and inculcate them with Euro-American standards, language, culture, and dress. As Utley wrote in his introduction to Pratt's letters, "He would establish enough Carlisle's away from the reservation and its influences to accommodate all the Indian children of the United States, and from these prep schools in civilization feed them into the public schools and thus into the mainstream of American life."[22]

Pratt wanted to do away with the reservation system. Many White Americans at the time thought that living communally and according to the seasons was not only heathenish and savage but also it set the Indians up to be targets of racist harassment and oppression. Both Pratt's and White Americans' thoughts led to genocide of tribes and tribal nations. Pratt very much wanted the American Indian to succeed and be the equal of White Americans. He was considered by many to be an advocate for the Indian. He was one of the first people to publish the term "racism" in the English language: "Association of races and classes is necessary to destroy racism and classism," he said in 1902.[23] However, his thinking was that it was the Indians who had to change their hearts, minds, languages, and especially their cultures in order to gain equality with the Whites. In an 1892 speech, he gave the famous summation of his educational philosophy: "A great general [referring to Sherman] has said that the only good Indian is a dead one. In a sense, I agree with the sentiment, but only in this: that all the Indian there is in the race should be dead. Kill the Indian in him, and save the man."[24]

Truly believing that he was helping Native peoples, Pratt went to Washington, DC, to advocate for funding for a boarding school. He campaigned to have Carlisle Barracks, an old Army post near the town of Carlisle, Pennsylvania—unused since the Civil War—turned into an Indian school. In late August and early September 1879, Pratt lobbied key officials within the Department of the Interior and the War Department to allow him to establish a school.[25] The old Carlisle Barracks appealed to him because the location was fairly close to Washington, DC, and was far enough away from the reservations that he could remove the children from their traditional culture and immerse them in the civilization of White America.[26]

On September 6, 1879, Pratt was ordered by the War Department to report to the Secretary of the Interior for Indian education duty.[27] He was asked to go to Dakota and Indian Territories to recruit students. At the insistence of Indian Commissioner Hyde, Pratt was to go to the Sioux chiefs Spotted Tail, at the Rosebud agency, and Red Cloud, at the Pine Ridge agency. Hyde wanted children from these reservations to serve as hostages, essentially, guaranteeing the good behavior of their people.[28]

At first, the chiefs declined to send their children, with Chief Spotted Tail saying:

> The white people are all thieves and liars, and we refuse to send our children, because we do not want them to learn such things. The government deceived us in the Black Hills treaty. The government knew that gold was there and it took the land from us without giving us its value, and so the white people get rich and Indians are cheated and become poor. The government let us keep this plains country and it agreed that the lines should be away out, and we should have a large district. Your men are out there now running the lines and they run lines a long way inside of where we agreed they should be. Some of our people who lived outside of these lines have been compelled to move inside. The government has always cheated us and we do not want our children to learn to do that way.[29]

Pratt responded by praising Spotted Tail and acknowledging the chief's fame and intelligence, but he also said to him, "You cannot read or write… You know very little about the large interests of your tribal property and what is best for the people over whom you are placed, simply because you have no education."[30] Ever paternalistic, Pratt told Spotted Tail that if he had been educated, he might have known about the Black Hills gold, and would have been able to keep his people's lands. Pratt then drove his argument home:

> There is no more chance for your people to keep themselves from the whites… Your own welfare while you live and the welfare of your chil-

dren demand that your children should have the same education that the white man has, that they should speak his language and know just how the white man lives, be able to meet him face to face and take care of themselves and their property without the help of either an interpreter or an Indian agent.[31]

Appealing to the persecution-weary Spotted Tail and the other headmen, Pratt dangled a tempting promise, saying he would not only educate the Native children the same way Whites were educated but also, "I shall send them out to work and to live among the white people… so that as boys and girls they will be coming into the same classes with white boys and girls and will so learn to know each other, and this will take away the prejudice of the whites against your people and it is the only way to remove such prejudice."[32]

The chiefs talked among themselves and ultimately agreed to send their children to the boarding schools. The chiefs may have had their own agenda and figured that the only way to outwit the Whites was to master their own game. They would learn English and study the laws so they might be used to force the United States to uphold its treaty promises. In the end, though, children who went through the boarding school system were traumatized. Many died from tuberculosis and other diseases. Others returned to their homelands only to realize they had been so assimilated into White culture that they no longer belonged, and they drifted into alcoholism and other self-destructive behaviors. Of the nearly 7,800 students from 500 nations who passed through Carlisle's doors between 1879 and 1918, only about 10 percent graduated with the equivalent of a high school diploma.[33] Most earned certificates for various skills such as masonry, carpentry, or, as was my grandfather Black Raven's case, wagon-making. A few who did earn diplomas went on to Dickinson College, also located in Carlisle.

Pratt headed next to the Pine Ridge Agency, in Dakota Territory, where he talked with Chief Red Cloud. Persuaded by the same arguments, Red Cloud also agreed to send children.

Eighty-four children arrived in Pennsylvania around midnight on October 6, 1879. The news of Pratt bringing "wild" Indian children to Carlisle made good newspaper reading. Several hundred citizens turned out to get a good look at them as they got off the train.[34]

Pratt left this group of children in the hands of his wife and proceeded on to Indian Territory in Kansas, where he had sent ahead two of his former prisoners whom he had assimilated to White culture at Fort Marion. He sent Etahdleah to the Kiowa and Comanche Agencies, and Okahaton to the Cheyenne and Arapaho Agencies, Oklahoma Indian Territory. Here they were able to recruit 52 more Indian youths.[35]

While the students had started traveling to Pennsylvania, it was months before the Carlisle barracks regimen was in order. When the Native youths arrived, the supplies that Pratt had ordered had not yet been received. There was little food and no bedding or blankets. The Native children continued using the blankets they came with, and they slept on the hard, cold barracks floors.[36]

Right away, Pratt ordered staff to cut the hair of the male students. This action caused one male student to spend the night outside and wail mournfully at the loss of his hair. He explained that when his people cut their hair, it was a sign of mourning, and he had gone outside to wail and show his grief. Upon hearing the wailing, some girls joined him, followed by other students, which woke the whole school. Mrs. Pratt asked that the wailing stop, so as not to wake the townspeople, saying "Something dreadful might happen."[37]

Luther Standing Bear, the son of Chief Standing Bear, was one of the first recruits from the Rose Bud Agency. He said initially that he wanted to get a haircut so as to be "in style" like the others who had received haircuts. But when his hair had been shorn off, he said "it hurt my feelings to such an extent that the tears came into my eyes. I do not recall whether the barber noticed my agitation or not, nor did I care." Standing Bear said that, after his hair was cut, "a new thought came into my head. I felt that I was no more Indian, but would be an imitation of a white man." Standing Bear must have reconciled himself to his situation, though, because he added that he soon "became anxious to learn all I could," but the memory stuck with him for the rest of his life.[38]

With their hair shorn, the Indian students next learned they would be getting White men's clothes. Luther Standing Bear described himself and others as being excited and anxious about the arrival of the clothes. The clothing arrived in wagons; the students all gathered around and then, one at a time, they were "sized up," with a whole suit handed to them. The items they received were dark, heavy, and scratchy gray goods, consisting of coats, pants, and vests. They were also given a dark woolen shirt, a cap, a pair of suspenders, socks, and heavy farmer's boots.[39] They were excited to try on their new clothes, even if some of them were too large. Luther Standing Bear remembers this about the trying on of clothes:

> As soon as we had received our outfits, we ran to our rooms to dress up. The Indian prisoners were kept busy helping us put the clothes on. Although the suits were too big for many of us, we did not know the difference. I remember that my boots were far too large, but as long as they were "screechy" or squeaky, I didn't worry about the size! I liked the noise they made when I walked, and the other boys were likewise pleased.

> How proud we were with clothes that had pockets and with boots that squeaked! We walked the floor nearly all that night. Many of the boys even went to bed with their clothes on. But in the morning, the boys who had taken off their pants had a most terrible time. They did not know whether they were to button up in front or behind. Some of the boys said the open part went in front; others said, 'No, it goes at the back.' There is where the boys who had kept their clothes on came in handy to look at. They showed the others that the pants buttoned up in the front and not at the back. So here we learned something.[40]

Because he could procure them inexpensively, Pratt ordered surplus army uniforms to be issued for the male students and dresses for the female students.[41] There was no money for supplies, however. One of his former teachers, Miss Longstreth, who was Quaker and had many friends in the community, requested that he make a wish list of the needed items. When Pratt had completed the list and given it to Miss Longstreth, she passed it along to some of her Quaker lady friends. They took the list and bought everything on it.

Pratt wrote in his request:

> This is to be an industrial school to teach young Indians how to earn a living among civilized people by practicing mechanical and agricultural pursuits and the usual industries of civilized life. I have nothing with which to begin mechanical training. I shall want to teach carpentry and will need… [then listed, with probable cost,] carpenter's tools and materials; blacksmith's tools and materials, including forge, anvil, etc.; tailor's equipment, including sewing machines; harness-making tools, painter's tools, shoemakers' tools, a printing press with type, etc., tinner's and coppersmith's tools.[42]

With teachers hired and supplied with tools for teaching, the Carlisle Indian School was up and running. Hearing of this news, it did not take long for other Indian agents to write to Pratt to ask him to take some of their youth. The agencies of Kiowa, Arapaho, Comanche, Cheyenne, and

Apache were not far from the Ponca Indian Agency, Oklahoma Indian Territory, where the Nimiipuu exiles were located.

While the Nimiipuu were in exile, First Lieutenant Richard H. Pratt visited the Ponca Agency. James Reuben was the first teacher to send students from Ponca Reservation, Indian Territory, Oklahoma to the new experimental American Indian boarding school. Pratt came to Indian Territory in the fall of 1879 and arranged for five Nimiipuu children to attend boarding school.[43] These Nimiipuu children were sent to the Carlisle Indian Industrial School in Pennsylvania.

Searching Carlisle's records, I learned that they arrived at the school on February 20, 1880. Among the five was my grandfather, Ka-khun-ne Black Raven, age 10. The other four were Luke Phillips, age 16; Harriet Mary Elder, age 13; Samuel Johns, age 15; and Sophia Rachel, whose age is unknown. On October 13, 1883, three more Nimiipuu children arrived at Carlisle: Dolly Gould, age 13; Charles Wolf—whose name was later changed to Charles Wolf Williams—age 15; and Rebecca Little Wolf, age 14. Rebecca died in 1885 at age 16, and is buried along with Luke Phillips, who died of tuberculosis on January 10, 1888, age 24. Samuel Johns also died at Carlisle, on February 11, 1888, at age 23.

Five Nez Perce children at the Carlisle Indian Industrial School, taken fall 1883 by Choate. The children were taken from the Nimiipuu exile camp at Ponca Reservation, Oklahoma Territory. Pictured standing, from left to right: Jesse Paul, Charles Wolf, Samuel Johns; seated: Dolly Gould, Rebecca Little Wolf. *Courtesy of Cumberland County Historical Society, Carlisle, Pennsylvania.*

We do not know under what circumstances Grandfather Ka-khun-ne went to Carlisle, but his mother, Phoebe, must have had strong feelings about sending her only surviving child to a far-off school, not knowing if or when she would ever see him again. She had already witnessed a war that was the result of the promises broken by Indian agents, military officers, and leaders in the US government. She must have sent him away with love, maybe saying, "Go and learn all you can and come back to help your people." I also thought, what would she send with him, food, medicine bag, blanket, something to remember her?

The youth traveled by train from the Arkansas City, Kansas rail depot to Carlisle, Pennsylvania. For the Nimiipuu, this train ride would be their second experience on the rails. The train passenger cars would not have been crowded like their exile train ride to Fort Leavenworth, Kansas three years earlier. I wonder if the train lavatory still emptied their waste onto the tracks beneath them. Did the youth wait until the train stopped to take on water and stop for meals? I imagine they got off the train to eat and to relieve themselves. We are not sure how many days it took the train to get to Carlisle, and the passenger cars did not have sleeping quarters, so the students would have had to sleep sitting up if they could. I wonder what the students were thinking, what they would find at this new school. Were they anxious, afraid, or excited?

The Carlisle newsletter, entitled *Eadle Keatah Toh* (meaning "Big Morning Star"[44] in Lakota), refers to children being brought by Indian Inspector William J. Pollock from the Ponca Agency on February 20, 1880. He was accompanied by the Ponca chiefs White Eagle and Standing Buffalo and interpreter Joe Esau. He brought eleven children from the Ponca and Nez Perce Tribes. There were five Nez Perce. The newsletter describes how White Eagle brought his son:

> White Eagle brought his only son, Frank, a bright-eyed little boy twelve years old. Nothing could exceed the tenderness and solicitude shown by this old warrior when leaving his boy. Tears streamed over the cheeks. To Mrs. Pratt he said, through the interpreter "This is my only one. His mother and three children have died within a year." The mother was a daughter of "Lone Elk" at one time a powerful Ponca chief.[45]

Grandfather Black Raven, age ten, was among this group of eleven children. He too was the only son left to his mother, Um-al-wat but known by then as Phoebe Lowry. She, too, must have had tears streaming down her face when saying goodbye to her only surviving son back in Indian Territory. Reading these accounts of how mothers would send their children off to school, not knowing if they would see them again, or if they would be ok. My heart tugged and tears came to my eyes, feelings perhaps similar to those Phoebe felt.

The *Eadle Keatah Toh* was published once a month and sent to the supporters and financial contributors of the Carlisle Indian School. Pratt would invite others of like thinking to contribute to the newsletter. In the second issue, he asked Indian Inspector William Pollock to write an open letter to the Honorable E. A. Hayt, Commissioner of Indian Affairs. In this letter, Pollack commented—using racist language typical of Euro-Americans at that time—on the merits of Carlisle Indian School after his recent visit, writing:

> I am fully impressed with the surest, cheapest and quickest ways to fully solve the "Indian questions" is to remove all Indian children of school going age, from the evil and pernicious influence, habits and surroundings of their parents and other adult Indians and place them at school remote from the locations of their tribes. The day school as conducted at the respective Agencies has proved an almost utter failure… During my residence among the Sioux, time and time again has "Spotted Tail" told me that their children could not learn English unless removed from their parents and camp surroundings.
>
> I was present when the Sioux children embarked at Rosebud landing for the Carlisle School, and there saw "Squaws" weep as only loving mothers can, at the thought of being separated from their children, and I presume the same devotion was shown in this Territory when the youths were being removed for the same purpose, but today the parents are contented and proud to know that their children are furnished with the same educational advantages as are those of their civilized white brethren; and nearly every mail brings the joyous intelligence that their children are rapidly learning the arts and habits of civilization.[46]

The newly arrived boys were housed in the same barracks as Luther Standing Bear. The girls went to the girls' barracks. They went through the same process that Luther Standing Bear and the other first arrivals had: hair shorn off, and dressed in American-style clothes. I am sure Grandfather Ka-khun-ne felt strange without his hair, as had Luther Standing Bear. To complete the transformation process, the students had to choose English names. The process was arbitrary, to say the least; Luther Standing Bear described it in this way:

> Although we were yet wearing our Indian clothes... one day when we came to school there was a lot of writing on one of the blackboards. We did not know what it meant, but our interpreter came into the room and said "Do you see all these marks on the blackboard? Well, each word is a white man's name. They are going to give each one of you one of these names by which you will hereafter be known." None of the names were read or explained to us, so of course we did not know the sound or meaning of any of them.[47]

Grandfather Black Raven went through a very similar process, and that is how he came to be called Jesse Paul, by pointing at a couple names on a blackboard. (Although my family never knew him as anything but Jesse, we are reclaiming his name as Black Raven because we want to honor his Nimiipuu heritage.) They were also assigned students from different tribes to be roommates, to reinforce that they were not permitted to speak their mother tongue.[48] The Dickinson College archivist, Jim Gerencser, told me that all the students wanted to learn Sioux, as there were so many Sioux children at the school.

In the early years, Pratt hired interpreters who would translate orders and lessons for the students who spoke many different languages. Luke Phillips, who had arrived at Carlisle with Black Raven, went back as an interpreter to the exiles' camp at the Ponca Reservation in 1886. He returned to Carlisle only to die of tuberculosis, in January of 1888, about a month before he was scheduled to leave. Luke is buried at the Carlisle cemetery.

Forced to change physically, all outward appearances of Indian identity were stripped from the children. The boarding schools also attempted to change the children mentally through the strict discipline of the Euro-American style of grammar school coupled with Christian religious education. The children were torn from their warm, secure family lives and forced into the highly regimented, non-nurturing environment of a military boarding school. Ever the military man, Pratt organized the students into companies as soon as there were enough students for it to make sense to do so, and named sergeants who were responsible for head and bed counts. We have Carlisle documents that say Grandfather Black Raven was in Company E in 1883 and was a private, and then in 1887 was in Company D and served as a corporal. During the early years the girls were not placed into companies but would line up to go to meals and their classes.

Large group of Native American children at Carlisle Indian Industrial School, taken circa 1884 by Choate on the school's parade grounds in front of the home of General Richard Pratt. Grandfather Jesse Paul is in this photo. *Courtesy of the Cumberland County Historical Society, Carlisle, Pennsylvania.*

Carlisle Indian Industrial School cemetery, October 2018: it is not used for the Army War College. *Paul Family Photo Collection.*

The regime for each day began with the students cleaning their space, dressing, and lining up to march to breakfast; indeed, they had to line up and march to every meal. They were expected to stand erect, like soldiers. Weekly inspections were conducted on Sunday before going to Sunday school. Pratt would come and look over everyone. Luther describes the inspection:

> First, Captain Pratt would "size us up" from head to foot, notice if we had our hair combed nicely, if our clothes were neatly brushed, and if we had cleaned our shoes. Then he would look the room over to see if our beds were made up right, often lifting the mattresses to see that everything was clean underneath. Often, they would look into our wooden boxes where we kept our clothes, to see that everything was spick and span.[49]

Pratt wanted to instill the meaning of a dollar in his students, so he set up a student savings program. The students would earn their money from working on the school farm, in the shops at school, and from the school's outing program.[50] As part of their education, the children were expected to learn a trade. They spent half a day doing classwork and the other half working at their assigned jobs.[51] Grandfather Black Raven's job was to learn wagon-making. Pratt introduced an incentive graduated-pay system, based on the difficulty of the task assigned. The students' savings were monitored and each student was to keep their own records. They could withdraw their funds but first they would have to make a price list of the items wanted and submit it for inspection.[52] In an issue of *Eadle Keatah Toh*, dated June 1887, I found a list that showed Grandfather Black Raven had donated twenty-five dollars to a building fund for new quarters at the school.[53]

Pratt also devised a system to help with discipline of the students. He involved the students themselves to enforce the rules. He used a court martial format, and selected cadet officers from the companies he had formed. The cadets were older students and they would sit as judges. Care was also taken to ensure that many tribes would be represented on the committee. The charges were brought before the court and witnesses gave testimonies and a defense was made, guilt or innocence was proven, and punishments handed out. Pratt reserved the right to overrule the court.[54]

One case presented to the committee concerned a young boy who had been caught stealing several items from the other students. He was found guilty, and the punishment to be meted out for this crime included whipping before all the companies, wearing a block of wood shackled to his leg with "thief" written on it for a period of one month; staying at the Guard house at night; and working hard labor for one month.[55] The committee chose not to whip the boy, but agreed to have a block of wood attached to his leg, stay in the guard house and hard labor for a month. For this case, they listed those students who were on the committee and Grandfather Black Raven is listed. This committee served in January and February 1887. What did Grandfather think of this manner of discipline? To me the punishment seemed very harsh. I am not sure if all the committee had to agree with the punishment. I wonder with this particular case if the committee came up with not as harsh a punishment and Pratt overruled their decision and imposed what he thought the punishment should be. Either way, I thought this to be too harsh a punishment for this young boy.

Jesse Paul at Carlisle, fall 1883. *Paul Family Photo Collection.*

Jesse Paul, circa 1886. Taken near the farm town in Bucks County, PA, where Jesse was a student with a farm family 1884–1886. *Paul Family Photo Collection.*

A large group of young men at Carlisle Indian Industrial School, circa 1887. Men pictured in the photo:

Front row, l-r: Samuel Dion(standing), Paul Boynton (seated), Eagle Little Hawk, Victoriano Gachupiu, Job Hunter boy, Nelson Caught the Eagle, Jonas Peace (?), Jose Nadilgodey, Outa Chief Eagle, David Turkey, Charles Hood, John Miller, Joel Cotter

Middle row, l-r: John Kitson (seated), Percy Zedoka, Paul Eagle Star, Frank Dorisn, Isaac Williams, Otto Sotom, Samuel Townsend, Eustace Esapoghet (?)

Back row, l-r: James Black Hawk (standing), Arrow Running Horse, Jesse Paul, Joel Tyndall, Wilke Sharp, Lorenzo Martinez, Charles Wolf, Roberta Matthew, Percy Kable

Photo courtesy of the National Anthropological Archives, National Museum of Natural History, NAA Photo Lot 73-8 INV 01200000.

Close-up of Jesse Paul from the group photograph.

The students could choose which church they attended, but whatever their choice, they had to attend every Sunday. They also had to attend a Sunday afternoon preaching service and an evening praise service conducted by the local pastors or professors from the nearby Dickinson College.[56] Since the Nimiipuu had been first influenced by the Presbyterian missionary Henry H. Spalding, and in exile it had been the lay Nimiipuu Presbyterian ministers who had come to them, I assume that Grandfather Black Raven attended a Presbyterian church in Carlisle. On my visit to Carlisle in 2004, I visited two Presbyterian churches that had been standing in 1880, the First Presbyterian Church of Carlisle and the Second Presbyterian Church in Carlisle. If he did attend one of these churches, how did Grandfather feel going to so large a church, especially when he would have been one of only a few Indians in attendance? These churches were large brick buildings and could hold several hundred people in the pews. Carlisle would have been more "civilized" than the towns of Baxter Springs and Arkansas City, Kansas, where the streets had been made of dirt and the houses mostly made of lumber.

During the students' first summer, Pratt held a summer camp, even though the teachers and many other staff left for the season. Summer camp was at Warm Springs, about 16 miles from Carlisle. They camped in tents and participated in fun activities, such as making bows and arrows, picking berries, and playing games. They each had a tin cup, plate, and silverware that they had to wash and take care of.[57] I find it ironic that the students were allowed to make bows and arrows and collect berries despite Pratt wanting them to abandon their culture.

The curriculum at the beginning of the second school year, in the fall of 1880, was more difficult, and the children were expected to participate in extra-curricular activities. I searched some of *The Indian Helper* newsletters and read in the February 18, 1887, issue that Jesse Paul (Black Raven) had been attending a debate at which the debaters discussed the question, "Resolved, that immigration from foreign nations should be stopped at once." The debaters presented their arguments and were judged, followed by general discussion. Jesse Paul (Black Raven) was the first to speak and was followed by other students. All made earnest speeches, some for and some against foreign immigration.[58] I would have loved to have been there and heard what Grandfather Black Raven spoke about. Was he for or against immigration?

In the issue of *The Indian Helper* dated May 25, 1888, I found that Jesse Paul, along with Kish Hawkins, had made a handsome drawing of a section of a telephone in a philosophy class.[59] The telephone had been invited by Alexander Graham Bell in 1870s and the patent was granted March 7, 1876. In the *Eadle Keatah tah,* February 1888 issue I found Jesse listed as a team member of the Invincible Debating Society. A debater! One topic for the debate team was "Resolved: That Indian Education Be Compulsory." I would have loved to hear this debate. Whichever side he had to debate, Grandfather Black Raven would have eight years' experience at Carlisle to draw upon. The debate took place in February 1888, the eighth anniversary of his arrival and just a few months before he was released and returned to Idaho.

Pratt thought that "[t]he contact of people is the best of all education."[60] Pratt had the students work on area farms and learn from farmers how to manage their own farms when they left school. These off-campus trips were called "outings." Pratt's outing system took on three forms. In the basic program, students were sent out for summer months only. They would be placed in middle-class farm households. This type of outing gave the Indian youth the opportunity to live, work, and worship alongside the host family members. The second version of the outing placed the students with the farming families for a period of one to two years. This gave them a broader experience and included attending the local school along with the host family children. This was Pratt's favorite version of the outing system. The third was to place students in industrial settings where they could learn skills other than farming. Pratt did not like this version as well, as oftentimes the students would be dropped to servant class and become victims of some degeneracy.[61]

Pratt believed the Outing program accomplished several objectives:

> It fostered acquisition of English by forcing the students to apply their new found language skills in practical work and family settings. It enabled them to earn money. It broke down prejudice: Indians came to appreciate the goodwill of their white patrons, while patrons gained an increased appreciation of the Indians' capabilities. Students learned the subtleties of civilized living, and little nuances of speech and behavior that could never fully be acquired in the superficial atmosphere of school.[62]

There were requirements of the students before they could be placed in an outing situation. They had to have a basic understanding of English.

The students were not forced to participate in the outing program, and had to formally request a placement. This request served also as a sworn statement. The students agreed to obey their employers, bathe regularly, attend their patron's church, refrain from leaving the farm without permission, avoid drinking, gambling, or smoking, and generally behave in a manner that would bring honor to Carlisle. The students also had to promise to write home once a month, detailing their progress and talk about their patron family.

The placing of students depended on the age and sex of each student, the nature of the work, the religious affiliation of both the student and patron. Pratt would also place the students far from the school to discourage runaways.[63]

According to Carlisle's records, Grandfather Black Raven went on two outings. The first began April 16, 1884, when he was sent to the family of Abdon Longshore of Dolington, Bucks County, Pennsylvania, and ended on his return to the school on September 6, 1886. How was Grandfather's experience? Was he lonely? Did he make friends with the family he was placed with? There had to be some basis of mutual likeness, given that he was there for two years. According to Pratt, Grandfather was supposed to be writing letters home. Was his mother able to read his letters? If so, was she able to write letters in return? I would give anything to see these letters and learn of the content and conversation shared between them.

On May 2, 1883, at the exile camp on the Ponca Reservation, the parents of Luke Phillips, Samuel Johns, Jesse Paul (Black Raven), and Harriet Mary asked Pratt for their children to be returned. The children had been at Carlisle for three years, and it had been agreed initially when their children left that they would return in three years. Both Pratt and the Ponca Indian Agent Woodin pressed the families to leave their children at Carlisle for more education. However, Harriet Mary's mother insisted her daughter be returned, because she was going to be returning to Lapwai with James Reuben in the near future. Harriet Mary was allowed to return. However, the other students remained at Carlisle, after much persuasion by Agent Woodin.[64] I also think the students had a say in this decision: I will share how Luther Standing Bear decided to stay later in this chapter.

Black Raven went on a second outing from March 22, 1887, to September 13, 1887. According to Carlisle historian Linda Witmer, "The policy for each boy and girl was that they were paid for his or her services while on the 'Outing' and the money was deposited in an interest-bearing bank account by the school, and turned over to the student when he or she graduated or returned home."[65] When Grandfather Black Raven returned from his last outing, he attended school for ten more months and was discharged on July 6, 1888, presumably with the wages he had earned.

What did Grandfather Jesse learn while at these farms? We can only surmise that the skills he acquired included basic farming, such as care of the farm animals and plowing, planting, seeding, and harvesting the crops. He would have learned the types of buildings needed on the farm to house the animals, store grain and foods, in addition to a tool shed, a wood shed, and a wash house for doing laundry. As we learned later, Grandfather Black Raven would be able to start a farm after he left Carlisle using the skills he learned while on his outing and he was able to build the buildings needed for a successful farm.

The curriculum at Carlisle was flexible, training each student according to his or her ability. The training eventually carried students through a tenth-grade level and included instruction in English, chemistry, physics, government, geography, history, advanced mathematics, and biology. Due to the fixed requirements, it would be ten years before the first graduation ceremony was held, in 1889, so the students who were first recruited in 1879-1880 did not acquire this training. Industrial certificates were awarded to those who gained proficiency in a trade, to provide recognition for those who did not graduate.[66] This would have included my grandfather, who earned his certificate in Wagon Making.

The usual length of stay for a student was three years. This period could be extended by two more years for a total of five. Grandfather Black Raven ended up staying eight years. The Carlisle records do not show why he was allowed to stay so long, and family oral history does not explain the length of stay either. There were many times when others who chose to stay were asked to tell the students why. Luther Standing Bear and the others in his group were eligible to return to Rosebud and Pine Ridge if they desired, because their three years had been completed. When asked if they all wanted to return to their reservations, most raised their hands, expect for Luther Standing Bear. He said he wanted to stay because he remembered his father telling him, "Son, learn all you can of the ways of the Long Knives (White people) as they are so thick in our country." So Standing Bear wanted to be brave and stay to please his father.[67] Several others in this first group also chose to stay, because Luther had spoken up. At dinner that night, Pratt had Luther stand, and Pratt complimented him for his bravery in remaining to learn more.[68] These testimonies had to have had an effect on those listening, one of whom was Grandfather Black Raven.

Pratt would sometimes take the entire student body to show the general public how well the Indian students had been transformed. He would parade the Native students to demonstrate how thoroughly they had been assimilated. One such occasion was the Bicentennial Parade held in Philadelphia in 1882. Pratt describes the day:

> During the school year 1882, Philadelphia had its great bicentennial exposition for which there was organized one of the most wonderful parades in all history. This parade covered miles and gave illustrations of the progress of the country. The Carlisle School was invited to participate with floats and marching by its cadet corps, headed by its band, and preceded by a mounted party of twenty painted and war-bonneted Indians brought in from western tribes. The managers of the parade gave me command of the educational division and placed Carlisle at the head of that division. The authorities of the Pennsylvania Railroad gave the school transportation from Carlisle to Philadelphia and return, but our seven floats, illustrating Penn's treaty and our mechanical and school work, had to travel the 120 miles by horse teams. It was a proud day when we marched and countermarched for hours through Broad Street in the presence of two million onlookers.[69]

Grandfather Black Raven was twelve when he marched in that parade and saw the truth in the saying that the Whites were as numerous as the stars in the sky. He really was a minority. The school paper published many sentiments of the students' experiences and observations of the bicentennial, with one Creek boy saying:

> While we were away we saw many wonderful things, large buildings. When I saw them I couldn't help but say to my self, 'Shall the Indians some day be able to build such buildings? Can they learn?' Then I said, 'Yes, they can learn, but as long as they are together all the time on reservations they never will be able but if they go out among the white people and work with them and learn there may be some hope.'[70]

Grandfather Black Raven would have read the school newsletter, though his reading skill after only two years might not have been fully developed. But I am sure he would have talked with his fellow students about what it meant to be an Indian student there at that time in history.

The Carlisle Indian Industrial Boarding School was the first of 25 schools that were funded and supported by the United States government. Soon after Carlisle opened in 1879, another boarding school was started in the Pacific Northwest: the Chemawa Indian Training School, established first at Forest Grove, Oregon, in 1880 and then moved to Salem, Oregon, in 1885. Chemawa is still operated as a Bureau of Indian Education high school. Other schools include the Chilocco Indian Agricultural School in Chilocco, Oklahoma (founded 1884; closed 1980)[71] and the Haskell Institute in Lawrence, Kansas (founded 1884, today called the Haskell Indian Nations University). The last government boarding school was the Sherman Institute, founded in 1902 in Riverside, California. This school is still open and is now called Sherman Indian High School.

I mention these schools because many of my family members have attended them. In all, more than 350 government- and church-run schools for Indians were established in the United States.[72] It is estimated that between 1869 and the 1960s, "hundreds of thousands of Native American children were removed from their homes and families and placed in boarding schools."[73]

Grandfather Black Raven (Jesse Paul) experienced eight years of assimilation policies that Pratt and others thought would turn a "savage" into a "civilized" Indian. He arrived a boy of ten and left a man of 18 years.

Over the years, my family has made many journeys to recover our stories and heal our wounds, as well as those of our ancestors. As I conducted the research to find the stories of my ancestors, I have felt them with me all along. I felt Black Raven especially strongly on my first trip to Carlisle. My sister, daughter Kim, niece Suzanne, and husband Phil went with me on this journey to Carlisle.

By searching the web, I learned that the Cumberland County Historical Society had a contact person, Barbara Landis, who worked with the archives of Carlisle student records. I contacted her via email and told her my family was planning a trip to Carlisle to do research on my Grandfather Jesse Paul. Ms. Landis responded warmly and helped put me in touch with administrators at Dickinson College, where there is a house they rent out to researchers.

I met several times with Ms. Landis, who helped me search for records pertaining to my grandfather. She also took my family and me on tours of the Carlisle School, which is now the Carlisle Army War College. We saw where students arrived, usually at night, and a large field next to a creek that would flood and freeze in the winter for ice skating. I also learned from her that the cemetery for the Native students was moved several times and some of the headstones might not match the person interred there. In any case, not all the bodies were moved. That was distressing to learn and made me sad. How were their descendants to find and honor their dead ancestors? When I visited the site of the present cemetery, my heart tugged and heaved with emotion; so many had been buried that were never allowed to go back home to their loved ones.

As I walked the grounds, I wondered how Grandfather felt living in such a regimented environment, forbidden from speaking Nimipuutímt, separated by a great distance from Nimiipuu tribal members, his mother and friends who were still in exile while he was living at Carlisle. I am sure he must have been lonely, especially at first, but perhaps over time he made new friends. He learned the ways of White people, which he would eventually bring home to help the Nimiipuu. He became one of the founders of the first Nimiipuu tribal government.

We made a second journey to Carlisle in the fall of 2018, for a commemoration of the centennial of the closing of the Carlisle Indian Industrial School in 1918. The Cumberland County Historical Society and Dickinson College hosted the event. The National Native American Boarding School Healing Coalition (NABS) was hosting its first conference at the same time.

I was honored to give a presentation at both events. I have been on this healing journey for many years and have written and talked about historical trauma and healing extensively. I offer workshops in which I present the healing model I have developed over the years, which has helped many of my family members as well as workshop attendees. I was happy to meet and speak with the descendants of boarding school survivors who had attended Carlisle. (There are no longer any living survivors of Carlisle.) This NABS conference was intended for all survivors and descendants of the boarding school era. Listening to the stories of the survivors was emotional and healing. When we listen to the stories, we validate the storyteller's experiences.

On this journey, my sister Jackie and my brother Jesse, both of whom had been to Carlisle before, my son Michael and niece Vonda came with me. For Vonda and Michael, this was their first time at Carlisle. We again toured the grounds and visited the gravesites of the three Nez Perce children who are buried there, and said prayers for all interred there. Some tribes are trying to repatriate the remains of ancestors, but so far, no relatives of the Nimiipuu children buried at Carlisle have requested that their ancestors' remains be returned.

The Paul Family at the 100-year commemoration of the closing of Carlisle Indian Industrial School, October 2018. The event was hosted by the Cumberland County Historical Society and Dickinson College. Pictured left to right are Vonda Schuld, Jackie Paul Inglis, Roberta Paul, and Mike Foiles. *Photograph from author's collection.*

We visited several of the buildings that would have existed when Black Raven was at the school: the parade grounds, the music pavilion, and the home of General Richard Pratt. Many of the buildings were built by the Carlisle Native students. One such building is the gym, where the famous Native athlete and Olympian Jim Thorpe trained during his years there, 1904-1913. There will be more trips to Carlisle with granddaughters and other family members.

The boarding school shadow is a long one, as evidenced by the actions Secretary of the Interior, Deb Haaland: "On June 22, 2021, Secretary Haaland announced the Federal Boarding School Initiative, a comprehensive effort to recognize the troubled legacy of the Federal Indian Boarding School policies with the goal of addressing their intergenerational impact and to shed light on the traumas of the past."[74] The Department's investigative findings were based on available US government records detailing the government's role in the Federal Indian boarding school system and subsequent outcomes. The report states that the United States had an obligation to correct and heal the wrongs wrought by the Federal Indian Boarding school system, because these wrongs continue to harm the Indian Tribes, Alaska Native Villages, and the Native Hawaiian Community. The report provided eight recommendations for meaningful actions that the US government can undertake to correct the wrongs.

1. **Apology:** The US government should acknowledge its role in a national policy of forced assimilation of Native children and issue a formal apology to individuals, families and tribes that were harmed by US policy.

2. **Investments:** The United States should invest in tribal communities in five key areas: Individual and community healing; family preservation and reunification, including supporting tribal jurisdiction over Indian child welfare cases; violence prevention and tribal lands; improving Indian education; and working to revitalize First American Languages.

3. **A National Memorial:** The US government should establish a national memorial to acknowledge and commemorate the experiences of Native people within the federal Indian boarding school system.

4. **Repatriations:** The government should identify children interred at school burial sites and help repatriate their remains.

5. **Return School Lands:** The government should work to return the federal Indian boarding school sites to tribal ownership.

6. **Tell the story:** The government should work with institutions to educate the public about federal Indian boarding schools and their impact on communities.

7. **Further research:** The government should study how policies of child removal, confinement and forced assimilation have impacted generations of families, particularly the present-day health and economic impacts.

8. **Advance International Relationships:** The government should work with other countries such as Canada, Australia, and New Zealand with their own similar but unique histories of boarding schools and assimilationist policies, to determine best practices for healing and redress.[75]

A few months after this report came out, US President Joe Biden issued an apology to the Native Americans for the trauma and abuse suffered at the US Indian Boarding Schools. President Biden made the apology at the Gila River Indian Community in Arizona on October 25, 2024. When I read that there would be an apology, I started to cry almost immediately. I thought of Grandfather Jesse Paul (Black Raven) and my grandmother Lydia (Woman of the Forest) Conditt and my father, Titus J. Paul (Mountain Lion) and his brothers and sisters who attended boarding schools. I thought of the instant transformation that my grandparents went through, the trauma of not allowed to speak their language or to practice their tribal culture and ceremonies. The apology will not take away the trauma of their boarding school experience but it is a good first step in the healing process. The acknowledgment that the trauma of abuse caused intergenerational trauma helps to heal the words of "Just Get Over It." The trauma was and is real. As a family we have suffered from intergenerational trauma; this apology gives validity to those harms.

It is my hope that the recommendations in the Investigative Report will be implemented with the passing of the Senate Bill 1723/House of Representatives Bill 7227 titled: "The Truth and Healing Commission on Indian Boarding School Policies Act."`

The time is now to heal our wounds.

Headstone of Luke Phillips in the Carlisle Indian Industrial School Cemetery. He entered Carlisle on February 20, 1880; died January 10, 1888. He was an interpreter for the younger Nimiipuu children.

Headstone of Samuel Johns. He entered Carlisle on February 20, 1880 and died February 11, 1888. Nez Perce is misspelled on the headstone.

Headstone of Rebecca Little Wolf in the Carlisle Indian Industrial School. *Paul Family Photo Collection.*

CHAPTER 14

Black Raven's Return

Black Raven returned to the Nez Perce Reservation in July 1888. He was reunited with his mother, Um-al-wat, who had remarried to Eugene Lowry and was using the English name Phoebe Lowry. There must have been tears of happiness, hugs, and looking each other over for signs of good health. For the first time he met the man his mother had married in Indian Territory, Eugene Lowry, and with whom she was now living in Lapwai. Very little is known of the activities of Eugene and Phoebe at that time. Oral family history says they joined the Indian Presbyterian Church in Lapwai, which would later be renamed the Spalding Indian Presbyterian Church.

The early years of Black Raven's return are also not well known. Administrators at the Carlisle School tried to stay in touch with students who left and follow their progress. About two years after returning home, Jesse Paul updated Carlisle with this letter:

Jesse Paul Nez Perce—at Carlisle 8 years
Age 19
Returned home 1888
Fort Lapwai, Idaho Terr.
June 20th, 1890

Dear Sir,

> I can not very well remember just the day and month I left my home, because I did not know then. I was quite small when I left home [by which he means the exile camp at Ponca Reservation, Oklahoma], and could not work at any thing. Now about working at school, I was about three years working on farms, and when I returned, I went to working at blacksmithing until I left Carlisle for home, and the time I spent at the trade is about eight months. I am employed as an interpreter for a surveying party which at work in the Nez Perce Reservation.

> Well most of the time since I returned I have been in some business. About two years ago I was out again with a surveying company and worked around here several places. The question, what particular trouble

have you had? I can not answer very well. I have not been in ill health for any time I have no farm at the present, but will have one when the reservation is surveyed.

This is all what I can think and will close.
Yours truly,
Jesse Paul[1]

In researching the *Indian Helper* newsletters, I found reference to Jesse Paul working for a land survey company. This statement was written about the two Nez Perce Men:

Charley Wolf who now calls himself Chas William, writes from Idaho Territory that he has found plenty to do since he went home. He visited the printing-office at Wallowa, Oregon, one day and they were glad he could help them for a day. They would have given him steady work and he would have stayed but as he was offered a place with a Surveyors' Company both he and Jesse Paul are working at that business for a while at $40 a month. He says one day they surveyed right through a wigwam and it made him think of Richard Davis's speech here when "Railroads through Indian reservations" was up for debate.[2]

My father told me Grandfather Jesse Paul helped survey allotments and also worked on the ferry at Spalding Crossing on the Clearwater River. The reservation was being surveyed in response to a new law that the United States was imposing on Native peoples to further "civilize" them: the Dawes Allotment Act, which became law on February 8, 1887. Slickpoo and Walker note:

Under this act, the president could, whenever he saw fit, divide up a reservation, and give each member of the tribe on that reservation a certain number of acres depending on the status and age of the individual. For example, each head of family was to be given 160 acres; and each single person over eighteen and all orphans, eighty acres, and every person under eighteen and single was to be given forty acres.[3]

"It is obvious," Slickpoo and Walker continue, "that this act was designed to force us to give up what was left of our traditional way of life. By dividing up the communal lands, attempting to break up tribal relations, and forcing everyone to speak English, this legislation was aimed at stopping us from being Indian."[4]

The US president ordered that the Nez Perce reservation would begin allotting parcels of land in 1889. In the early 1890s, a Harvard University anthropologist, Alice Fletcher, began surveying allotments.[5]

Fletcher and Pratt had similar ideas concerning the need to assimilate Indians into White civilization. Her convictions were formulated as a result of her experiences among the Omahas and the theory of social evolution developed by Lewis Henry Morgan. Morgan, an early anthropologist and a railroad lawyer, suggested that human societies everywhere had evolved through developmental stages from savagery to barbarism to civilization. He believed that most Native Americans were still at the level of Lower or Middle Barbarism, from which, in time, they would move up to Civilization.[6]

Fletcher also had a close relationship with Pratt, and she visited Carlisle Indian Industrial School several times. She was an official "correspondent" of the school paper in 1887.[7] She wrote about the Dawes Allotment Act, and her articles described the implications of this act for the tribes. Jesse Paul was still a student there when these articles were written. He would have had an opportunity to read these articles and learn what to expect of the Allotment Act prior to his return.

Soon after Fletcher's arrival in the summer of 1889, she found she would need help with communication between tribal members and government officials. The tribal council formed a committee of nine men from the various reservation communities.[8] The committee was dominated by Protestant Christian Nimiipuu leaders—not one representative from the non-Christian groups was given a seat on the committee.

There was a lot of opposition to the allotment process. Early in the process, Fletcher received no cooperation in surveying allotments. She met with the members of the Kamiah First Indian Presbyterian Church, explaining— with the Native pastor translating—that she wished the people would see the wisdom of the great change that allotments would bring and how she wished they would help her with the process.[9] She was met with silence, and after a while, Khip-khip-pel-lehk-kin spoke, saying, "We do not want our land cut up in little pieces: we have not told you to do it. We must wait for our people in Lapwai to consent."[10] She replied that they had no choice: the Dawes Act was law and was best for them.[11] She returned to her camp site, thinking that no one would work with her to pick out their lands. The next day, however, Pastor Robert Williams came and said he was ready to register, along with his wife, along with the couple's parents and siblings.[12]

The process of allotting the lands began in Kamiah Valley, the old homeland of Ut-sin-malikan, and now the home of his daughter Wa-le-won (Jane), who had married Tin-tin-nae-khom-kan (Jason Conditt). The

Conditts had four children: Ma-sats-nean (Homer Conditt), born around 1867; Tawlikitsanmay (Woman of the Forest, Lydia Conditt), born 1871; William Conditt, born 1875; and Watkins Conditt, born 1878. The latter two died in 1885, prior to allotment.

Fletcher devised a system of recording family genealogy to aid in determining who was entitled to an allotment. Each applicant for allotment had to name his or her parents and grandparents, as well as their aunts and uncles and children. She used this list to cross reference her land registry, so that every person could be traced throughout the tribe to the remotest kin. Fletcher also noted that if the Indian were to own land in "fee simple," the line of inheritance must be established.[13] These genealogy charts are on file at the Bureau of Indian Affairs, North Idaho Indian Agency. From these first records, our family has been able to trace our history. Although not all names, births, deaths, and relations match up, it is a good beginning. The genealogy charts also list individuals' degree of blood and tribe of origin. Some of the charts include Indian names, but there is often no meaning given.

Alice Fletcher brought with her a close friend, Jane Gay, who cooked and ran the camp. Fletcher also hired a surveyor named Biggs. To help with the surveying, she hired newly returned students from boarding schools who spoke English well,[14] including Jesse Paul. These students were known as "chainmen."[15] Fletcher took four years to complete the allotment process, always taking a break in late November and returning in June to work. During that period, Jesse Paul chose his allotment, on the Camas Prairie between present-day Craigmont and Reubens, Idaho. His mother Phoebe Lowry chose land in Lapwai. Fletcher completed her work in the late fall of 1892, having surveyed nearly 2,000 allotments.

The newly-allotted lands totaled 136,000 acres.[16] The Dawes Allotment Act allowed for the sale of remaining reservation lands to settlers. The leaders of the Nez Perce and officials of the US government agreed to the terms of sale. "The Nez Perce Tribe had to cede, sell, relinquish, and convey to the United States all their claim, right, title, and interest in and to all the unallotted lands within the limits of the reservation, except for 34,000 acres reserved for timber lands, agency, school, mission and cemetery in 1893."[17] 542,000 acres were ceded to the United States, for which the tribe was to be paid $1,626,222. There is controversy about this transaction, as it appears that it was never paid in full:

Of this amount, the sum $626,000.00 was to be paid out as soon as possible after the ratification of the document. The remaining million dollars was to remain in the treasury and one year after the date of ratification, $50,000.00 was to be paid to the tribe, and semiannually thereafter $150,000.00 plus interest was to be paid the tribe until the entire amount owed was paid. To this day few Nez Perces can recall benefiting from any such transfer of funds.[18]

The effect of the Dawes Allotment Act directly affected the Nimiipuu for generations. On November 8, 1895, the reservation lands were opened for White settlement, creating a land rush like the Oklahoma land rush in Indian Territory when it was opened for homesteading.[19] Grandfather Jesse's allotment was on the Camas Prairie and soon after the allotment process had ceased and opened for homestead, the Jesse Paul ranch was surrounded by several White homesteaders.

Black Raven and Woman of the Forest

Prior to the Nez Perce War of 1877, missionary work was still being conducted. Reverend Henry Harmon Spalding had returned to the Nimiipuu Reservation in October 1871. He continued his duties of preaching, baptizing, and accepting into membership many Nimiipuu. In July 1872, due to poor health, he was removed from his duties by the Presbyterian Mission Board.[1] Spalding decided to move to Kamiah and remained there until just prior to his death. He was brought back to Lapwai to receive medical attention in mid-summer but died August 3, 1874.[2]

A year prior to Spalding's death, the Presbyterian Mission Board had sent Sue McBeth to serve among the Nimiipuu. She arrived on October 9, 1873.[3] Her work was primarily teaching the young Nimiipuu men to become ordained ministers[4] and she helped prepare twelve men to become pastors.

One of her first Nimiipuu ministers was Robert Williams, who was ordained in 1879. Prior to becoming ordained, Williams had helped McBeth start a church at Kamiah, now called the First Indian Presbyterian Church of Kamiah. The first service was held December 25, 1871, and the church is still active to this day.[5] This church was where Ut-sin-malikan's daughter—my great-grandmother—Wa-le-won (Jane Parsons Conditt) worshipped along with her husband, Tin-tin-nae-khom-kan (Jason Conditt) and their four children.

Sue McBeth worked with the men, but soon realized the women needed education also. She sent for her sister, Kate McBeth, who arrived in October 1879.[6] Kate was given the responsibility of teaching the women to sew, clean house, and cook, and she also started a Sabbath school. There was a condition concerning who could attend: the women must have husbands who were Christian.[7] Also, women wearing native dress would not be accepted. Both Sue and Kate believed in these conditions for their converts:

> The men must be taken out of their blankets and cut their flowing locks; the women out of their straight, shift-like, immorally short (knee length!), native dresses. To clothe her pupils as properly dressed Christian women became one of Kate's main objectives. She measured, fitted, and cut out dozens of newspaper patterns for the long sleeved, high-necked, flowing, elaborately gored-skirted Victorian dresses.[8]

I am not sure if Wa-le-won attended Kate Macbeth's school, but those who did shared their newly acquired skills.

Kate McBeth introduced the first Christmas celebration at Kamiah. She decorated a tree and had gifts for everyone.[9] This event must have caused much excitement and wonder among the Kamiah churchgoers.

The Christian Nimiipuu grew in strength and were evangelized to give up all manner of the traditional ways, not only of dress but also of worship. Sue McBeth believed "there could be no Christian citizenship in any tribe, until the tribal relations were broken up, and that churches could not long exist that were not established on the purity of the home."[10] Kate McBeth describes what Sue was trying to accomplish:

> The two objects to be attained were clearly before her. The first, the power of the chiefs over the people must be broken, and the man must feel his individuality, instead of feeling he was a part of a band. Second, the moral tone of the people must be raised.[11]

Kate served first at Kamiah, then was required to move to Lapwai in 1885, the year the exiles returned. There was a large celebration to welcome the returnees, described by Reverend G. L. Defenbaugh, the minister of the Lapwai (Presbyterian) Church. He writes that as the wagons bringing the returning women and children arrived, the members of the community all gathered in a semicircle to greet them, "116 in all." The return speech and the greetings of everyone was shared earlier in Chapter 12.

The Nimiipuu had held Fourth of July celebrations for many years, with the Kamiah (and Lapwai) Christians being controlled by the missionaries, who hosted picnics, speeches, and encampments.[12] The Lapwai group, which was considered to be the more "heathen" group by the missionaries, hosted a more traditional feast, which included wearing Native clothing, gambling, horse racing, and drinking.[13]

The Fourth of July celebrations escalated tensions between the Christian and non-Christian Nimiipuu.[14] When he returned in 1888, Black Raven and his mother Phoebe lived in Lapwai, and, it being a small community, they could not have completely ignored the celebrations. Black Raven must have been tempted to go in order to see and celebrate with old friends and relatives.

During the Fourth of July camp of 1897, a new directive was issued by the elders of the church. They decided to camp separately from the non-Christians and decreed that if members chose to go to the "heathen" camp, they must stay there and not be allowed to cross back and forth.[15] I don't know what Phoebe did, but it must have been yet another trauma for her to have to choose which group of her people to be with. I do know from something my father told me that Phoebe had a small cabin next to the Spalding Indian Presbyterian church, where she attended services. Black Raven, given his Christian education at Carlisle, probably stayed in the Christian camp.

All along, more and more children were being "recruited" into boarding schools. Sometimes recruitment meant kidnapping, or it meant the Native parents sent their children because they were being coerced by authorities. Clearly, American authorities wanted to destroy the future of tribes by removing and assimilating all the children.

In 1883, great-grandmother Wa-le-won's son and daughter, along with several other Nimiipuu, were sent to a boarding school in Oregon. My father always told us his mother had attended Chemawa, near Salem, Oregon. In my quest to find my grandmother's records while attending Chemawa, I went to the National Archives and Research Center located in Seattle, Washington. I have since found the school records for my grandmother and great uncle. First, they went to Forest Grove, west of Portland, and then finished at Chemawa. My father's mother, Tawlikit-sanmay (Woman of the Forest, Lydia Conditt) was 12 years old when admitted. Her brother, Ma-sats-nean (Homer Conditt) was 16. They were at the boarding school for five years. The recordkeeping of the early years at Chemawa was limited, so little is known of the activities they took part in. However, I found hospital records kept by the physicians at the school, which helped to show how long they stayed.

Woman of the Forest went to Chemawa, where she was given the name Lydia. She and other students kept autograph books. I suspect these were writing assignments, but they read like yearbooks. Two of Lydia's books survived, and I found them in Black Raven's trunk. The cursive handwriting is wonderful to look at. One student's name was Daniel Boone, and he had fancy writing with lots of loops. A student would start with the greeting "Lydia Conditt, No. 119," and then write a few words, mostly along the lines of "remember me and I will remember you." And they sign with their name and their number. The students also received Victorian calling cards. The cards were small, with a hand holding a bouquet of flowers printed on a flap. When you lifted the flap, there under the flowers would be the student's name. Both men and women had these Victorian floral calling cards that they exchanged with each other. Grandmother's collection includes over 50.[16]

A large group of Native American girls at Chemawa Indian School in Salem, Oregon, circa 1888. My grandmother Tawlitkitsanmay' (Lydia Conditt) is first from the left in the back row. *Paul Family Photo Collection.*

Tawlitkitsanmay' (Lydia Conditt) while at Chemawa Indian School, in Salem, Oregon, circa 1888. *Paul Family Photo Collection.*

Chemawa Victorian calling cards given to Lydia Conditt while she attended the school. She first attended boarding school at Forest Grove in 1883–1885, but it closed and the new Chemawa Indian boarding school was started near Salem, Oregon. The floral hands hide the names: lift up the floral part and the name of the student is underneath. Both men and women students had these Victorian calling cards. They would exchange them with each other. Lydia attended Chemawa from 1885-1888 along with her brother Homer Conditt. They also each had an autograph book, which was a home-work assignment, to learn how to write in cursive *Paul Family Photo Collection.*

It was probably during one of the Fourth of July celebrations that Black Raven met and courted Woman of the Forest. The annual camps were one of the few times that Kamiah and Lapwai groups would gather. Black Raven and Woman of the Forest were married on August 6, 1894. Our family Bible does not state where they were married, but I am assuming it was at Kamiah. They moved to Black Raven's 120-acre allotment on the Camas Prairie. Here they began to raise a family and develop what eventually came to be called the Paul Ranch.

My father, Titus Paul, told me this about his parents' early efforts: "They started out with a tent near a creek on the ranch property; they carved out a ranch and began farming the land. They rented an additional hundred acres that was turned into farmland for growing wheat. They also raised cows, horses, ducks, turkeys, and chickens. We had about a dozen horses to help run the plows. We had a three-bottom plow, which required five horses to pull, and a one-bottom plow, which required three horses to pull.

Another story was recorded by my mother, Maxine S. Paul, who got her information from my father, Titus Paul, for their grandson (and my nephew) Bruce Paul's senior history project. Histories of several local families were collected and published in a book titled *1984 Highlands of Craig Mountain*, edited by Jo Thomason. Here is an account of the early days of the ranch beginnings, with Black Raven called by his boarding school name, Jesse Paul:

> Jesse's early farming operations were primitive, pioneer ones. He broke out forty acres with a sod buster walking plow behind a team of horses and cleared land by sawing down trees and skidding them with this same team to be made into firewood for the winter or to sell a few as saw logs to local mills, such as the Click Mill, which was about two miles away. His early crop was flax, which was good on new land. Later, Marcus wheat, a spring variety, was raised and the grain was hauled by wagon to Culdesac, the terminal point for the Camas Railroad at that time. Besides Jesse's original 120 acres, land nearby was rented on which were raised Forty-Fold club wheat varieties, barley, oats, and hay for cash crops as well as feed for the livestock. Jesse hired his crops threshed by those who did this as their profession.[17]

This humble beginning launched a hundred years of living on and working the Paul Ranch. All Black Raven and Woman of the Forest's children were raised there. Most, and maybe all, were brought into the world with the help of Woman of the Forest's mother Wa-le-won at her place in Kamiah. Woman of the Forest bore eleven children over a 22-year span, with two dying in infancy (Simon in 1909, and Rachel in 1911): first born, in 1896, was Richard. Richard was followed by Esther in 1897; William, in 1899; Bessie, 1901; Rose, 1903; Alta, 1905; Titus James (my father), 1907; Alexander, 1910; and Reuben, who was born in 1918.

Around 1912, that first tent was replaced by a small four-room kit house purchased from the Sears Roebuck catalog. As the family grew larger, this building, too, was replaced. The family moved from the creek to higher ground and expanded into a two-story building with five bedrooms, kitchen, dining room, and a large porch on two sides. The ranch house was the first on the prairie to have electricity, running water, and all the modern conveniences of the time. Farming operations continued to expand, and several outbuildings, which included a granary, woodshop, pantry, laundry house (I still have the wash tubs they used for their laundry), smoke house, and garage were added. Below the house were two chicken houses and a large barn for horses, cows, and pigs.

Elder Paul children of Jesse and Lydia Paul, from left to right: Richard, William, Bessie, and Esther, in 1901. *Paul Family Photo Collection.*

Younger Paul children, 1907. From left to right: Rose, Alta, Titus, and Bessie. *Paul Family Photo Collection.*

Around this same time, a White couple named Patton came to the Camas Prairie late in the fall and did not have time to build shelter. Jesse and Lydia let them stay in their granary for the winter. They subsequently bought land near the Paul ranch and the two families remain friends today. In fact, most of the White Americans in the area accepted the only Native family living in the region.

The Paul family tried to be self-sustaining. A family story, recorded by my mother, describes their efforts:

> There was always a garden with a root cellar for storage for winter and produce that could not be raised on the prairie could be obtained from the grandparents living in the Kamiah valley. Jesse planted an orchard near the house, and there were wild berries, such as service, huckleberries, and elder berries, to be gathered and dried. Items that could not be raised were often purchased from the peddlers that flourished from about 1910 to around 1940. Driving a light wagon, they brought fresh fruit and vegetables, melons, spices, and drug items to the isolated farms, where they were welcomed and often put up for the night. The farm also furnished milk and butter, with poultry, pigs, and calves for meat. The pork was put down in a salt brine, but the beef was dried as only the Indians knew how, in a tepee over non-resin wood. Few deer were killed because one had time to go to the mountains for this game, and Jesse did not have time for hunting.[18]

Woman of the Forest was a good seamstress and made most of the girls' clothes, with dresses made of bright calico. She also made gloves and moccasins from home-tanned deer hides. The boys bought overalls and shirts for everyday wear as well as suits for church. Black Raven dressed in good dark suits.

Each year more land was tilled and gradually they were able to lease land nearby to increase the size and income for the growing family. Before the railroad arrived on the reservation, Black Raven hauled the bundled sheaves of wheat to Lapwai to be threshed and ground into flour.

In 1895 the reservation opened to homesteading, and Black Raven and Woman of the Forest had several White settlers as neighbors. Because of more demand by the settlers to bring their harvest to market, the railroad to Reubens, Idaho, was completed by late 1899. This town was about seven miles from the Paul ranch and became the Paul's post office and trading center. Several of the family members would catch the train from there to go down to Lapwai, and on to Lewiston if necessary. By 1908, the railroad had extended across the prairie through Craig Junction, Ilo, and Vollmer, and on to the communities of Nez Perce, Ferdinand, Cottonwood, and Grangeville. The towns of Ilo and Vollmer eventually grew together and became the town of Craigmont in June 1920.

In 1910, the Carlisle Indian Industrial School sent out a form requesting an update from Black Raven. I found the form, filled out by Black Raven (responses in italics below) dated May 10, 1910, in the National Archives.

Name: Jesse Paul

1. Are you married and if so to whom?
   Yes, married Lydia Conditt, ex. student of Chemawa Ind. School.

2. What is your present address?
   Reubens, Idaho

3. Did you attend or graduate from any other schools after leaving Carlisle?
   No

   Give names of schools and dates if possible.
   [Left blank]

4. What is your present occupation?
   Ass't Ranger on the Nez Perce Indian Timber Reserve.

5. Tell something of your present home.
   We have a three room frame building for living purposes. And all the other buildings necessary for farming.

6. What property in the way of land, stock buildings or money do you have? Own 120 acres of land. 20 head of cattle and work horses, all told have $400 loaned out.

7. Have you been in the Indian Service? In what positions? How long each?
   NO

8. What other positions have you held since leaving Carlisle?
   Held a position as a ferryman on a Government ferry boat for two years.

9. Tell me anything else of interest connected with your life.
   I worked with the Oregon Railway and Navigation Company when surveying a location for railway. And also worked for the Northern Pacific Railroad Company as an interpreter for making settlements on damages done on the Nez Perce Indian Lands.

   We have lived on my land and family about 10 years. I have at present about 100 acres of winter-wheat and beside this have about 60 acres more *in crops. In my present work, I am under the Interior Department as assistant Ranger, drawing $75.00 per month.*[19]

As a forest ranger working for the tribe, Black Raven's duties required that he travel the reservation to check on the number of trees being harvested and sold to either Nimiipuu or the local lumber mills on the reservation. The towns with lumber mills he visited on the reservation were Winchester, Kamiah, Orofino, Sites, Kooskia, Green Creek, and Ferdinand. He carried a gun, because there were men who would try to steal lumber from the tribal reserves. I asked Father if he knew whether Black Raven ever had to use the gun. He replied, "No, but he did know how to use it and folks wouldn't want to bother him when they saw he had one." My father also told me the following story:

> Dad also had a large Morgan horse he rode around a lot. He was the only one who could ride it. If we kids tried to ride him, he'd buck us off. Dad never tied the horse when he dismounted. He would lay his gloves down and the horse would stay. When he was ready to go, he would pick up his gloves, hop on and take off. He was quite a horse, a good-looking horse.

Some of Black Raven's duties as a forest ranger included issuing permits for grazing cattle and cutting timber and measuring the harvested trees to make sure the right amount was paid for. These permits were issued to Whites as well as Nimiipuu. He watched for forest fires, and his call, "Fire on the reserve!" brought farmers with teams, shovels, axes, and wet gunny sacks to extinguish it. He held this job until he retired in 1935. Aided by his son, Titus, Black Raven also surveyed allotment boundaries.

The Paul family was known to go to church, which required a whole day of travel. They either had to come down off the Camas Prairie to the Spalding Presbyterian Church, or travel across the Camas Prairie to the Meadow Creek Indian Presbyterian Church near present-day Ferdinand, Idaho—about twelve miles from the Paul Ranch. Sometimes they went all the way to Kamiah, but only on special occasions. The family Bible records that the children were baptized at Kamiah Second Indian Presbyterian Church. They also attended services on the Camas Prairie in their neighborhood at the Cold Springs School, sponsored by the Presbyterian Church of Reubens. There were often tent revival meetings that Grandmother Woman of the Forest attended, bringing the children along. Grandfather was not always along due to his own travel for work.

The family participated in the annual Fourth of July celebrations. When the elders at the 1897 Fourth of July celebration declared that the

Christian camp was to be separate from the non-Christian, they started hosting the Christian camp meetings at different Indian Presbyterian churches. At the 1909 celebration, the camp directors decided they needed to find a permanent place in the higher elevations to get away from the heat of the valleys, and to offer privacy for worship. An elder and the minister from each of the six Presbyterian churches made up the site-selection committee. It was mentioned in the minutes that since James Stuart and Jesse Paul had done the surveying of the Reservation and knew the lands well, they were appointed to assist the selection committee.[20]

The following summer, a location near the top of Mason Butte was selected, with the help of Jesse Paul and James Stuart. The location had tall timber, water, pasture for the horses to graze, and enough open space to erect the large tent where meetings were held. The site became a permanent place for the annual gathering of the Talmaks Camp Meeting Association, which is still going strong today. Talmaks means "thunder over the buttes" in Nimipuutímt. Black Raven was a volunteer caretaker for the camp, helping to keep the place in good condition, and he was often assisted by his sons. Father told me many times of the happy memories he had of Talmaks.

The Paul Family at Talmaks Presbyterian summer camp, near Craigmont, Idaho, circa 1911. Pictured left to right in the front row are Bessie, Rose, Lydia holding Alex, Titus, and Alta; standing outside the tent are Richard and Esther. *Paul Family Photo Collection.*

The ranch took a lot of time to manage, and the whole family worked together in this endeavor. However, they did find time to have fun. Some of their activities included riding cows, hiking, playing horseshoes, hunting grouse, fishing, and playing baseball with a ball handmade by their mother out of deer hide. In the winter they cleared the snow from Click Mill Pond so they could ice skate. (One time they cleared the snow away for skating, but before they could enjoy the fruits of their labor, someone came and sawed out the ice for their supply of refrigeration.) The children rode on a homemade sled with two sets of runners: a front set for steering and another in back for leverage. There were also side adventures to Lewiston on the train.

Their school basketball teams would travel to Gifford and Reubens and play in halls lit by a single lantern at each end of the large room. Baseball was another sport the people in the area played. Teams would travel by train to sporting events, which was faster than traveling by car at the time.

The Paul children, along with their White neighbors' children, attended Cold Springs School, a one-room schoolhouse that went up to the eighth grade. The school was two miles west of the ranch.

The Cold Springs one-room school house, near Reubens, Idaho, n.d. The Paul children attended school here with the children of area White farming families, from 1st to 8th grades. They were the only Native American family attending this school. *Paul Family Photo Collection.*

Oral stories circulate among the Nimiipuu about the government school at Lapwai and how they would send school officials around to bring in the children of Native families. Black Raven and Lydia did not want their youngest children sent off at such a young age, especially since the school required students to board there. Black Raven and Lydia, having had their own experiences of being sent off at a young age, were determined to keep their two youngest daughters at home until they were older. One day they heard that a government school official was coming to take the two youngest girls. The ranch house sat on a hill about a quarter mile from the county road, and Black Raven and Lydia could see when someone was approaching. The family had bought an upright piano, which was delivered in a wood crate. Once the piano was uncrated, they put the crate to use to store wood out in the wood shop. Black Raven and Lydia hid the girls in the piano box, with wood stacked gently and carefully on top of them. When the agent asked where the girls were, Black Raven and Lydia said the girls were at the neighbors for a while and would not return that day.

The Paul family did allow their children to go to boarding schools, but only when they were teenagers. In 1915, Richard, the oldest, went to Cushman Training School, located on the Puyallup Reservation near Tacoma, Washington, where he learned to be a carpenter. William also attended Cushman in 1915, but he did not stay long. He went to Alaska to work on the fishing boats, but soon returned and remained to help with the ranch. Esther and Rose went to Chemawa from 1919 to 1922. My father Titus went to the Chilocco School in Oklahoma, just south of the Kansas state line, in 1922. Alta married either in late 1922 or early 1923, but she died giving birth in May 1924. It is not known why Bessie did not go to Chemawa; maybe she was needed to help at the ranch. Alex also attended Chemawa, from August 1924 to February 1925. Reuben, the youngest child, attended Sherman Institute at Riverside, California from 1928 to 1936.

The family's transportation improved with the times, as the ranch prospered. Father said that the first car in the family was a Willys-Knight, a sedan with a three-speed transmission. "It didn't last very long," my father told me. "Another car we had was a Nash. This one we had a while, and in the winter, it was put on blocks so the tires wouldn't wear out and go flat. The car I learned to drive was a Studebaker. It was a touring car with an open top, and we had to buy curtains and fasten them to the frame. There were no windows, but it did have a windshield. It was kind of a fun car."

Black Raven and Woman of the Forest were living the "Progressive Indian" ideal: they owned a successful working farm on which they raised crops; they sent their children to school; and they lived in a two-story home with electricity, running water, and all the modern conveniences of the times. The future looked bright and all was well.

Black Raven was active in the affairs of the tribe. In 1922, the tribe was authorized by the office of the Bureau of Indian Affairs to conduct a survey of the social, economic, and industrial conditions of the reservation. This work became part of the Merriam Report, a collection of surveys carried out on all the reservations throughout the United States. With the information collected from the surveys, local Indian Agencies were to develop a five-year program to meet local needs by addressing the conditions of each tribe.[21]

The Nimiipuu Reservation survey showed the Allotment Act had further reduced the land base of the Nimiipuu, many of whom sold their lands because they did not understand the laws or were swindled out of their land title. There was a growing number of younger Nimiipuu who were not as thrifty, industrious, and temperate as the older generations. The Bureau of Indian Affairs officials who conducted the survey asked themselves what they might do to reduce the idleness, poverty, vice, and intemperance that seemed to be growing in the tribe. Their answer was to form a Nez Perce Indian Home and Farm Association. This association would be made up of the adult members of the tribe in general council and would act in conjunction with the superintendent. The council consisted of James Stuart, President; Jesse Paul, Vice-President; Corbett Lawyer, secretary; and members Ellis Khip-khip-pel-kehken, George Peo-peo-tah-likt, Steve Reuben, John Seven, Silas D. Whitman, and Ralph Armstrong.[22]

The council members worked to form a working government system for the tribe. It was decided to form two tribal governmental divisions: one a general council, composed of all the adult members of the tribe, and the other a business committee to represent the tribe in activities in which the Nimiipuu were participating. The tribe wanted a permanent representative body, and whenever the opportunity for participation in tribal affairs presented itself, the business committee was quick to respond. The committee gradually developed into a well-organized and nationally recognized governing unit.[23] Black Raven served on this committee as the vice president for at least four years, according to the records I have found. In 1927, he helped write a constitution to move the tribe closer to becoming self-governing.

This business committee was used in an advisory capacity to the Superintendent of the Agency, which was not what the Farm Association wanted. It took several more years before the tribe was able to become a totally self-governing body. This process evolved over two decades, which eventually led to formation of a Tribal Executive Committee elected by the tribe at large, and these elected council men and women would manage the affairs of the tribe.[24]

Richard Paul, circa 1916.
Paul Family Photo Collection.

William Paul, seated, and unidentified friend, circa 1918.
Paul Family Photo Collection.

Rose, on left, and Esther, seated, circa 1919. *Paul Family Photo Collection.*

Alta Paul, taken at Cold Springs School circa 1922. *Paul Family Photo Collection.*

Reuben Paul, in his University of Idaho graduation photo, 1949. *Paul Family Photo Collection.*

Titus Paul (left), Andrew Red Duck (center), and Alex Paul (right), standing on the front porch of the Paul Ranch house, circa July 1925. *Paul Family Photo Collection.*

The wooden piano crate where Rose, Esther, and Bessie were hidden from the Indian agent, to avoid being taken to boarding school. *Paul Family Photo Collection.*

CHAPTER 16

Enough Death!

By 1923, several of the now-adult children were living at home: two girls, Esther, 25; Bessie, 22; and one boy: William, 24. They lived with their younger siblings Alexander, 13, and Reuben, 5. Titus, age 15, had left in September 1922 to attend Chilocco Indian Agricultural School in Oklahoma. Richard, now 27, was living in Lapwai. Alta, 18, had married and was living with her husband, Pete Samuels. The third oldest daughter, Rose, had died on February 1, 1922, at the age of 22, due to pericardial effusion.

Esther was a nurse at the Lapwai Sanitarium for Tuberculosis, having studied nursing at Chemawa. Bessie helped with the chores of running the kitchen and food preparation, while William worked the ranch grounds and helped supervise Alexander with the plowing, harvesting, and other chores. Reuben was too small to help, but I am sure he had chores. Black Raven was busy with work and tribal affairs and was often away from the ranch and traveling around the reservation. Sometimes he would stay at a hotel in Winchester if the roads became impassable due to mud or snow. This left Woman of the Forest busy with keeping the ranch and house in order, church activities and being a mother.

The month of November brought sickness to the family. It was the month that changed the lives of the Paul family and nearly broke their spirits. Several of the family members contracted typhoid fever, and three of the older children were hospitalized: Esther, William, and Bessie. The younger two, Alexander and Reuben, remained at home, but a nurse was brought in to care for them while Jesse and Lydia rode the train from Craig Junction to Lewiston, taking turns to be with their sick children. The *Lewiston Morning Tribune* ran this account in the November 30, 1923, edition:

3 CHILDREN DEAD: Typhoid Fever Ravages Jesse Paul Family. Two Daughters Ill. Bodies of William, Bessie, and Esther to be taken to Kamiah today for burial.

One of the most pathetic sorrows ever coming to the attention of the residents of this city and section is that involving Mr. and Mrs. Jesse Paul of Reubens, well known and influential members of the Nez Perce tribe of Indians, who since last Tuesday at 2:30 o'clock in the afternoon, have lost three children by death. William age 24 years, died at St. Joseph's Hospital Tuesday afternoon from typhoid fever, and when his end came his two sisters, Bessie, and Esther both grown, were occupying beds in the same hospital and suffering from the same disease that had removed their brother. Yesterday morning at 7:30 o'clock Bessie passed away, and at 8 o'clock last night Esther died. And to make the sorrow of the parents more poignant at an hour when their heads are bowed in deepest grief, two others of their children both at home 4 and the other 1 year are in their beds at their home in Reubens, today according to yesterday's reports they too being afflicted with typhoid.

The mother and father of the stricken children, three of whom have passed away within 24 hours of each other, have been spending their time between the sick ones at home and those in Lewiston hospital and yesterday when the end came to Bessie and Esther the mother was being borne to Lewiston on the Camas Prairie train, arriving here several hours after Bessie died, but about nine hours before Esther passed away, and the comforting words of a mother were hers until death entered upon the scene. Richard Paul, a brother, and a married sister of the dead children were also present when Bessie died. Mr. Paul spent Wednesday here with daughters, returning to Reubens so that his wife could leave her two little girls who are sick at Reubens and be with Bessie and Esther.

This afternoon when the Clearwater Short Line train departs for Kamiah the bodies of the three children will be aboard, the burial party to be formed by the mother, sister, and brother now in Lewiston and possibly Mr. Paul if it is safe for him to leave his sick girls at his home.

Burial will take place in the Indian burying ground at Kamiah, the date of the funeral not yet being made known.

Mr. Paul is chief forester of the Nez Perce Indians forest area, and at this time is in charge of logging operations at Reubens, where recently the Craig Mountain Lumber company purchased many millions of feet of timber belonging to the Indians from the government.

Reading this newspaper article brought me deep pain. Every November, I experience deep sadness and sorrow. I never understood why until I found this article and noted that the date of the three children's deaths corresponded with my depression. A great weight lifted from me, though I feel robbed of my aunts and uncles, and the ancestors my family lost then as well as in the 1877 war.

There are two errors in the newspaper article. First, it states that two daughters were ill at home, but it was the two youngest boys, Alexander and Reuben. The second mistake is the children's ages were given as being one and four, but the two boys were 13 and 5 years old.

Another newspaper account from the *Lewis County Review*, dated December 12, 1923, describes the character of the children and the funeral service:

> The news of their deaths comes as a shock to their many friends. Willie, Bessie, and Esther were young people well known and well-liked by their white friends and fellow tribesmen, and their loss is deeply felt, especially among the younger people.
>
> They leave to mourn their loss, Jesse Paul, their father, who is chief forester of the Nez Perce Indians forest area and is one of the most respected men of the tribe and a highly respected citizen of the Reubens country. Lydia their mother, Alta Samuel of Craigmont, a sister, and the following brothers, Richard; Titus, who is a student at an Indian school in Chilocco, Okla; Reuben and Alex.
>
> The bodies of the deceased were taken to Kamiah Friday and the funeral services were held at the Second Presbyterian church at 10 o'clock Saturday morning, Reverend James Hayes conducting the services. Interments were made in the church cemetery.
>
> One of the largest groups ever gathered at the church honored the dead and the floral offerings were profuse and beautiful. Expressions of sympathy for the family have been current over the entire district where they have lived for so many years.

The two younger boys, Alexander and Reuben, did survive. The deaths of her other children took a toll on Woman of the Forest—she died five months later, on May 2, 1924. Then Alta died in childbirth May 17, 1924, just 2 weeks later. All the girls were gone; the only remaining children were the four boys, Richard, Titus, Alexander, and Reuben.

Woman of the Forest was in such grief and shock she died before being able to heal from these losses. She has kept coming to me in dreams, urging me to remember her children and to somehow heal the gaping wound their deaths had opened. I could now see how these deaths shocked my family into silence, how historical trauma spread numbness across the generations and was passed on to me.

With Richard out on his own, and Titus away at school, Black Raven was alone in his grief while having to raise his two youngest children. Soon after his wife died, he realized he was not able to take care of his two surviving sons, and so asked for an application from Chemawa Indian School to be submitted by the Agency Superintendent O. H. Lipps. In a letter written by Lipps at the National Archives Pacific Alaska Region (Seattle) he describes Black Raven and the reason for seeking admittance:

Department of the Interior
United State Indian Field Service
Fort Lapwai Indian Agency
Lapwai, Idaho
June 18, 1924

Mr. Harwood Hall
Supt., Salem Indian School
Chemawa, Oregon.
Dear Mr. Hall:

> I am enclosing herewith the application of Jesse Paul for the enrollment at your school next year of his son, Alexander Paul. The mother of this boy was an old graduate of Chemawa. She died a few months ago. Jesse Paul has lost during the past few months three grown children and his wife. I regard him and his wife as the best examples of successful returned students I have ever known. He is an Ex-Carlisle student and started out as a prisoner of war when a small boy, and as such General Hugh L. Scott conveyed him with the other Nez Perce prisoners from the head waters of the Yellowstone River of Montana to North Dakota, and there put them on the train to Fort Leavenworth. This was forty-five years ago. Two years ago, General Scott was here and Jesse returned the compliment by taking the General in his fine touring car over the reservation. We lunched at Jesse's home, which is a nice seven room modern house, with telephone, electric lights and most all modern conveniences. It is located on a two hundred and fifty acre farm, owned in fee, and on which he pays taxes. He and his wife as soon as they were married moved on to his allotment located over twenty miles to their nearest Indian neighbors. They lived there for two years in a tent, not having money to build a house. Both received fee patents to their lands, but instead of selling them have bought other lands. Also, instead of mortgaging their own lands they own mortgages on other white neighbors' lands. They bought about three thousand dollars of Liberty and Victory bonds during the war and paid cash for them. Also, they have considerable money in bank and loaned out.
>
> This is my idea of a successful returned student considering what the government starts out to do with the Indian—that is, to give him an education and training, allot him a piece of land, have him go on that land and establish a home, take his place in the community as an industrious progressive citizen and become a useful and self-supporting member of society. These two peo-

ple did that thing and did it so well that they have been outstanding example of what Indians can do if they would only take advantage of the opportunity the government offers them. The opportunity of these two Indians was no better than that of thousands of others of their race, and what they have accomplished practically all others of their school-mates might have accomplished. The *Saturday Evening Post* of May 31ˢᵗ contained an article on the American Indian by Secretary Work. In that article special reference is made to a successful and thrifty Nez Perce Indian. Jesse Paul is that Indian.

Since the death of Mrs. Paul, Jesse finds it impossible to keep his two children together here, so he has decided to send Alexander away to school He will be able to pay tuition for him and will pay his expenses to the school. He would like to take him down there about August 1st. Please advise whether or not you can enroll him.

Very respectfully,
O.S. Lipps Superintendent

The response from Harwood was affirmative, and Alexander arrived at Chemawa in September 1924 at age 14. He was admitted into the 6th grade. Within a short time, Alexander wrote home complaining about his treatment, saying he had been whipped unmercifully and the other students did not like Nez Perce students. When he received this letter, Black Raven went to Superintendent Lipps requesting an investigation, which Lipps conducted by sending a letter:

Dear Mr. Hall:

Jesse Paul, the father of Alexander Paul enrolled at Chemawa, has asked me to write to you about his boy. This boy has written his father that he cannot get along at Chemawa, that he has been whipped unmercifully, etc., and that the Nez Perces are not liked by the other tribes.

Jesse seems very much concerned about the boy, as he has always taught his children to obey, to be industrious and to keep out of trouble. He thinks that if the boy is dissatisfied and is unable to get along that he had better bring him home and arrange for his schooling elsewhere....

This boy Alexander lay at death's door for several weeks and it may be that he has not fully recovered from that illness and the shock caused by the deaths of his older brother and sister and his mother.

Please call Alexander in and have a talk with him and find out the nature of his trouble, and then advise as to what you think should be done.

Very sincerely,
O.H. Lipps Superintendent

Mr. Harwood responded quickly with a letter dated October 18, 1924:

> I talked with the boy and he says he has no reason to complain; that he has not been punished, etc. I find that complaints are largely made when students are homesick and make statements through homesick eyes. The boy is all right and says he is very happy here.

I really have doubts that Alexander was homesick, and why would he lie about being harmed? Mr. Harwood made light of Alexander's situation. This response seemed to satisfy Black Raven, however. Alexander was allowed to stay in school and life went on. The month of November was fast approaching, the anniversary dates of his children's deaths. Early in January 1925, Black Raven became ill and was sent to the hospital on January 14th. The Agency Superintendent was so moved by his hospitalization that he wrote a letter to the Commissioner of Indian Affairs in Washington, DC, telling him about Jesse Paul. The letter is dated January 15, 1925:

The Honorable
Commissioner of Indian Affairs
Washington DC

> Sir:

> I have to report that Jesse Paul; Scaler at this Agency, is in poor health and that yesterday we sent him to the hospital at Lewiston, Idaho. I have arranged with a local scaler, who, Mr. Paul had recommended as competent and reliable, to do the log scaling for us temporarily until it can be determined whether or not Mr. Paul will be able to return to duty.

> In this connection I desire to explain that Jesse Paul last year lost by death his wife and four adult sons and daughters within a few months' time. In fact one son and a daughter were buried in the same grave. These and one other died of typhoid fever. The other daughter died of childbirth and his wife died probably of a broken heart. Through all this trouble Jesse Paul maintained the stoicism of a Spartan and only recently had he shown signs of failing health. He now appears possessed of the feelings that he will not recover and has given instructions of the management of his property in the event of his death.

> Jesse Paul is the Nez Perce referred to by Secretary Work in his article in the *Saturday Evening Post* of May 31, 1924, as an example of the thrifty, capable and progressive Indian. Starting life as a prisoner of war of Chief Joseph's band of Nez Perces, his achievements make an inspiring story worthy of publication in the American Magazine. He is the most com-

petent full blood Indian I have ever known and one of the gentlest, finest characters, either white or Indian, it had ever been my lot to deal with. I should deeply regret the protracted illness of Mr. Paul and his death would be an irreparable loss to this Agency and to the Nez Perce tribe. We are giving him the best possible care and treatment and it is hoped that a favorable report as to his early recovery can be made within a few days. I shall keep the Office advised of his condition and should he fail to make early recovery the Office will be requested to appoint or transfer a scaler to take his place.

Very respectfully,
O.H. Lipps Superintendent

Finding this letter in the family papers helped piece together the story of the tremendous loss that the Paul family experienced. The full tragedy was not over, however. While Black Raven lay ill, he asked his oldest son, Richard, to bring Alexander home. He had heard that Alexander was not well and wanted him home with him. It was not easy to go and get the boy; again, a letter had to be written by the Superintendent asking permission to release Alexander to Richard. This was done, and they both returned. Alexander arrived with a 102-degree temperature and was put to bed immediately. Alexander died of tuberculosis on the morning of February 20, 1925. Grandfather was still in the hospital. I learned this one night as I was working on my dissertation—by coincidence, it was also February 20—and I stopped and screamed, **"ENOUGH! ENOUGH DEATH!** Grandfather, you had to feel this was enough! How did you survive?"** That night he came to me in a dream and said, "I have not been there for my surviving sons. I need to live so I can help them." I could finally feel Grandfather's grief and understand why he came to me on the night I tried to take my life. It was he who was saying "enough death!" and not just me screaming when I was writing his story. He was screaming with me. I now recognized the importance of him coming to me that night and telling me to *"Go home"*—go home and reconnect, heal my broken heart, and begin to help heal the soul wounds of the generational wounds of the Paul family.

Somehow, despite this latest loss, Black Raven recovered. Perhaps he remembered how his life as a small child had been without his father, and now he realized he needed to be there for his youngest son Reuben. It is not known how much longer Grandfather stayed in the hospital, but eventually he returned to the ranch, only to leave it and lease the land. He had had enough. He moved to Kamiah, where he remained. From family stories, I have been told he did not fully live life as before, that there was a "sadness" about him. He did remarry and had another daughter named Joanne, born in 1931. His youngest son, Reuben, who was 8 years old, was sent to the Sherman Institute in Riverside, California, in 1926.

Black Raven left behind his boarding school trunk, which he'd been given at Carlisle to stow his possessions. When he returned home to the reservation, the trunk came with him. Over the years many items had been stored in the trunk. Probably in 1926, after his children and wife died, he packed up his wife's belongings along with several items that belonged to his daughters, Esther, Bessie, Rose, and Alta: baskets, shawls, colorful silk head scarfs that Grandmother Lydia had worn, bead work, including cornhusk bags, and beaded purses, belts, moccasins, and gloves. There were also the two autograph books and calling cards that Lydia had while attending Chemawa, as well as the autograph book belonging to Esther when she attended Chemawa. There were photos of Esther's friends, and family photo albums. There were also old blankets, bed linens, and some wool rugs. When my father Titus Paul married my mother Maxine Caster in 1931, Grandfather Black Raven shipped the trunk to them in Arkansas City, Kansas. Every time my parents moved; they brought the trunk with them.

Grandfather's Trunk: Jesse Paul received this trunk while attending Carlisle Indian School in 1880. This trunk has held many family treasures throughout the years. The items in the trunk helped me find and tell our family's generational story. It held photo albums, Native baskets, beaded items made mostly by Esther Paul, such as beaded bags, belts, moccasins, and gloves. It held Grandmother Lydia's Chemawa autograph books along with the Victorian calling cards; also, the autograph book of Esther Paul from when she attended Chemawa and the Lapwai Sanitorium. The trunk had shawls, blankets, and Grandmother Lydia's silk head scarves. I am so thankful that Grandfather held onto these items, put them in the trunk, and gave it to my father, who in turn, along with my mother, valued and saved the items. It was as if the trunk was holding the Paul family story until it was time to tell our story and heal the generational wounds. *Paul Family Photo Collection.*

As a child, I would search through the trunk and wonder who had worn the beautiful scarves and shawls, who had done the bead work, who were these people in the photos? Father did not speak about his family unless asked, and even then he would give only minimal answers. My mother knew some of the history and would share it, but as a child I did not understand the trauma caused by so many children dying in such a short time.

Black Raven could have destroyed Woman of the Forest's belongings but chose to keep them. My parents honored and respected these items. The many items in Grandfather's trunk have helped me to find our family stories. Each item has a story to tell that helps piece together the puzzle of the family intergenerational trauma.

Black Raven continued to serve on the Farm Association committee as vice president for a few more years. He also remained the tribe's forester until he retired in 1935. He and his new family still attended Talmaks and were active in church affairs. In late February 1936, Black Raven became ill again and was admitted to White's Hospital in Lewiston. He died on March 2, 1936, at the age of 66. He is buried next to his children and wife in the Kamiah Second Indian Presbyterian cemetery.

Three surviving Paul Brothers, taken after WWII at the Paul Ranch. From left to right: Reuben, Richard, and Titus. *Paul Family Photo Collection.*

Mountain Lion, My Father

My father, Titus Paul, was born in a tepee under a Ponderosa pine, assisted into this world by his grandmother, Wa-le-won, on August 11, 1907. His birthplace was the homeplace of his grandparents in Kamiah, Idaho. He was the seventh child of Black Raven (Ka-khun-ne, Jesse Paul) and Tawlikitsanmay (Woman of the Forest). Our family Bible notes that Father was baptized August 18, 1907, at the Kamiah Second Presbyterian Church.

My father's Nez Perce name was given to him later in life. His friends always called him Tiger, which evolved into Mountain Lion, and that led to Koo-ya-mah, a phonetic spelling of the Nimipuutímt word meaning "mountain lion." In the *Nez Perce Dictionary*, it is spelled k̉oỷamá.[1]

Painting of Titus Ko Yamá (Mountain Lion) Paul in his headdress. *Painting by Patty Reid, 1986 and gifted to the Paul family. Paul Family Collection.*

Father had happy memories of being the youngest child for a while. But as he grew, other children came along: his brothers Alexander and Reuben. Two other children, Simon and Rachel, died in infancy and he barely remembered them.

The Paul Ranch had grown over the years, but the family was still living in a small house down by the spring. Titus remembered when the little house was moved up to higher ground and remodeled, adding a second story. He thought this happened in 1912, when he was about five.

Father recalled speaking both Nimipuutímt and English at home. They would sing hymns in Nimipuutímt, and he told us about the sweats the family would attend, both at home and at the Nez Perce Indian Church summer camp. Later, though, after boarding school, he lost much of his Native language.

He liked to go for walks around the ranch to discover things. He would make bows and arrows out of thorn bush because the branches were reasonably straight. He had learned to milk the family cow at an early age. He would also help feed the chickens, turkeys, and domesticated ducks. When he grew older, he helped plow with a single-bottom plow pulled by three horses. His older brother Bill (short for William) ran the three-bottom plow behind five horses. At the time they had 100 acres in crop. I can't even imagine walking behind the plow and guiding the horses on so many acres.

Father had fun, too, playing with his siblings, hiking, hunting grouse, fishing, and playing baseball with the handmade ball of deer hide. He told us when the snow would be up to the tops of the fence posts, he'd make skis from barrel staves. By attaching a leather strap to the curved stave, he could slip his feet in—and off he would go down the hill in front of the ranch house.

The family often visited his maternal grandparents, Jane and Jason Conditt, at their Kamiah Valley home. Titus remembered the stories his grandfather told him, saying that Grandfather Jason could tell a story and bring it to life. His uncle Ma-sats-nean (Homer Conditt), his mother's brother, also told many Coyote stories, which he liked hearing the most. These Coyote stories were told in Nimipuutímt.

When Father was considered old enough to go to school, he joined his older sisters and brothers, walking to the one-room Cold Springs School. Thirty children from the area joined them. Before he could go to school, he had to have a haircut. His father Black Raven told him, "Now that you're a schoolboy, you must look like one." He was seven when he had his first haircut. He attended school for eight years. In addition to homework, he would still have his chores to do at home. Keeping a large family clean and fed, not to mention running the day-to-day activities of the ranch, required a disciplined household.

When asked how his parents handled discipline, Father told me, "They were pretty strict, so I had to do everything just so, but that was alright, didn't hurt a thing." His mother taught the children about various plants and how to prepare dried meat the Indian way. His parents had rules which were expected to be obeyed. These rules were to "keep our rooms clean, ourselves clean, no fighting among ourselves and to treat everybody nice. We had to be that way." When asked what happened when the rules got broken, he replied, "That didn't happen very often, but we would get a switch across the behind. We conducted ourselves in a polite manner, saying please and thank you."

As a child, my father learned how to listen to the sounds in the woods from his father. Black Raven also taught my father the daily devotions, which Father practiced by walking the ranch grounds and the forests that surrounded it and listening to the wind and animals. This gave him the time and experience to listen closely to what the robins and other birds were singing and saying about the weather, which he could predict by listening to the birds. I know I am biased, but this is a great example of how being raised in a culture that values close listening connects us to the earth, the seasons, and to all the life around us.

The family sang hymns, accompanied on piano by Father's sister Esther. They must have been a rousing choir there on the hilltop ranch house, because the neighbors told my parents they could hear them from a couple miles away across the prairie. The family attended church in many places. Sometimes, during the harsh winters on the prairie, they would stay home or go to the Cold Springs School where church was held for the farming families in that area. In the summers, they trekked to the summer encampment at Talmaks.

Father attended Cold Springs School from 1914-1922, from first through eighth grades. Then it was time for a decision. Black Raven said the children needed not only a book education but a skill to earn a living. Here's how my father said it developed, "One evening at the dinner table Dad was going around the table, asking where we would like to go to school. As we went around the table Bessie was first to say she wanted to go to Chemawa, where Mom had gone. Alta wanted to go to Chemawa, too. Esther had already attended Chemawa, and when my turn came, I said, 'As far away as you can get me,'" Father chuckled. When he told me this, I was surprised he wanted to be that far from his family. "Really?" I asked and he said, "Yes, I wanted to explore the world."

"Far away" turned out to be the Chilocco Indian Agricultural School in Oklahoma.

The Chilocco Indian Agricultural School was developed soon after Chemawa and was a government-funded school based on the ideology that Richard Pratt had implemented at the Carlisle School. Chilocco was located on the border of Oklahoma and Kansas, about 25 miles south of Arkansas City, Kansas. Congress authorized construction of the school on May 17, 1882.[2] Construction took two years, and Chilocco started recruiting students in 1884. Some of the children were the exiled Nimiipuu who lived only 30 miles away.

The school operated almost 100 years, from 1884 until 1980. Most of the students came from Oklahoma, and from tribes in Kansas, Missouri, and Nebraska. During the years that Father was there, the student enrollment was between 800 and 1,000 students.[3] By 1922, when young Titus arrived, it had grown into a large campus with several dormitories, a dining hall, classroom buildings, various vocational buildings, a hospital, steam plant, several barns, a gym, athletic fields, and housing for the staff. The entrance had an arch over the road with the school's name, and a tree-lined two-mile road to the campus that seemed to go on forever, lined on both sides with orchards and fields of crops. The school land base was 8,640 acres.[4]

My father, 15 years old, left for Chilocco in early September. When I asked him if he was afraid of leaving home, he replied, "No, I was a rascal that way, I liked to see different things, and I was never homesick." Two young girls also left for Chilocco with him: sisters Pauline and Ruth Corbett. The trio, my father told me, traveled from Lewiston by ferry on the Snake River to Riparia, Washington, then took a train to Pendleton, Oregon, where they changed trains to Cheyenne, and then on to Newton, Kansas, and finally to Chilocco.

The Chilocco Indian Agricultural School entrance arch. *Paul Family Photo Collection.*

When they arrived at last in Chilocco, the trio was met at the train station and Titus was taken to Home 1 for large boys. As historian Lomawaima writes, "Each home had a disciplinarian [a role similar to that of a resident assistant] who explained the rules and regulations."[5] According to Father, the disciplinarian said, "There is no foolishness; do everything just so-so, such as keeping your room clean, keeping yourself clean, and no speaking of your Native language. They were pretty strict. We were given regular army uniforms, which were expected to be worn on Sundays."

Father was assigned to the eighth grade again; his previous teacher at Cold Springs had not prepared him well enough to enter high school. He took US history, civics, arithmetic, English, general exercise, agriculture, and auto mechanics. His first year at Chilocco, his grades were average; he had some catching up to do. When I reviewed his school records, I found his grades improved every year. The school was run much like Carlisle: students went to classes for half a day and then worked half a day. Father's job was working in the auto mechanic shop. Lomawaima describes the daily schedule:

In accordance with Chilocco's vocational charter, students spent half the day in academic classes, half in vocation work/classes or on work details…. In 1910, the Indian Education office in Washington directed its superintendents to abandon the split-day plan for younger students, who should devote their time to academics until they were older, when industrial work would be more meaningful. This removed younger students from the vocational track for several years but did not exempt them from the work details necessary to the upkeep of the school in the dining room, kitchen, sewing and mending rooms, dormitory, butcher shop, and bakery. Institutional needs dictated administrative efficiency, and reveille awoke Chilocco students at 5:30 A.M., the first of twenty-two bugle calls punctuating the daily schedule. Weary students were released after Assembly at 9:05 in the evening.[6]

Father's day was long. When I asked him about that, he replied, "I just did it." Time was not wasted. However, there was time for fun activities in the evenings after dinner and before bedtime. Down along Chilocco Creek, Father and his friends would hunt rabbits with bows and arrows, then build a fire and roast their game along with parched corn. This was not an approved activity; they just did it.

"The teachers were pretty good," my father told me. "They made sure you did your homework, whatever they assigned you to do. A lot of 'em would help you if you couldn't do it. They were willing to help you. They were pretty good teachers, all of 'em."

Other times boys from the school would go to Chilocco Creek and do "stomp dances." This was a boys-only activity. The boys would go around stomping in a circle, with one boy in the middle beating a small drum. I asked if they got in trouble for doing Native dances.

"Well, I had to walk around the flagpole one time with a rifle on my shoulder for going out stomp dancing," he replied with a laugh. "For about an hour or so, I think, or something like that. I don't know, sometimes [the disciplinarian] made me sweep the halls for punishment, a lot of 'em."

"Did you keep doing the stomp dances?" I asked him.

"Yes," my father said, "we would get caught, and so we marched a lot around the flagpole."

There was a sort of low-key underground, at least among my father and his classmates: they played stick game and danced. And, if there was another Nimiipuu around, they'd speak Nimipuutímt.

Even though he was hundreds of miles from home and had no family or friends to talk with, my father enjoyed his high school years. Father helped at the post office, where he was a mail carrier. At the train stop, there was a hook where the outgoing mail would be hung up. As the train approached the station and slowed, the conductor could snag the bag and pull it aboard. Then the conductor would throw a sack of mail onto the platform, which Father would catch—or get knocked down. He also worked in a store that sold candy and bakery items. He worked there a few hours every day and earned between 25 cents and a dollar a day.

His favorite job, and the one he talked about the most, was being the bus driver for the sport teams. Father had learned to drive back at the Paul Ranch. He was working in the mechanic shop and had to drive the school vehicles to the shop, and when they noticed that he was a good driver, they asked him to drive the school bus. That he did. He also drove other students to activities, too. He would meet students at the train stop where he was often the first one to greet the new students.

The bus driving duties led to him being a chauffeur for school officials. "I knew how to drive, I was a good driver, and they trusted me," Father told me. "I knew that I had to keep their trust and I kept it. I drove a 16-passenger bus and a Ford Model T sedan." He told me that "the teams of Chilocco had to play junior colleges because the high schools wouldn't play them on account that they were too good of athletes. These teams would even out-play the junior college teams."

My father also got some free time out of the deal: "I also drove the 'Big Shots' around when they came from Washington, DC. I mostly took the single women teachers to town every Saturday afternoon. They would shop or do their errands and I would play pool or see a movie. I had money because I worked in the school store that sold candy and bakery goods."

Communication from home was sparse. When asked how he found out about the death of his sisters and brother, he said he had received a telegram. He was not able to go home for the funerals; the cost and the distance were too much. He couldn't afford to return home when he received word his mother had died. He never talked about the deaths of his siblings and his mother.

He did manage to return home for two consecutive summers, 1925 and 1926. His younger brother Reuben was left under the care of Black Raven. In the summer of 1925, Black Raven took Titus and Reuben on a pleasure trip to Glacier and Yellowstone national parks. They traveled by car and drove first to Spokane, where they took a train to Glacier National

Park, because there was no road across the mountains yet. The car was put on the train. They had a wonderful time visiting the parks, where they camped in tents.

Father's class of 1927 was the first to graduate from Chilocco with a four-year high school diploma. In the yearbook published for the class of 1927, he was nicknamed Ty. He had joined the school's Sequoyah Literary Society, of which he later became vice president, and the glee and debate clubs. He was the class vice president in 1925 and acted in a school play. (He played Sailor Boy in a production of *The Captain of Plymouth*.)

My father would later say his years at Chilocco were the best thing for him. His teachers thought highly of him and commented on his character and abilities. They described him as "quiet, earnest, worthwhile, not very forceful, honest, high ideals" and he was "a very trustworthy and dependable young man. Have always found him willing and a very good worker. Is an extra good car driver and takes better care of a car than the majority his age" and "he could and should go to college."

After graduating, Father went to Sweeny Auto School, in Kansas City, Missouri, for auto mechanic training. After that, he said, "I bummed around for a couple of years, doing odd jobs, helping one family plant and harvesting a crop of corn."

Titus Paul's high school graduation photo from Chilocco Indian School, 1927. *Paul Family Photo Collection.*

Titus and Maxine

In the fall of 1929, Father was hired on at the Shell Oil Refinery in Arkansas City, Kansas. An acquaintance recommended he stay at a boarding house run by a Mrs. Caster. She had a daughter named Susie Maxine, who would become my mother. The story of how they met was described to me in 1972 by my mother, who went by Maxine:

> I met my husband-to-be when he came to board at the boarding house my mother opened up when I was sixteen. She had asked a friend to send her some boarders; three young Indian boys were among the first that he directed to her accommodations. My girlfriend was staying with us at the time, and we two teenagers were very much impressed by these good-looking young men. I set my cap for the handsome one with the two first names (Titus Paul). It took me two weeks to get him to ask me for a date. It was almost two years later that we married.

Even though Maxine liked Titus, some of her family members did not. I heard that her uncles beat up Titus, telling him to stay away from Maxine. When asked how she was able to continue seeing the man she'd set her cap for, she replied, "I told them that I loved him and I was going to continue seeing him and this is how it is going to be."

Maxine Caster's high school graduation photo from Arkansas City, Kansas, 1931. *Paul Family Photo Collection.*

Titus Paul and Maxine Caster on the front porch of her mother Bessie Caster's boarding house in Arkansas City, Kansas, 1930. *Paul Family Photo Collection.*

The marriage of Titus, a full blood Nimiipuu, to Maxine Caster, of Irish, German, and English heritage, took place July 2, 1931, in Arkansas City, Kansas. Mixed-race marriages were frowned upon and, in fact, in many states it was illegal and remained so until the 1960s. The Supreme Court ruled in 1964 that bans on interracial marriage violated the 14th Amendment, but that didn't actually change any state laws. That finally happened in 1967 when the Supreme Court overturned an 1883 decision and ruled that state laws banning interracial marriage violated the Constitution.

Most of the state laws were aimed at forbidding Whites to marry Blacks or Natives, but there was plenty of anti-Asian sentiment, too. Lots of lives were damaged by those old trauma-inducing laws. In any case, there were many instances of White men marrying Indian women, which gave rise to the derogatory phrase "squaw man." For a White woman to marry an Indian was rare.

My parents married during the Great Depression and employment was often temporary depending on the availability of jobs. The Shell Oil Refinery laid off employees, which left Father temporarily unemployed. He was able to find work at Chilocco. The school had a stone quarry, and Father was hired to cut the stone that was used to build a girls' dormitory. For this work, Father earned $80 a month but for whatever reason he only worked every other month. They had to stretch that $80 to cover two months' rent on their duplex, which was $20 a month, as well as pay for groceries, bills, and the payments on their Model A Ford coupe.

When this job ended after 15 months, Mother and Father decided to take a trip to Idaho. Mother would finally meet her husband's family.

They made the journey west in the Model A, which, my father told me, "Really got the miles from a gallon of gas, but it took quite a bit of oil. I remember we stopped in Denver and bought a five gallon can of oil and filled it before going into a service station for gas. We cooked our own meals in motels" where they stayed while traveling—when they could get a room. Often my mother was the one who would go into the motel office because sometimes, if they saw Father, they would be denied a room. Several times they camped along the roadside.

They arrived in Idaho in the fall of 1932, and Mother described her first sight of the hills and mountains of Idaho:

He was happy to see his homeland and feasted his eyes on the fall foliage along the Salmon River. I thought this was the longest road in the world since it followed the river and was wedged between the hills on both sides. People were panning for gold along this stretch of the river.

> When we got to Grangeville, Titus thought he knew the short-cut to Kamiah and took off down an old dirt road that followed the hillside and was not wide enough to pass a car when one met another vehicle. We did make it to Kamiah and found his father's house and wife and little Joanne. Jesse was on the road but came in time for supper. I admired these digni-fied people but thought them a little short on manners since they talked in a language I did not understand in my presence. Jesse wanted his children to know their native tongue so Nez Perce was spoken in the home, they used English only when they wanted me to know what was said.

They stayed at the Paul Ranch for six weeks. Father's family was reserved about his new bride, and at first didn't totally embrace her into the family. Father cut a load of wood, which he took down to his father in Kamiah. Mother met some of the neighbors whose children had gone to school with the Pauls and enjoyed hearing stories of the family. Black Raven, who had moved to Kamiah after his first wife died, still travelled around the reservation as part of his forester job and stopped by regularly to bring groceries. Mother thought a man doing the marketing strange, but, as she later told me, "It was natural for Jesse since he was the one away from home and it was convenient for him to stop at the stores and do the shopping."

On their way back to Kansas, Mother later wrote, "We stopped in Salt Lake City, Herbert Hoover drove past our car on his way to the train after making a speech at the Mormon Tabernacle that morning. He was in an open touring car and his cheeks were rosy. This was the day before the election which Franklin D. Roosevelt won the next day."

Back in Kansas, Father was hired back at the Shell Oil refinery. Their first child, Jesse LaRue, was born on July 29, 1933. Two years later came Warren Gilbert, on August 24, 1935. Jacqueline Kay was born on November 29, 1937. In between Warren and Jackie, Titus' father Black Raven died, on March 2, 1936. The Depression kept taking its toll, and once again Shell Oil laid off people.

Father had been yearning to return to Idaho, and the couple decided to head for Idaho for good. They sold part of their furniture, bought a Model A Ford for $85, and a little trailer for $15.

The ranch, with all its land and buildings, had been leased to a White man who had done little to keep up the house. When Father and Mother arrived to set up their new household, there was little furniture, no cook stove or beds, and the ranch house itself had become rundown. This was not the way Father had left it sixteen years earlier.

There were few jobs to be found, so, to make ends meet, Father drew unemployment insurance. Because there was not enough money for gas, every other week he would walk 17 miles to Nez Perce, the county seat, to sign up for work and collect unemployment. On the return 17-mile trip, he would stop and buy groceries for the family—that's how dedicated he was to providing his family with food. I don't know if he sometimes got a ride or if he had to camp somewhere along the route or if maybe there was a family he could stay with, but the 34-mile roundtrip must have taken two days to complete.

Despite the disappointment with the conditions of the ranch house and not having jobs, my parents were glad to be there. The children could roam over the ranch in safety, as long as they stayed off the cultivated fields. Father could touch the ground of his youth and listen to the birds. Mother described their first winter in Idaho: "We were so isolated at the ranch we lost a day some place and never knew where it went. We stayed at the ranch all winter with few contacts with the outside world but the children were healthy and had no colds."

They spent the summer and winter at the ranch, but the White man who had leased the place decided he didn't want Father there and asked him to leave. Even though the land belonged to our family, the lease was in the man's name, so Father honored the lease and left.

Father moved the family to his grandparents' place in Kamiah, the place where he had been born. There, the living conditions were even grimmer than at the ranch. All that was left of his grandparents' home site was a shack that needed a new roof. Under the porch lived a family of skunks. But my parents were determined: they replaced the roof, coaxed the family of skunks out from under the porch, and made the shack livable. How he did that I've always wondered. If I'd thought to ask, he probably would have answered, "Old Indian trick."

They lived there for three years, from the summer of 1939 to spring of 1942. During that time Father worked for road construction crews, helping to put in the road from Greer to Kamiah. He also spent a summer working in the lumber camps at Pierce, Idaho. Mother planted a large garden. Father supplemented the food supply by hunting wild turkeys and pheasants, which were plentiful. He also took up fishing at night. He and a friend, Eugene Wilson, would take a small boat out on the Clearwater River and, by the light of a torch, spear salmon.

After the bombing of Pearl Harbor in December 1941, Father tried to enlist, but he was told he was too old. He decided to go to Bremerton, Washington, to the Navy shipyards. He left in January 1942, and the rest of the family joined him in June, after school let out. Father started a job as a mechanic, but he soon realized he wanted to become a welder. He badgered his foreman to let him learn welding. Finally, the foreman gave in, saying, "If you can find someone to teach you, go ahead." Father said of his training:

> I kept asking my shop foreman to get me a welding toolbox. He finally got tired of me asking, and one day I came to work and he said here, take this order and go get your toolbox. I went over to the supply store and handed them the order and got the toolbox and hood and a leather apron and gloves and whatever else I needed. I came back to the shop and had to get the table ready to lay out the equipment. I had an Indian friend from Wisconsin who was a welder. He only had a half-hour lunch and I had an hour. I'd eat my lunch and then I go over and sit by him. He'd show me how to do this and I kept at it. When I left Bremerton, I was an expert welder.

Father valued learning, and he insisted on always studying something during his years as a welder in the Navy shipyards. He told many stories where he had to figure out how to weld something that no one else could.

One day, the foreman needed mine detectors welded to the bottom of a ship in dry dock. To do this properly required that my father lie flat on his back and weld carefully. To weld too fast would result in a sloppy seam, leaving the mine detector insecurely attached to the hull. While my father was lying on his back and carefully welding mine detectors, the captain of the ship happened to walk by. Seeing my father lying down on the job, he said to himself, "That Indian is loafing. I'm going to report him to the foreman." The foreman came over and said that the captain had complained about him loafing. My father simply waved the foreman in closer so he can examine his welds, which were perfect. The foreman nodded, appreciating the fine work, and said, "Forget I ever said anything."

After that, whenever there was a tough job, the foreman would send for Titus. He worked on repairing the battleship U.S.S. *Nevada,* which had survived the Pearl Harbor bombing. He welded in the submarine detectors and figured out how to weld the "Big Guns" onto the battleships.

Another time, my father was ordered to weld armor around the bridge hatch of a ship. The welders worked in pairs for this job. The world was at war and time was of the essence, but my father and his partner were proceeding slowly and carefully. On the other side of the bridge, another pair of welders were moving quickly. Again, the captain of the ship came around, and saw one fast team and one slow team. "That Indian, he is loafing again," the captain said to himself, and again spoke to the foreman. The foreman approached him, "The captain is complaining that you are loafing." My father motioned the foreman to the side that finished welding first. Father pulled on the bridge hatch handle but the hatch wouldn't open. Then he went to the other side where he had been working—and the hatch opened just fine.

When I first heard this story, I thought the moral was "haste makes waste." But as I began to look deeper, I could see, feel, and understand something about my father that I was missing in my own life: that of being true to myself. My father defied the captain's internalized stereotype of Indians being lazy and unable to do things in a timely manner. In Nimiipuu culture, you take the time to do things properly, which might take a little more time, but then they don't have to be done again.

Throughout his life, my father set himself goals. He always wanted to learn something new. At the age of 65, he started to golf; at the age of 72 he rode his first bicycle; at the age of 82 he went swimming in the Pacific Ocean; at the age of 85 he danced to rock n' roll at his granddaughter's wedding; and at the age of 87 he became serious about golf. His goal at the age of 94 was to win a gold medal in the Senior Olympics. He had already won a bronze and a silver. Although he never did win a gold medal, to us, he won the gold medal of life.

In Bremerton, the family lived in a tent house until permanent housing could be finished for all the workers in the Navy yard. Mother helped with the war effort by operating a crane, being a nurse's aide, and various other jobs. When the war ended, Father was hired at the submarine Navy yards, but he and Mother decided it was time to return to the ranch.

Father and Mother bought a used pickup truck, packed up the family, and drove back to the ranch on the Camas Prairie in June 1946. During World War II, the ranch had been in probate after the death of Black Raven. The land had been leased out, but the lease had expired and the estate settled. Father made some trades with his brothers Reuben and Richard, so he could have full ownership of the ranch. This had been a life dream and ambition of my parents, to farm and own their own land.

The ranch itself sits in the middle of the Camas Prairie at an elevation of 4,100 feet. The prairie has rich, volcanic soil ideal for growing wheat, lentils, barley, peas, canola, bluegrass seed, and many other crops. The ranch at that time had about 100 acres of tillable land, the rest being forest and pasture, for a total of about 160 acres. A creek cut across the property. The closest town was Craigmont, Idaho, about seven miles away. Father also owned another 140 acres of farmland near Ferdinand, Idaho—his mother's allotment, which he had inherited.

Father and Mother settled into bringing the ranch back to life. They put a new roof on the house and papered the rooms. By the fall of 1946, they had electricity. With an eye on becoming self-sufficient, they planted a garden, purchased a small cleat tractor and a 3-bottom plow, a team of horses, a milk cow, and some chickens. Mother said, "He worried himself to death trying to get the 114 acres plowed at the Ferdinand place and the 160 acres at the home place [the Camas Prairie ranch]. He also bought a little combine that was always breaking down, but we survived by faith and hard work."

After a cold and snowy December, I was born August 30, 1949. There is a twelve-year age difference between my older siblings and me. We all were born in a hospital, the first generation not to be born in a tepee. Father and Mother decided I needed a sibling closer to my age, so two years later Wayne Richard Paul was born, on October 21, 1951.

Discipline changed from one set of children to the next. The two oldest, Jesse and Warren, were spanked or switched, depending on the circumstances and the severity of their infractions. Jackie, on the other hand, never received a spanking in her life and was considered the family's little angel. Then, when the next set of children came along after twelve years, the roles were reversed. I received spankings from Mother, but Father never laid a hand on me. I remember only one time when he said a cross word to me. I was about four. We were at the table eating dinner when I threw a temper tantrum. He removed me from the table, took me out to the front porch, and scolded me, saying, "You are too old to be acting this way." I never did it again!

Mother was 36 when I was born, and Father 42, so they had aged and matured by the time the second set of children came along. As with most families, the youngest were accused of being spoiled. We didn't know how good we had it.

The Titus Paul family, 1953. Front row: Titus Paul with Richard on his lap and Maxine Paul holding Roberta; back row (standing, left to right) Jesse, Jackie, and Warren. *Paul Family Photo Collection.*

Mother saw to it that her children went to worship services and Sunday school at the local Presbyterian church in Craigmont. There were many social gatherings at the church, too, which Mother and Father attended. But Father was less likely to go to worship services. He continued to take walks alone in the woods on the ranch. This was his spiritual connection. I could always tell how the walk went after his return: he had a cheery tune that only he could whistle.

Father used his welding skills to build machinery needed to run the ranch. The other thing that helped him run the ranch was his problem-solving: his determination to figure out how things worked, could be fixed, or just get done. He developed a weed sprayer he could tow behind his tractor. He made trailers to carry equipment on. And when equipment broke down, he was able to fix it.

Initially farming 300 acres, Father leased tribal land to increase the size of the operation to about 2,000 acres. He was one of the first farmers on the Camas Prairie to try to raise green peas. He was trying to improve the soil with peas, which fix the essential nutrient nitrogen that is depleted after so many years of tilling the soil to grow wheat. He used "green manure" by growing peas and clover so he didn't need to buy fertilizers and avoided the use of chemicals. By raising a crop of peas, which he'd plow under and plant a second crop, this time clover, which also got plowed in, the quality of the soil improved. This method is still used today by farmers.

Father was the first in the area to get a wheat crop of 100 bushels per acre. The highest yield he achieved was 116 bushels, a yield that, for our part of Idaho, is still considered wonderful. And this was without chemical fertilizers. He was also one of the first farmers to plant lentils, which are also good for the soil. For much of the 20th century, a few counties in northern Idaho and eastern Washington produced most of the lentils grown in the United States My mother helped form the Pea and Lentil Association in Lewis County, Idaho, which promotes the raising and use of lentils, which led our family to learn many ways to prepare lentils.

Father was also a member of the Lewiston Grain Growers, serving on the board of directors for several years during the 1960s. Our parents were also active members of the Grange, which provided socialization and fun for all the family.

Father's success using natural fertilizer to increase grain production and his early adoption of lentils contributed to his being inducted in 1999 into the Chilocco Indian Agricultural School Hall of Fame, his alma mater. At the ceremony there were 400 people in the audience, and it was the first time any of us—my brother Jessie, sister Jackie, and I, along with four grandchildren and our mother—had seen him talk to a large crowd. He gave a moving speech, and my heart swelled with pride at watching this dignified 92-year-old man causing us all to swipe the corners of our eyes.

Titus Paul displays his medal on the occasion of his induction into the Chilocco Indian Agricultural School Hall of Fame, June 12, 1999. *Paul Family Photo Collection.*

The Paul Family at the awards banquet for Titus Paul's Hall of Fame induction, June 12, 1999, in Oklahoma City, Oklahoma. Pictured are (seated) Maxine and Titus Paul; (standing, left to right) J. R. Inglis, Kim Enz, Jesse Paul, Roberta Paul, Mike Foiles, and Jackie Paul Inglis. *Paul Family Photo Collection.*

Titus and Maxine on their 70th wedding anniversary, July 2, 2001. *Paul Family Photo Collection.*

He had this to say, "I have always done the best that I could; if I didn't understand it, I would study it and figure it out. I learned a great deal from the teachers of Chilocco, and to them I give respect." There was much more that he spoke that day, but it is those words that have stuck with me. I have heard those words spoken before about my father from friends and family, and I will continue to speak those words in my story as part of my healing journey.

Life at the ranch for Mother was at times difficult: she felt so isolated. In reading her stories, I often see this word "isolated." I think because we were a biracial family we didn't fit in to the local community. My White mother did not always feel accepted by the locals: she was too White for the Nez Perce community, and for the White community, well, she'd married an Indian. So, we became a family onto ourselves.

Winters in that part of Idaho are harsh. There were times when school would not be held for a couple of weeks because of so much snow. The winters the family did stay at the ranch, Father had to plow a path over the farmland to the closest neighbor, where the school bus was able to arrive. This was about two miles from the ranch house. We were indeed isolated. I think that's why she convinced Father to move to Craigmont for the winter a few times before I even entered school.

One bone of contention existed between our parents (one that I am aware of, at least). During the spring, summer, and fall, the whole family helped plow the fields, plant, and then harvest the crops. During the winter months Father had extra time on his hands. He liked playing cards, which led him to participate in card games at the local tavern in Craigmont. He would stay late, upsetting Mother. She was left at the ranch with no car—what would she do in the case of an emergency? Furthermore, Father's card playing on a few occasions did cause some loss of cash flow—often enough to cause friction.

Mother wanted to move to Craigmont, and eventually she convinced Father that they needed to provide more social activities for us children. My three older siblings were grown, gone, and living their own lives. I had lived on the ranch for ten years, free to roam and explore. Richard and I were not in favor of the move—we'd be losing our playground. Now we would be confined to a house on a small lot with only one tree. We couldn't see the advantages Mother was talking about.

But the ranch house was sixty years old and showing its age. Our old home, creaky, drafty, and cold in the winter, couldn't compare with homes built in the late 1950s. Finally, Father agreed with Mother and, in the spring of 1959, the move was made.

For a couple summers, we would move back out to the ranch for harvest. We didn't live in the ranch house after 1961. We continued to farm the land and care for the ranch—but because no one was living there, people began to steal things. Father had to build a shop in town to store his farming equipment and tools. The ranch house itself began to deteriorate.

While Father was alive, he would never allow us to talk about tearing down the house. Over the years, family members would take things from the ranch house to use in their own homes as memories of the ranch. But the house continued to deteriorate; weather was not kind to the place. The roof was falling in, and the porch was caving in, too. About a year after Father passed away, we as a family agreed it was time to tear down the old ranch house. In the fall of 2005, we finished taking what we wanted: doorknobs, windowsills, doors, siding, porch flooring, and even some of the boards used as interior walls. The rest of the usable lumber was given to someone who did the work of taking it down.

My brother Warren then pushed the remaining lumber into a pile along with the other outbuildings to be burned. It was hard to watch everything go up in flames. Where once our house stood tall and majestic, there was now just a smoking pile. Even the bull pine tree that stood behind the pantry outbuilding had died in the spring of 2005. I always felt this tree was watching over us, but now it was being burnt with the house. I called that tree Grandfather Pine; it was so large and strong, I am sure it was well over 500 years old. It survived a fire that had burned part of its trunk, creating a hiding place for us children. I so miss that tree.

When I was there at the ranch, taking what I wanted from the house, I walked to the back forty where I could sit and look back at the ranch house. I did this a couple of times. The first time was in the early stages of the house being taken apart, when you could see through the upper level of the house, and it looked as if you could see into the house's story, its history laid bare. This house witnessed the married life of Jesse Black Raven and Lydia Conditt Paul; they gave birth to 11 children, only three of whom survived to adulthood. This house witnessed the deaths of eight children and my grandmother Lydia.

As the old, dry wood went up in flames, I could feel the heat as well as the spirit of the house and its memories going up in flames and smoke. The old ranch house and Grandfather Pine were gone in a matter of minutes. It was sad, but, at the same time, the fire released old memories, and a sense of peace settled over the land.

The Paul Ranch house in 1998. *Paul Family Photo Collection.*

Grandfather Ponderosa Pine Tree, at the Paul Ranch, circa 1985. *Paul Family Photo Collection.*

Grandfather Ponderosa Pine Tree had died just as we were preparing to burn the ranch house. *Paul Family Photo Collection.*

The Paul Ranch house in Craigmont, Idaho, just prior to being burned down, October, 2005. *Paul Family Photo Collection.*

The Paul Family's ranch house burning, October 2005. *Paul Family Photo Collection.*

With the death of Titus Paul, a generation had come to an end. Now, current and future generations continue to explore the past as we walk into the future. This land will always be here. With Father's passing and the end of the old house, a time has come to sing a new song, to move forward and weave together the warp and weft of our family's history.

CHAPTER 19

Am I Indian or Am I White?

When I was going through my divorce, I wrestled with recovering my Native identity. But I also struggled with my Euro-American identity. One of my questions was, am I Indian, or am I White? I am both, of course, but more importantly, I am a human being.

My mother was White and she had been married to my Indian father for a very long time. She chose to marry him despite what society and her family thought. How is it that their biracial marriage worked, but mine did not? My father and mother stayed together as a biracial couple through the Depression, World War II, and into the post-war civil rights era—for 71 years! Their marriage was not perfect, but their "Come hell or high water" attitude kept them working things out over many decades. They were not perfect, but they respected each other—and they didn't have affairs!

As I worked my way through divorce, I was supported by both of my parents. I returned home more often and traveled with them to the many battleground sites as well as to family functions. As we drove, my father would tell stories about how he grew up, how he learned manners, how he learned respect for elders and for himself. My mother, too, was respectful. Their marriage, I noted, was one of respect for each other. Mother did not become the "Indian wife" nor did Father not become the "White husband": they each held on to and shared their cultural values. One cultural difference that did sometimes cause arguments was their sense of time. Mother wanted things done "on time" and Father did things "in time." But they managed this difference through mutual respect.

I needed to find out more about Mother's side of the family to understand both her and myself. My mother's mother had married five times. During our many drives, I discovered Mother came from a long line of strong women, many of whom had survived difficult times.

Susan Cody was one such ancestor, a great-great-grandmother who came to the United States in 1837 from County Kilkenny, Ireland. Susan arrived in the United States as a child of three with her widowed mother, Ann Cody. There's some mystery here: why would widow Ann come to the

United States at all? This was before the potato famine of 1847, that resulted from the Irish being forced to export all the food they grew. The English had, after all, been perpetuating a slow-motion genocide against the Irish for centuries, so she might have been trying to escape someone or some condition in Ireland. But how did a widow with a small child have adequate funds to purchase passage from Ireland to the United States? She may have been following a dream based on what she heard about the United States, but that doesn't explain how she realized the dream. Or perhaps she was a mail-order bride? In any case, we simply don't know her full story.

Family records suggest that Ann and Susan disembarked in New Orleans and settled in Baton Rouge, Louisiana. Ann soon met a Mr. Moran and they married. The marriage produced several infants who did not survive—and then the husband died. Ann was a widow a second time and, having to provide for her daughter and herself, was looking for opportunities to support herself and her child. This was around 1849; the California gold rush was in full swing. Groups of friends would often pool their resources and travel together to seek their fortunes in gold.

Ann sought passage on a wagon train for Susan and herself, which was unusual for two unaccompanied women to do. At first, they had a team of mules to pull their wagon, but the mules weren't strong enough and were traded for a team of oxen. In California, they panned for gold and made enough money to set up a boarding house in the San Francisco area. But Ann soon died, leaving 16-year-old Susan an orphan.[1] Family letters suggest she didn't want to remain alone in San Francisco and thought about returning east to enter a convent.

With money saved from the boarding house business, Susan booked passage to New Orleans. Before leaving she purchased a beautiful and expensive $100 embroidered silk scarf, a carved rosewood box inlaid with mother of pearl, and a steamer trunk to hold her clothing and belongings. But when the ship arrived at the Isthmus of Panama, she was told that she could only take what she could carry on a donkey. She tied what she could of her belongings into the silk scarf, hiding the gold vials in her clothing, and leaving the carved box and steamer trunk on the beach.

After reaching New Orleans, she traveled by riverboat up the Mississippi River. Onboard, she met a Mrs. Bell and her daughter. Mrs. Bell's husband was president of the Pleasant Retreat Seminary for young women. Susan changed her mind about entering a convent and went to the seminary instead. While in seminary school, she met two sisters, Victoria and Laura Barnett of Lexington, Missouri, who invited her home for Christmas. There she met her future husband, Edwin Ryland Barnett. They married August 30, 1855, in Booneville, Missouri. Susan was about 20 while Edwin was 30 years old. Together they had nine children, the forebearers of my mother. Susan settled into being a farmer's wife and raising her children. She died at the age of 71 and is buried in the Springfield Cemetery, Cowley County, Kansas.

Both sides of my family, White and Indian, crossed the Isthmus of Panama heading for the East Coast. In those days, it was one of the few ways to go from the West Coast to the East. I find it amazing that both families traveled similar routes.

In 2014, my sister Jackie and I decided it was time to retrace the footsteps of both sides of our family. We wanted to walk the same path as they did as much as possible, and we decided to book a Panama bus tour with a travel group. The tour encouraged stops to get out and explore. While our ancestors had travelled via steamship, we flew to Panama. Arriving in early January 2015, Jackie and I were excited to see the land our forebearers had crossed.

Great-great-grandmother Susan Cody had been the first to cross. We often wondered why she took this way back to the East Coast, and not a train. The reason, it turns out, was simply that transcontinental train service was still ten years in the future. Additionally, in the 1850s, there were no wagon trains returning east from the gold fields of California.

At a museum of Panama history, we learned the steamship companies advertised that it was faster to travel by ship to Panama and cross the Isthmus of Panama rather than travel around Cape Horn through the cold and stormy Southern Ocean. Ads to that effect had been plastered all over San Francisco, appealing to the gold miners who, having either made their fortunes or given up, wanted to return to the eastern United States. Steamship companies also promised that travel across the Isthmus of Panama was safe, as voyagers were accompanied by guards.

That didn't mean the trip across was easy, though. We knew Susan Cody had to leave her trunk and most of her belongings on the west coast of Panama and was only able to take what she could bundle into her silk scarf. She rode a donkey to the Rio Chagres, with vials of gold dust and a few nuggets hidden on her person. Travelers then had to travel on the river in a dug-out canoe, before disembarking in the rain forest and proceeding on foot to the Atlantic Ocean. From the Pacific side to the Atlantic side of the Isthmus is about 60 miles. All along the way the travelers would have heard and seen many species of monkeys, birds, snakes, crocodiles, and other wildlife.

We cruised up the Rio Chagres in a small motorboat from which we gaped at the monkeys and birds, hearing and seeing many of the same things as our ancestors before us. While we had the luxury of air-conditioned buses and hotels most of the time, the heaviness of 100 percent humidity got to us. I tired easily and was sweating all the time, so much so I could—weird as it sounds—taste the metal fillings in my mouth. I wondered what Susan would have worn—a dress, or maybe pants and shirt, or perhaps she donned multiple layers of clothing to save what she could despite the heat.

We visited Old Panama City, which had been destroyed by the privateer Henry Morgan in the late 17th century and is now a World Heritage site. Viejo Panama had been established in 1519, making it one of the oldest European enclaves in the Americas. Now the old town is part of modern Panama City, with its buildings and brick streets slowly being refurbished. We were able to walk on the same streets in 2015 as Susan Cody had in 1852 and our great-great-grandfather Ut-sin-malikan 16 years later.

We visited Iglesia de San Jose, a church built in 1675 and known for its ornate floor-to-ceiling gold altar. Had Susan or Ut-Sin-malikan seen this church? As we walked the narrow brick streets, the beauty of the colorful buildings, with their yellows and pinks popping out of stark white walls, must have impressed them as it did Jackie and me.

Another part of our tour took us to the rain forest, where we met some of the Indigenous people of the region. A replica village gave insight into how they had lived for hundreds of years. When Susan Cody was guided through the jungle, the path had been narrow and obscured by thick layers of trees and plants. The humidity must have left them exhausted by the time the party reached the Atlantic Ocean.

Ut-sin-malikan's journey across the Isthmus of Panama in 1868 was markedly different. By then, a railroad spanned the Isthmus. A large build-ing that took up a whole block, the old railroad station was still in Panama

City when my sister and I visited, but now it housed a farmers' market on the weekends and was used as an event venue at other times.

Ut-sin-malikan would have seen large buildings in San Francisco, but the train station in Panama City would have been impressive. This part of the journey would have been his first train ride. The train followed the course of the Rio Chagres as well as going through jungle. A new adventure for a 75-year-old man who had already had lots of adventures and hardships. Translator Robert Newell noted in his journal that both Ut-sin-malikan and Lawyer became ill while in Panama. It was only later determined that they had contracted typhoid fever, either from mosquito bites or bad drinking water. Lawyer did recover. Ut-sin-malikan died in Washington, DC, perhaps of typhus, though it does appear he was murdered.

Eventually, I married again, but the time between marriages was priceless, as I was able to spend a lot of time with my parents, something that would not have happened if I had stayed in the first marriage. Mother helped me to move forward and to not stay stuck and feeling sorry for myself. She traveled to the battle sites with Father and me, and other family members came when they could. When Mother passed away in October 2002, I witnessed the deep grief of my father for the loss of his wife.

The healing journeys with my family continued, but there was one who was not able to heal all his wounds: my younger brother Richard. He started drinking when he was young and became addicted. Even though I shared with him some of the process of healing, he chose not to hear or accept help. When he went into an alcoholic coma, the whole family hurt. Lying in intensive care, he would come in and out of the coma, and I could see some resemblance to the little brother whom I had grown up with.

I asked his doctor how Richard was, and he said my brother was in bad shape. The doctor never made eye contact when talking with me. To me, it seemed this White doctor was just treating another alcoholic Indian. We set up a family meeting to discuss Richard's future care with this doctor. When 25 family members showed up, the doctor's jaw dropped—and his attitude towards Richard seemed to change for the better.

At one point, I just knew I had to perform a ceremony for Richard. I know I should have, but I didn't even ask the ICU people if this would be

OK. I knew not to try smudging, but I did prepare a medicine bundle and placed it on his bedside table. The nurses, at first, walked around it, as if they were afraid of it. Finally, a nurse's aide asked what to do if they had to move him. I told her, "Please take it with him, and handle it with care and respect."

He died in September 2000. The family was at his bedside when he crossed over; I sang a song to help him go and said prayers to help heal us all.

Father continued to live with assistance at home. When his health began to fail again, the family all gathered to be near him and to thank him for all he had done for us. Our father crossed over in October 2004, on the anniversary of Chief Joseph's surrender at Bear Paw.

Another wound that had been difficult to salve is the grief of my grandmother Tawlikitsanmay,' Woman of the Forest, Lydia Conditt Paul. As my family and I traced the steps of our ancestors, I have heard her voice calling to me, but I did not know how to heal the hurt of the loss of her five children over her lifetime. This wound cannot be healed by traveling the Nez Perce Trail. In writing and researching the family story, I wanted to stop and cry, but then I would push the feelings back. One can only put off fighting the feelings of such a horrific loss of children. I kept saying to myself, it didn't happen to me, and saying to Grandmother, I will honor your children and not forget them. However, there came a day that I broke down and wept and cried uncontrollably for a long time, I had the deep cry. I felt the pain of my grandmother's loss of children. I somewhat understand their loss, but the loss is also my loss and our present family's loss. We lost having aunts and uncles who would have married and had children. We lost grandparents too early, never to have learned from their wisdom.

The sadness I have felt since I was a child around Thanksgiving and Christmas is Woman of the Forest asking us to not forget her children at the time of year when the three older ones died. Great-grandmother Um-al-wat, Phoebe Lowry, calls to me as well. "Help with healing the loss of five children and a husband because of genocide." I needed help to heal these very deep wounds—but how?

In March 2004, I attended the "Healing Our Wounded Spirits" conference on the Umatilla Reservation near Pendleton, Oregon. It was there I learned about the idea of a "soul wound," a wound that afflicts all Native people. I wanted to find out how to heal the "soul wound" of the Paul family. The next year, the Wounded Spirits conference was held in Klamath Falls, Oregon. My father had died during the intervening year, and I was feeling the sadness of being without parents.

Um-al-wat and Tawlikitsanmay' were nudging me to go to Klamath Falls and to participate this time in the Wiping of the Tears ceremony. I kept hearing the poem my grandmothers inspired me to write, "Sounds of Silence," and the line, "It is time to hear and heal." So off to Klamath Falls I went.

I joined the circle for the Wiping of the Tears ceremony. The ceremony involves participants telling and identifying their wounds. I shared the story of Grandfather Black Raven and his mother Um-al-wat. I shared the loss of Black Raven's five siblings and his father, Seven Days Whipping. I said that Black Raven and Um-al-wat were the only family members who survived the Nez Perce War. Then I told how Black Raven and his wife Tawlikitsanmay' lost five of their nine children—all within a single year. Black Raven then lost his wife. In the circle, all the witness-participants heard these stories and could pray with those who had shared their stories. Spiritual leaders from the Native community sang healing songs. It did not matter whether we practiced Christianity, or Wasat, or Seven Drum Religion. A weight was being lifted.

As part of the process of healing, I began telling these family stories to others. I have been honored to share my research and stories at an international conference that celebrated South African Archbishop Desmond Tutu on his 75th birthday and for his role in forming the Truth and Reconciliation Commission, the program that helped start South Africans on a path that might heal them of the horrors of the apartheid regime. Called "Memory, Narrative, and Forgiveness: Reflecting on 10 Years of South Africa's Truth and Reconciliation Commission," the conference had two major aims, according to the conference report. One was "to assemble an interdisciplinary group of scholars from over 40 countries to reflect upon the achievements of the Truth and Reconciliation Commission," while the second was to "recommit the nation to a psychotherapeutic process of reconciliation, with Archbishop Desmond Tutu as an exemplar, mentor, and guide."[2]

The conference was in Cape Town, South Africa, and at the gathering I had the honor of meeting Archbishop Tutu. In full regalia, I presented him with gifts that I had brought to thank him for being a leader in forgiveness and reconciliation. These included a pair of medallions I had made for the bishop and his wife; a cloth bag with a Nimiipuu design; sweet grass and sage; and a letter of introduction from my people and signed by the tribal chair, inviting them to come to the Pacific Northwest. I also gave bags with sweet grass and sage to members of a group called the Mamas. Among other questions, the Mamas wanted to find out what had happened to their sons who went missing during apartheid. One Mama misplaced the bag I gave her and was distraught, and when it turned up, she was overjoyed.

I had already had a dream I would meet Bishop Tutu. When I was in South Africa, I met one of the bishop's PR people, who arranged for me to meet him personally. I was there with my sister and niece. I had no idea he would be surrounded by a large entourage when we met: there were body-guards, his assistants, and a gaggle of media. As I was introducing myself, a TV camera moved right up into my face. I started stuttering—Ah, ah! —and my sister had to step in to say how honored we were to meet him. Every time I think of that experience, I still glow: Bishop Tutu was a role model and has inspired me and many others.

Archbishop Desmond Tutu meeting with my sister Jackie Paul Inglis and me in our regalia during the conference entitled "Reflecting on the 10 Year Anniversary of the Truth and Reconciliation Commission" in South Africa and celebrating Archbishop Tutu's 75th birthday at the University of Cape Town in South Africa November 2006. *Paul Family Photo Collection.*

Archbishop Desmond Tutu meeting with Jackie Inglis and me at the Truth and Reconciliation conference at the University of Cape Town. Jackie is presenting a beaded medallion made by Raynel Olney Begay (Yakama) to Archbishop Tutu. *Paul Family Photo Collection.*

The conference presenters were from many countries around the world. They came to share stories about using the truth and reconciliation model in their countries. People from countries who have suffered from genocide and violent conflict shared a great deal of research which offering many insights.

As I listened to these presenters, they affirmed for me that we begin to heal as we share our stories. It's more complicated than it sounds, but listening to the stories of those damaged by violence—whether from war or systemic racism or domestic violence—opens a path which, when we travel together, we all begin to heal. It's as my father said all those times for all those years: You must learn to listen so you can listen to learn.

CHAPTER 20

Signs from Black Eagle

One day in Oregon, while attending a conference on the Warm Springs reservation, I was sitting outside next to the pool, enjoying the sunshine. I experienced a daytime vision: a black eagle was pointing at me, which I felt was a warning of the impending death of a loved one. A black eagle in the Pacific Northwest is a young bald eagle that hasn't yet developed its white feathers. The eagle hovered over me as if protecting me. Soon after this vision, I visited the Warm Springs Museum. There I found a print that looked exactly like the vision I'd just had. I bought the print and had it framed. On the drive home, again I passed a black eagle sitting on the side of the road. When back home, I hung the print on the wall in my bedroom.

The night my brother Richard died, my brother Jesse, sister Jackie, and I were with him. We sang songs and prayed. After he had taken his last breath, I asked the staff to detach him from all the life-support machines and tubes. I could then pray for him to be taken by the Great Spirit. When we went to tell Mother and Father, I once again felt the black eagle hovering over our family. I knew then our brother was safe and would not be taken by the bad alcoholic spirits, and he had safely crossed over into the spirit world.

When death is near one of my immediate family, I frequently have the dream of the black eagle hovering over us, protecting and guiding us. And then, too, we will know to sing and pray to the creator to welcome our relative into the spirit world. I have had other powerful dreams when people cross over. When my nephew Willie died, I dreamed many birds were singing, welcoming him into the spirit world. At Richard's graveside service, a family friend sang "On Eagle's Wings" as an eagle circled overheard. When we buried my father, we all stood together praying and, again, an eagle soared over our heads.

The black eagle print hanging squarely on my bedroom wall became crooked one day, apparently without having been touched. At first, I thought it was Richard asking about his family. I said, *They are doing well; you would be proud of them.* I straightened the print so it hung squarely again. But the next day the print was again askew. *Is that you Richard? Or you brother Jesse?* Who else might be asking for attention? I straightened the print once again. But the next day, the print was crooked a third time. I was a little irritated. *What do you want? Is that you, Great-grandfather Seven Days Whipping?* I'd felt him nudging me when I visited Fort Buford in 2008 and then again when, in 2021, I read an article about a Nimiipuu warrior dying before reaching Fort Buford. I felt a sense of affirmation wash over me, and a mystery revealed: it *is* Seven Days Whipping, about whom we know so little. I feel in my gut he is buried near the site of the old fort. One of our family's next healing journeys will be to commemorate his death at Fort Buford, along with the three other Nez Perce who are mentioned in the article I read as being buried there as well.

Drawing of a Young Bald Eagle by the author.

In July 2017 I took my family to the Wallowas for the beginning of the Appaloosa Nez Perce Trail Ride and the annual Tamkalits Pow Wow. Tamkalits means "from where you can see the mountains" and is located in the town of Wallowa. The trail ride retraces the 1,170-mile path of the Nimiipuu retreat during the War of 1877. Each year, riders cover a section of about 100 miles. The Trail starts in the Wallowas, the homelands of our ancestors, the Chief Joseph Band.

My children had never been to the beautiful Wallowas and I wanted them to experience the birthplace of their Nez Perce family, the land where great-grandfather Seven Days Whipping and his son Black Raven were born.

There were several places in the Wallowas where the Nimiipuu camped during the summer, including one called the Place of the Peeled Bark or Indian Village Grove. This site has many tall Ponderosa pine trees and a meadow with a creek running through it. I had visited this place a couple of years earlier with visiting tribal elders descended from Joseph's band, who now live on the Colville Reservation in northeastern Washington. On that trip, I had felt the presence of ancestors, as if they were touching me. I knew in my heart I needed to bring my sister and as many of our children and grandchildren as we could wrangle. I also wanted my family to participate in the Tamkalits Pow Wow.

With all that in mind, I made all the women cotton wing dresses with matching shawls and new high-top moccasins. For the men, I made ribbon shirts. I reserved a duplex cabin for our families to stay together on Wallowa Lake. After we first explored the town of Joseph and surrounding area, I took them to the Place of the Peeled Bark. I knew this was where my ancestors' spirits were waiting to be introduced to their descendants.

I cried happy tears when my family gathered at this ancient home of our ancestors. They wandered through the grove of tall Ponderosa pines, looking for the trees with peeled bark. We then gathered to sing a song. Through tears, I introduced each family member to their ancestors as the wind blew through the trees, as if our ancestors were ready to hear the names of their descendants. My heart filled with gratitude to be in the place where Grandfather Black Raven and his siblings had played as a child. That precious time before the War began must have been happy for Great-grandfather Seven Days Whipping and his family. How hard it must have been to leave this beautiful place, never to see it again!

The Place of the Peeled Bark is now part of the Wallowa National Forest. No camping is allowed, but you can visit the site and see the trees from which bark had been peeled away. The Nimiipuu peeled back the bark to get the underpart of the bark to eat. This was done in a manner to not destroy the tree, but also to provide needed food for the people in lean times.

An official sign at the Place gives some information about why the Nimiipuu peeled these trees:

> While little evidence of the campsite remains, the Nez Perce people did leave a record of their stay. In the early spring, the Nez Perce peeled the outer bark… with a scraper. This created the large oval scars on the trees which you see along the trail. Archeologists speculate that the inner bark was used as a supplemental food. Other possible uses may have been fiber baskets, clothing, or medicine…
>
> [P]eeled trees are a living record of the Nez Perce's interaction with the environment. Due to its cultural significance, the Indian Village Grove had been placed on the National Register of Historic Places.

My sister and I discussed how much the Paul Ranch looked like this Place of Peeled Bark. The Paul Ranch had tall Ponderosa pines, a meadow, and a creek running through the property. Now we understood why Grandfather Black Raven chose the Ranch allotment on the Camas Prairie. We could easily imagine a young Black Raven running through the meadows with his friends.

With happy hearts, we returned to our cabin to get ready for the grand entry of the Tamkalits Pow Wow. We had never danced as a family group in the grand entry. We did so now with pride and happy tears.

A peeled bark pine tree in Indian Village Grove near Joseph, Oregon, in 2016. *Paul Family Photo Collection.*

The Paul family in regalia at Tamkalits Friendship Pow Wow, July 2018, in Wallowa, Oregon. Pictured in the front row, from left to right, are Bella Foiles, Amanda Enz, and Elizabeth Enz; in the back row, left to right, are Kim Enz, Roberta Paul, Mike Foiles, Vonda Schuld, J.R. Inglis, Jackie Inglis, and Suzanne Gebhards. I made all the wing dresses for the women and ribon shirts for the ment. I also made several high-top moccasins for the girls. *Paul Family Photo Collection.*

It is by the four winds that the Great Spirit moves. To get my attention, to get me to take notice of something in my life, the Creator often must knock the wind right out of me. On one particular day, the Four Winds were moving, all right: it was raining, there was lightning and thunder, there was hail mixed with sunshine, and the winds came from every direction at once: north, east, south, and west.

It was a day in September 1994. The place was Wellpinit, Washington, on the Spokane Indian Reservation, at their Long House, where they hold ceremonies, honor elders, and receive guests. The occasion for the gathering was an agreement between Washington Water Power and the Spokane

Tribe. The Little Falls Dam, which is located on the Spokane Indian Reservation, is owned and operated by Washington Water Power (WWP; it is now called Avista). When the dam was built decades ago, there had been no agreement, just a seizure by the state. But now a wrong had been made right and a wound between the Spokanes and Washington Water Power had begun to heal. My boarder and friend Charlene, a Spokane tribal member, was instrumental in getting the two sides to come to an agreement.

I had gone to Wellpinit to witness this event and the beginnings of healing. In addition to knowing Charlene, one of the key negotiators of the agreement, I had been working off and on at Wellpinit with Spokane youth and knew a few tribal members. It did my heart good to see, witness, feel the power of this ceremony. I had enjoyed the ceremony and was just about to leave when a man came up to me. As I was walking out, he walked beside me.

"You're a pretty lady," he said with a tip of his cowboy hat.

"Thank you," I reply.

"Might you be a single lady?" he asked.

At that, I smiled. "Yes, I am."

"Would I be out of line to ask how old you might be?"

"How old do you need me to be?" I replied, a little sarcastically.

"I'm getting off on the wrong foot here."

I took pity on him. "I have a 24-year-old daughter and a 17-year-old son, and I just turned 45."

To which this stranger said, "You're old enough that we might just be able to get along. But you're kidding, you don't look that old. How is it that you're able to look so young?" Hardly a silver-tongued devil! But he later said he felt like he'd been hit by a bolt of lightning and that his ears were ringing from a clap of thunder. "When the smoke cleared," he'd say years later, "there we stood, a bit dazed, but both aware that a tremendous power was at work in our lives."

"It's in my genes," I say, laying on the snark. "My parents don't look their age, but beauty is only skin deep."

"I do know that," he said. "Do you think you'd consider going out with me?"

"Maybe, but I'd need to talk with you to get to know you better."

"Well yes, would you have time right now to talk a little bit?"

"Yes," I replied, though I suddenly felt like I was in a daze.

"My name is Philip Wise," he said, and asked me to come over to his pickup. "I'll show you why it is that I'm here for the signing." He opened the driver's side door, leaned over his seat, and retrieved a piece of paper. He handed me the sheet, saying, "This is why I'm here today."

When WWP had announced the agreement, they asked people with interesting stories to submit them. Phil had sent a story about his father, who owned some Spokane tribal land; his father had homesteaded on the land years before. Phil's father had traded a corner of his land to a Spokane named Richard Peone. Peone had given him a Winchester rifle, a hundred dollars, and a cow in exchange. Sensing that this man might be sensitive to Native Americans, I replied, "Very interesting." Phil leaned back into his truck and pulled out a rifle. I stepped back—I don't like guns one bit.

"Is this the rifle in the story?" I looked with interest, not really sure what I was looking at.

"It is," he replied. "I was a year old when my dad made that trade. This rifle has been in my family for 53 years now."

Later Phil would tell me that, indeed, he had always had a respect for and liking of Native ways and history. He'd read about us a lot and had even hiked many of the old trails and visited battle sites.

Phil started asking me direct questions: "Do you drink?" "No." "Do you smoke?" "No." Is this guy vetting me, I wondered.

I noticed the parking lot was nearly empty and I had to go to Cheney, a few miles to the south, to pick up a paycheck. I suggested we meet later for coffee and pie. I'm not sure where this came from, but I was attracted to Phil from the moment I met him.

Phil countered, "How about dinner. You set the time."

We decided to meet at 7 p.m. at my place. As I said goodbye and walked to my car, I realized I had just made a date. I giggled, and said, "A date!" and pinched myself. Now what have I done? I just made a date with a man I do not know who has a gun. The next thought that came to mind was, "What am I going to wear?"

The sun broke through and everything looked beautiful. The day had begun so cold and rainy, and I almost didn't leave the house. But something inside of me pushed and said go, so I obeyed and went.

I picked up my check in Cheney and started back to Spokane. I decided I needed something to wear, so I stopped at Macy's downtown to try on some clothes. Nothing seemed right, though, and I realized how ridiculous this was. I had a closet full of clothes this man had never seen me in. Besides, I couldn't afford new clothes: I was a poor just-graduated master's student with no full-time job yet.

Just as I was crossing the Monroe Street bridge, the rain poured down, until there was a river streaming down the road. What's going on, I thought, this crazy weather: first, cold rain and wind, then sunshine, and now more rain.

At home, I realized I had butterflies in my stomach because I was going on a date. I told my roommate Charlene that I had met a man who worked for Washington Water Power. I told her a little about him; she had already met him during the process of negotiations between the tribe and the company.

"He seems like a nice man," Charlene said, which made me breathe a little sigh of relief.

I tidied up the house and wondered if this man will be early or late. I kept repeating to myself, "I'm going on a date, what have I done?" In the shower, I told myself, "You're okay, just be yourself. Never mind that you haven't been on a date in four years. That's been your choice." I liked how I looked in a dress, so I slipped into a black knit turtleneck dress with long sleeves. With it I wore my turquoise jewelry and belt, with my black hat and beaded head band.

I told my son Mike that I was going out—with a man. About then, the doorbell rang. I greeted Phil and introduced him to Charlene and Mike. Mike sat in a chair, arms crossed over his chest, and gave Phil a once-over before nodding and saying hello.

As if our roles had suddenly been reversed, on my way out the door Mike instructed me to not be late getting home. Phil smiled at that and gave Mike a nod of acknowledgement.

Phil said he wanted to take me some place special. His friend owned a restaurant in Spirit Lake, about 50 miles from Spokane and just over the state line in Idaho. I felt touched he wanted to take me to a special place and to meet his friend. Tears came to my eyes. "That would be lovely," I said.

Phil drove the back roads to Spirit Lake, and we talked the whole way. Rain and hail poured down. At the Spirit Lake Lodge, owners Rod and Nancy Erickson were just about to close but were glad to accommodate us. Rod played guitar and sang. Still full of the huge salmon meal the Spokanes had served at Wellpinit, we both ordered chef salads from Nancy.

Rod had a great voice and coaxed Phil into playing a number with him. For some reason, I was surprised he could play the guitar. It wasn't the best guitar picking, but he played for me. We ate and listened to Rod play and sing. He then came over to our table and talked with us for a while.

We finally left the Lodge. It wasn't that late, and I hoped Phil would suggest another place to go. As we were driving back toward Spokane, he asked if I would like to go country dancing. "Oh! I love to dance," I told him.

Phil drove to a place called the Slab Inn. In those days, you could still smoke in bars. We went as far back in the place as we could, so we could still hear each other and be out of the smoke as much as possible. I felt dazed, my stomach full of butterflies, salad, and salmon.

Phil asked me to dance. He took me in his arms and we twirled around. It didn't take long for me to get into rhythm with him. I felt like I was in a whirlwind.

Finally, midnight rolled around, and Phil asked if he should be getting me home.

"Yes," I sighed, "we should be starting back." In his pickup, I had a strong urge to kiss him, so I did: I leaned over and gave him a kiss. But then suddenly I had to stop and jerk open the door, just in time to throw up the contents of my stomach.

"Do you always get this emotional?" Phil asked.

I shook my head. *No!* "No, there has been the 24-hour flu going around at the daycare where I have been working this past week. I'm pretty sure that is what I have." Which (partly!) explained the butterflies in my stomach all day.

"Can I take you to the hospital?"

"No, no, just home."

He pulled out of the parking lot but didn't get far before I had to ask him to stop so I can throw up again. This happened one more time before we got to my house. Phil asked if there was anything he could get me, and I said, "Yes, could you go to the store and get me 7-Up and soda crackers?" This was at two in the morning. While he was gone, I laid on the couch, and when he returned, he asked again if there was anything he could do for me.

"No, I just need to rest. I hope you don't get this."

Phil left then, and I crawled into bed.

When I finally awoke the next morning, I wondered if I would ever hear from Phil after all the commotion. What a way to make a first impression! But I didn't have to wonder long, as Phil called to ask how I was doing. "Better," I said, "but now I'm really hungry." He asked me to call him later in the day. I slept off and on most of the day and did finally eat some food.

That evening, I called Phil to thank him for getting me home safely and for going to the store for me in the wee hours. Phil invited me to come to his ranch the next day; although he worked at Washington Water Power, he did so to support his ranching habit. Much to my surprise, I said "Yes!" It was uncharacteristic of me to agree so spontaneously to visit a strange man at his home.

Four months later, Phil proposed to me on bended knee, wearing his Stetson cowboy hat. "Yes," I said. We were married July 1, 1995, beneath a circle of tall Ponderosa pines, with loving family and friends as witnesses, in a traditional Native/Christian marriage. I was in Native dress and Phil was in his Western suit.

Phil Wise and I at our wedding, July 1, 1995. We married outside at the Whitworth Presbyterian Church, under ponderosa pine trees, with lots of family and friends attending.

I made and beaded my dress and made the fan from a Black Raven. *Paul Family Photo Collection*

The same week I became engaged to Phil, I was offered a job that I really wanted at Washington State University, in their School (later College) of Nursing. It was to me a sign of good relationships to come in both work and marriage.

One of my first responsibilities at WSU was to begin a summer nursing camp for Native high school students. The idea behind the camp was that if young people got a taste of the health care profession, they might be inspired to pursue nursing or medicine as a career. And while the entire health care system was then—as it is now—in dire need of more diversity, the Native American community especially needed more caregivers. Native Americans have a much shorter life expectancy than Euro-Americans, and suffer disproportionately higher rates of heart disease, diabetes, cancers of all types, and accidental injuries.[1] When I started at WSU, the nursing population was 83 percent White, with Native Americans making up only 0.4 percent of the work force. Bear in mind that Native Americans make up about two percent of the total US population.

To get the camp up and running, I had to establish relationships with tribes in the area, to begin building trust between them and the university. However, the funding for this new program came through grants—it was temporary "soft" money, as opposed to "hard" money that comes through a permanent state allocation. Grant funding, I learned, was not highly valued by the tribes. Their experience had been that grants were written without their being consulted. After receiving the funds, researchers would "helicopter" in to do their research with a tribe, then leave without sharing results or even ever telling research subjects what the researchers were up to.

When the university announced a grant designed to help recruit Native students, I was as first greeted with distrust. In fact, one of the first questions I got at a meeting with tribal educators was, "Is this soft money or hard money?" To try to create some momentum to help establish permanent relationships and earn the trust of tribal members, I created a Native American Advisory board. The board was composed of tribal folks appointed to the task by tribal councils, in addition to faculty and staff from WSU who had written the grant.

The board helped us all gain insight into our various institutions and policies, and the faculty members who wrote the grant committed to making the new program a permanent item in the nursing school's budget. That happened over the next few years: my position was "hard" funded by the State of Washington. Additionally, an endowment was established specifically for scholarships for Native American students as well as to help fund the summer healthcare camp and other activities.

The camp grew over the years, but I was horrified to hear from the summer-camp students that they thought they were too "dumb" to be nurses. I knew I needed to help these young people understand the depths of their capabilities. One way I did this was by helping them connect (or in some cases, reconnect) with their culture and history. I began telling the Nimiipuu creation story of Coyote and the Monster of Kamiah. I witnessed a blossoming of pride as they learned of the rich history of Native peoples. We brought more Native cultural stories to the table, connecting students with their proud heritage and helping them to unlearn the stereotypes that had held them back.

The camp was eventually named Na-ha-shnee Native American Health Science Institute by the student-participants. Na-ha-shnee, the students thought, sounded Native without actually meaning anything. (We checked, as we didn't want to inadvertently take a sacred or profane word as the name of our camp.)

The students were taught basic nursing skills as well as anatomy, chemistry, and math. We also studied cultural leadership styles. I helped to develop and teach a class called "Plateau Tribes Culture and Health." This class was first taught to nursing students, but it is now part of WSU's curriculum for all healthcare students, doctors, and nurses. The class involved "didactic" instruction (book learnin,' as we used to call it) as well as a week of hands-on learning in the health clinics of the various Plateau Tribes. The class was taught by guest Native Health care professionals and Native elders. We wanted students to have a basic understanding of how the Indian Health Service system works, especially since so many Euro-American doctors help pay for their education by working for a year or two at a tribal clinic under the auspices of the IHS. We hoped that by making it clear that, when doctors come and go like that, and are just using their service to pay a debt, no bonds of trust are formed. What all communities need, whatever their ethnic backgrounds may be, are healthcare professionals who are permanent members of the community.

We also introduced students to the history of the Plateau region and its peoples, as well as how Native peoples of the Plateau used traditional plants as medicines. We introduced the concept of intergenerational historical trauma, an idea new to many students but which is the source of so many health disparities in Native American communities.

There were "nay sayers" who thought that, since I wasn't a nurse myself, I didn't belong in a nursing program. But I wasn't teaching nursing, obviously; I was helping young people see there was a path for them into the profession.

There were also those who didn't understand racism, which left me feeling alone and abused at times. Because I was the one and only person of color in the nursing program, I was asked to be the chair of a diversity committee. I embraced the task and researched workshops to enlighten staff and faculty. And while the workshops were mostly well received, I did learn a valuable lesson at a retreat for nursing faculty and staff one year. After small group discussions about how to promote leadership, one person mentioned there were "too many chiefs, and not enough Indians." Talk about awkward. The good news was the collective gasp that ran around the room. Then everyone turned to me, and I was the one who had to say, "Please don't say that." I was crushed that, after all the workshops on how traumatizing stereotypes are and how important diversity is, incidents like this were still happening. I almost quit that day. Fortunately, my allies gathered around me to calm me down. I learned something important and made sure folks I worked with understood what it meant when I said, "It is not my job to make your thinking diverse. That is *your* responsibility." Diversity activists now say that this responsibility is a critical part of "doing the work" of being anti-racist. From then on, my allies had my back and would speak up when the situation called for it.

After 22 years as founding director of Native America Health Sciences, I retired a few years ago. During my time at WSU, I helped graduate 65 Native Americans with their Bachelor of Science degrees in nursing; eight Master of Nursing students; two students with PhD's in nursing; and four students who earned Doctor of Nursing Practice degrees. At the time, there were fewer than 20 Native American PhD's in nursing. When I retired, a scholarship fund was created by tribal members and named after me. It earned enough interest to come to fruition in 2020 and the first scholarship was awarded in the spring of 2022. The name of the fund is the Robbie Paul, Ph.D., Native American Health Sciences Scholarship at Washington State University Foundation. Anyone who wants to contribute to this fund, please do!

Through Facebook and other means, I remain in touch with many of my former camp students and nursing students. Many are now practicing nurses, doctors, and hospital directors[2] and they often tell me they are still telling the stories I taught them.

I was fortunate to have my personal story and my family's healing journey intersect so well with my professional life. It was and continues to be my passion to help bring understanding and healing to both Native and non-Native communities.

I'd finished a master's degree in psychology in 1994, and my thesis was a first foray into writing a personal history of my family and my Nimíipuu people. But even then, I knew the ancestors were not finished with me. In dreams, they were very clear to me I was not done with healing our family's historical trauma, and that I would need to continue researching and telling the stories of our family and our people. I figured I'd take a year off and then start applying to Ph.D. programs. But as happens so often, life got in the way. I married Phil, started the job at WSU—and five years blew by.

My friend Terrie Ashby Scott and I were recruited by Gonzaga University to their doctoral program in leadership. Gonzaga wanted more diverse students in their program. Terrie, who is African-American and Japanese, and whom I knew from WSU, was contacted first, and she thought of me as a likely co-student. When we were offered graduate assistantships that would help pay for the program, we seized the opportunity. I prayed to the ancestors and asked them if this was the program for me. I started in winter 2000 and, at first, I wasn't so sure this was a good idea. As I advanced in the program, though, it became very clear that I'd found a good fit. My professors were instrumental in helping me define the scope of my research into historical trauma.

My doctoral degree journey had many ups and downs. I was in my second semester when my brother Richard died. That hit me hard, but I carried on. Two years later, my mother died, right when I was reading a lot about historical trauma. The literature was too close to home, so I took a semester off. I started again in the summer of 2003, but then my father died in the fall of 2004. This loss was especially hard because now we as a family had to deal with the estate, selling off property and belongings as well as contending with the grief of losing our beloved father. So, I took another semester off to grieve and to help my family settle our father's estate. I continued my classes again in fall of 2005.

I continued gathering research until spring of 2006, at which time Gonzaga University encouraged me to submit an abstract for the conference being held at the University of Cape Town, South Africa, in celebration of the 10th anniversary of the Truth and Reciliation Commission and in honor of Bishop Desmond Tutu's 75th birthday. Much to my surprise, my abstract was accepted, and so now I was preparing to go to South Africa. I was also entering my seventh year in grad school: I needed to complete the program by spring 2007. Phil was saying, "Get the dang thing done," as he wanted his wife back. I was working full-time at WSU and my evenings were spent in my basement office researching and writing my dissertation.

I returned from South Africa full of enthusiasm, and my ancestors were pushing, nudging, and cheering me on. I spent that winter writing my heart out. My husband would come to the basement to make sure I was still alive, and sometimes would bring me food. My dissertation committee kept cheering me on and helping with suggestions and edits. Finally, that spring, I completed the massive, 500-page dissertation. I had completed the requirements for a degree of Doctor of Philosophy! My doctoral committee and I had a party to sign off on the Ph.D.

I had known all along that I'd want to throw a graduation party to thank and honor all those who had supported me through the doctoral journey. I had been making small gifts whenever I had spare time, and so had a little something for the 75 people who attended. It was a full house, with so much fun and celebration. I felt a pat on my back from the ancestors. And though I shed some tears because my parents had died before I finished my dissertation, I was comforted knowing they were with me in spirit.

My father's main regret about going to a boarding school was the loss of his mother tongue. As a child, he had been fluent in Nimipuutímt, but at school he was forced to speak English only and so, as he told me, "I lost my language; I don't understand much anymore, and I would like to relearn the language." He was not able to fulfill this goal before his death. One of my goals has long been to learn and speak Nimipuutímt fluently. Bringing the language back to the family is an important part of our collective healing. By learning the language, I will know our culture at a deeper level. Nimipuutímt is not an easy language, so I listen daily to a lesson offered by a Nimiipuu teacher on Facebook.

The process of finding our stories has brought our previously silent history to life and made it real. The journeys, the research, the telling, and the listening all have helped to bring a deeper understanding and healing of our family's and our people's wounds. In their article "Utilizing Traditional Storytelling to Promote Wellness in American Indian Communities," published in the *Journal of Transcultural Nursing*, Hodge and colleagues emphasize the power of telling and listening in curing ceremonies. Healing arises when we acknowledge our grief with the knowledge offered to people through the Creator.[3] What I learned from Desmond Tutu is that telling one's truth—and listening closely to the telling of others' truths—is a first step towards reconciliation. From reconciliation flows introspection, empathy, and understanding. With this perspective, I realized that if my grandmother Um-al-wat could survive the atrocity of a war and the murder of five of her children, then I most certainly could survive a divorce. My troubles, as trying as they have been, pale in comparison.

I realize now my ancestors did the best they could, given their circumstances. I have learned forgiveness has many levels, and the work and the time required to forgive. When the descendant of the cavalry soldier assisted me down to the pipe ceremony at the Bear Paw battle site, I was not yet ready to let bygones be bygones. He talked of wanting to make amends, and I wondered what amends he could possibly offer. I thought then it was far too late for making amends. Later, I was able to forgive, even if my heart remained heavy and I refused to forget. Many Americans are the descendants of people who performed ferocious acts of violence out of obedience—to a commanding officer or to a priest and what they thought a certain book required of them. Just as I had to first acknowledge the power of the "dumb Indian" tape that kept replaying in my head and heart, so too do most Americans need to acknowledge the racist and genocidal tapes that have been handed down to them by their forebearers.

The offering of amends is a topic that needs further research. What does it look like? Are the sins of the fathers passed on to their children? If not, then how can the process of offering amends help Native Americans with the loss of lands, tribal languages, ceremonies and a way of life, and the genocidal loss of millions of lives? As I dwell on these questions, I hope you will too—we who are recovering from traumas inflicted over many generations, but also those who are the children of the perpetrators. We are all recovering from a kind of poison, I think, and I am moved by something Heather McGuire wrote in her book *The Sum of Us*: that Black thinkers from "Baldwin to Toni Morrison have made the point that racism is a poison first consumed by its concocters."[4]

In discovering my family's stories, and in listening to my ancestors speak to me through dreams and visions, and by in turn telling these stories, I find I am becoming a good Native leader! I would also say Truth Teller, like my great-great-grandfather Ut-sin-malikan; he was a Truth Teller. Somehow, I have gone from "dumb Indian" to sought-after speaker, someone who can bring the past into the present in ways that reveal and heal. Much as described in the book *The Sacred Tree*,[5] I first learned to relate my ancestors' stories to the four directions: spiritual in the east; emotional in the south; physical in the west; and mental in the north. I can't just sit down at the keyboard and type. I must first pray to the Creator. I face the east asking for the spirits of my ancestors to connect with me and the Creator. From the east, I remember the sacrifice of my ancestors, and the love that has always been there for me and others who find their stories. I then turn to the south and ask for the emotions that need to be felt in the telling. I turn to the west to ask the Creator for help with finding the purpose of these stories, and it was from the west that I learned that healing comes from knowing truth, and that truth helps reconcile us to the bitter deeds of the past. There is no side-stepping, no going around: I needed to feel the burn at the bottom of my heart so that the wound is cauterized. I then turn to the north and ask the Creator and the ancestors for the wisdom and insight to find the words of these stories. It is the ancestors who have encouraged me to tell and share these stories with others, in hopes that the stories inspire their own healing process.

The healing method our family developed as we researched and travelled to battle sites and boarding schools came to include some steps I hope you can take as your own to use on your own healing journey.

1. Recognize healing is a process and takes time—maybe the rest of your life. Know, too, that you are your own best physician for this type of healing.

2. Because you are the primary healer of your wounds, take personal responsibility for your healing.

3. Pray to your Creator for the time to go to those places in your family's or your people's history that have affected you and your loved ones; take small steps, as these journeys are not going to heal all the traumas at once.

4. If you can discover and relearn your history, on or near an anniversary date of a traumatic wound, go to the place where that wound was first opened.

5. Participate in a ceremony or create one that has meaning for you.

6. Share the story of what you know. Listen to your ancestors when they tell you "It is time to heal, time to tell the stories."

7. If your journeys are solo ones, pray, smudge, and ask for healing and the ability to forgive.

8. If you are able, begin to let go of the wound so as not to be held captive and continue to be overwhelmed. This is an evolving practice and, like an onion, there are many layers of forgiveness.

9. It may take more than one visit to a site to feel any improvement but, remember, generational wounds are deep and may take time and several trips to heal. Especially for younger people, it may take many visits, many ceremonies, and much introspection and listening to the stories of others before understanding comes.

10. Practice behaviors that help empower yourself and others to grow in empathy.

This last step is the combination of all the previous ones: you are behaving in an empowering way when you listen, when you research, when you go to sacred sites or the sites where trauma and deaths occurred. For me, this began with my trips home to the Paul ranch. There, I learned to listen to the earth, to lie on the earth and let the earth help heal my wounds. While I am not able to go to the ranch, there is a place near the home that Phil and I have made together that is sacred to me. This sacred place is important for helping me to stay on the path of harmony and balance, of healing and reconciliation. In this sacred place, I have learned to listen, to be still— so still and quiet I can hear a bird take a drink of water on the other side of the mountain. Then I know I am in harmony with the earth.

The thing I wish for most is that we learn respect. We have different opinions, religions, even different sciences, but none should reign over the others as the only way to be. I tried to put this thought into a poem.

Respect

R Respect begins with your relationship with the Creator.

E Elevate and look to the Creator for you answer to prayers.
Expect excellence of yourself.

S Strengthen yourself by loving yourself, your family, your
community, and that you are
Special, so recognize that you are unique.

P Prepare yourself for whatever challenges you face, and
know that your
Purpose in life is a personal responsibility.

E Educate, be a lifelong learner, and know that
Earned respect is earned over time.

C Create an honoring space to be with the Creator.
Create and contribute to the world.

T Trust the Creator to lead and guide you.
Trust and treasure the uniqueness of the life that is within
yourself.

In this decades-long journey of healing and sharing, of learning, listening, and crying, I have found a spiritual depth within myself that is cleansing and, I believe, hopeful. Having had the opportunity to share this story in South Africa with celebrants of that troubled nation's truth and reconciliation process helped me realize there is hope for humanity. As we share our stories across the world, we learn we all have suffered, but we do have a choice to confront the atrocities and heal those wounds. We validate each other by listening, and by listening we gain empathy for one another, and strengthened with that empathy we can find the capacity to forgive and to halt the cycle of inhumanity. As it has been for my family, my hope is for the world to:

Listen to the Birds

Listen my relatives of the world, children, grandchildren, great-grandchildren, I pray for you for continued healing.

Listen to the birds, the birds that can bring guidance, like the red-tailed hawk that guided me on my first journey home to the ranch.

Listen to the birds sing songs of praise for a new day.

Listen to the birds that sing a song for the end of daylight.

Listen to the birds for when your spirit is ready to go to places of unhealed wounds.

Listen to the birds to learn mourning songs.

Listen to the birds to learn healing songs for the soul.

Listen to the birds sing songs of when it will rain and songs when the rain stops.

Listen to the birds to hear your ancestors guide you, to protect you,

to lift your soul to the great spirit above.

As the song "On Eagles Wings" says,

the eagle will carry my spirit to the ancestors

and I will always be with you in spirit.

Acknowledgements

Imust first acknowledge my ancestors, who through dreams and other means have led me to the place I am now. To be clear, I am not the only descendant of the ancestors I write about in this book. I don't know, nor does anyone know, how many descendants of Ut-sin-malikan (on the matriarchal side of my family) and Seven Days Whipping (on the patriarchal side) there are and how much they know of their ancestors. As I began to know my family's story, I realized how we became disconnected from our history and who our co-descendants are.

Obviously, I do not speak for all those unknown-to-me descendants, nor do I try; I speak only for myself and my family. However, the path I have been on has resulted in a small mountain of research. I have shared the research I have collected with some of my cousins, siblings, nieces, nephews, and distant cousins who have asked for it. It is my hope that this book will help motivate those who do not know their ancestorial history to find their own healing path.

I am thankful for my brother Jesse, who began to find our family ancestors' history and begin to reclaim our ancestorial history and knowledge. For me it was an unhealed wound of not knowing who we were and are that led me to find as much as I could about our family ancestorial history. The journey of listening to the ancestors has been rewarding and healing and is a journey that never ends.

I am grateful, too, for my family, especially my parents, Titus J. Paul and Maxine S. Caster Paul, and my children, Kimberly Ann Enz and Michael Paul Foiles. A source of ongoing sustenance has been the joy my granddaughters bring me, and so I thank Amanda, Elizabeth, and Isabella. My sister Jackie Paul Inglis has been a close companion on this healing journey for which I am forever grateful; and, too, for the joy of her children: JR Inglis, Vonda Schuld, Suzanne Gebhards, Patrick Inglis, and Christopher Inglis. My brother Warren Paul and his wife, Donna, and their children, William and Bruce, as well as my brother Richard Paul and his sons, Silas and Dallas: all have helped me in ways tangible and in ways spiritual.

To my friends, allies, and counselors who saw me through difficult times and were helped on my healing journey, thank you to Randy Mickelson,

Terrie Ashby-Scott, PhD, Carol Allen, RN, PhD, Janet Katz, RN, PhD, Jenny Ferguson, Joyce Kohler, Phyllis Beran, Rosalee Saad, Gwen Cater, John Thomas, and Rita Spinal.

My invaluable allies at WSU include Barbara Aston; Emma Noyes; Ruth Bindler, PhD; Thelma Cleveland, RN, PhD; Marian Sheafor, RN, PhD; Anne Hirsch, RN, PhD; Pat Butterfield, RN, PhD; and Lisa Brown, PhD.

The writing of this book began years ago with my master's thesis at Eastern Washington University where my committee members were Joan Niemann, PhD and Valerie Appleton, PhD. This book grew in scope and courage under the generous and spiritually sensitive tutelage of my doctoral committee at Gonzaga University: Shann Ferch, PhD, Sandy Wilson, PhD, James Beebe, PhD, and James Hunt, PhD.

This book would not have come to fruition without the excellent help of Brian Clark. Thanks, too, to Kay Dixon for her comments on an early draft of the book and to Trevor Bond, PhD, for his careful reading of an early draft and to Janet Katz for helping with revising key chapters.

Finally, my wonderful husband Phil Wise has pushed and encouraged me to write and get this book published for many years. He has been my main cheerleader!

Notes

CHAPTER 2
1. Slickpoo and Walker, 1972, pp. 201–206
2. Brave Heart et al., 2011, p. 282
3. Rogers, 2001, p. 1513

CHAPTER 3
1. Pinkham and Evans, p. 30
2. Haines, 1955, p. 9
3. Haines, 1955, p. 10
4. Slickpoo and Walker, 1973, p. 47
5. Slickpoo and Walker, 1973, p. 46
6. Educator's Guide at https://www.nps.gov/
   nepe/learn/education/upload/isaaptakay-les-
   son-plan_web.pdf accessed July 21, 2021
7. Haines, 1939, p. 18
8. Haines, 1939, p. 18
9. Slickpoo and Walker, 1973, p. 31, 32
10. Slickpoo and Walker, 1973, p. 31, 32
11. Swayne, 2003, p. 8–9
12. Swayne, 2003, p. 8–9
13. Slickpoo and Walker, 1973, p. 68
14. Haines, 1955, p. 10
15. Slickpoo and Walker, 1973, p. 47
16. 17. Slickpoo and Walker, 1973, p. 67

CHAPTER 4
1. Aoki, 1994, p. 747
2. Josephy, 1997, p. 38
3. Haines, 1955, p. 58
4. Swayne, 2003, pp. 16–17
5. Slickpoo and Walker, 1972, p. 68; Swayne,
   2003, pp. 17–18
6. Swayne, 2003, p. 19
7. Haines, 1955, p. 29
8. Jefferson quoted in Prucha, 1984, pp. 21–22.
9. Locke, 2003, pp. 113–14
10. Josephy, 1997, p. 48
11. Haines, 1955, pp. 40–50; Josephy, 1997, pp.
    48–68
12. Josephy, 1997, p. 69

CHAPTER 5
1. Drury, 1979, p. 28
2. Drury, 1979, p. 28
3. Slickpoo and Walker, 1973, p. 71
4. Haines, 1954, p. 56; Drury, 1979, pp. 28–29;
   Josephy, 1997, pp. 96–97
5. Josephy, 1997, p. 69
6. Josephy, 1997, p. 97
7. Josephy, 1997, p. 98
8. Josephy, 1997, pp. 99–100
9. Josephy, 1997, pp. 126–128
10. Drury, 1979, p. 39
11. Drury, 1979, pp. 39–42
12. Josephy, 1997, pp. 151–155
13. Drury, 1979, pp. 41–44; Josephy, 1997, pp.
    147–157
14. *Treaties: Nez Perce Perspectives*, 2003, p. 8
15. *Treaties: Nez Perce Perspectives*, 2003, p. 8
16. Slickpoo and Walker, 1973, p. 72
17. Drury, 1936, p. 186
18. Drury, 1936, p. 186
19. *Lewiston Morning Tribune*, December 16,
    1927
20. *Lewiston Morning Tribune*, December 16,
    1927
21. Drury, 1958, p. 122
22. Drury, 1958, pp. 123–124
23. Drury, 1958, pp. 123–124
24. Slickpoo and Walker, 1973, p. 75
25. Josephy, 1997, p. 210; *Treaties: Nez Perce
    Perspectives*, 2002, p. 10
26. Drury 1958, p. 190
27. Drury 1958, p. 197
28. Drury 1958, pp. 197, 198
29. Drury 1958, p. 197
30. Josephy, 1997, p. 113
31. Drury, 1958, p. 197
32. Drury, 1966, p. 181
33. *Lewiston Morning Tribune*, December 16,
    1927

CHAPTER 6

1. Brouillet, 1869, pp. 23–24
2. Trafzer, Sherman, 1986, pp. 25–27
3. Mann, 2009, p. 94
4. Mann, 2009, p. 94
5. Haines, 1955, p. 92
6. Mann, 2009, p. 102
7. West, 2009, p. 49
8. Mann, 2009, p. 101
9. Mann, 2009, p. 100
10. West, 2009. P. 50
11. West, 2009, p. 50, Josephy, 1997, p. 252, Trafzer, Sherman, 1986, pp. 26–27
12. Josephy, 1997, pp. 253–257
13. Josephy, 1997, pp. 256–257
14. Josephy, 1997, p. 256
15. West, 2009, p. 50
16. Josephy, 1997, p. 284
17. Karson, 2006, pp. 64–65
18. Karson, 2006, p. 64
19. Karson, 2006, p. 65
20. Phinney, 2022, "Families of the five Cayuse men executed by the government for the 1847 killing of Marcus Whitman are still searching for their graves." Retrieved from https://www.underscore.news/reporting/uo-students-advance-the search-for the cayuse-five on May 20,2023.
21. Josephy, 1997, p. 286
22. Karson, 2006, p. 65
23. Pevar, 1992, p. 37
24. West, 2009, pp. 60–61; Drury, 1979, pp. 89–131; Josephy, 1997, pp. 292–338
25. Richards 1993, p. 190
26. West, 2009, p. 62; Drury, 1979, pp. 89–131; Josephy, 1997, pp. 292–338
27. *Treaties: Nez Perce Perspectives*, 2003, p. 38; Josephy, 1997, p. 316; Drury, 1979, p. 94
28. Karson, 2006, p. 77
29. Slickpoo and Walker, 1973, p. 85
30. Haines, 1955, p. 54–55
31. Slickpoo and Walker, 1973, p. 85
32. Slickpoo and Walker, 1973, p. 101
33. Slickpoo and Walker, 1973, p. 137, West, 2009, pp. 65–67
34. Josephy, 1997, p. 334
35. Josephy, 1997, p. 337, West, 2009, P. 70
36. Manring, 1912, pp. 88–126; Drury, 1979, pp. 154–155; Josephy, 1997, pp. 380–381
37. Drury, 1979, pp. 156–157; Josephy, 1997, pp. 381–382; Manring, 1912, pp. 158–171
38. Baird et al., 2015, p. 500; Josephy, 1997, p. 383
39. Quoted in Baird et al., 2015, p. 500
40. Drury, 1979, p. 159; Manring, 1912, pp. 211–215; Kip, 1859, pp. 69–71

41. Manring 1912, pp. 213–214
42. Drury, 1979, p. 159; Manring, 1912, pp. 211–215; Kip, 1859, pp. 69–71
43. Kip, 1859, pp. 116–117
44. Quoted in Baird et al., 2015, p. 501
45. McWhorter, 1953, p. 105
46. Baird et al., 2002, p. 53
47. Drury, 1979, pp. 169–170; Josephy, 1997, pp. 402–403; McWhorter, 1952, pp. 100–101
48. Baird et al., 2002, pp. 215–245
49. Baird et al., 2002, pp. 215–265
50. Baird et al., 2002, pp. 315–324; Josephy, 1997, pp. 408–416
51. Baird et al., 2002, pp. 330–333
52. Baird et al., 2002, p. 348
53. Baird et al., 2002, p. 356
54. Baird et al., 2002, pp. 360–361
55. Baird et al., 2002, p. 361
56. Baird et al., 2002, pp. 365–366
57. Baird et al., 2002, pp. 368–375
58. *Nez Perce Treaty Perspectives*, 2003, p. 42
59. Baird et al, 2002, p. 383.
60. Josephy, 1997, pp. 428–437
61. Slickpoo and Walker, 1973, p. 179, West, 2009, p. 97
62. Baird, 1999, p. 4
63. Smith, 2001, p. 85

CHAPTER 7

1. The federal neglect of the Nimiipuu is well documented in Baird and Swagerty, 2002.
2. My brother Jesse obtained Newell's diary on microfiche from Bob Wiggins, a great-grandson of Newell. Jesse then had a copy typed up from the handwritten original; it is this typed copy that I read. Newell's diary is also quoted from extensively in Drury, 1979, esp. pp. 248–253
3. Newell diary
4. Drury, 1979, p. 248; Josephy, 1997, pp. 438–439
5. Drury, 1979, pp. 248–249; Josephy, 1997, pp. 438–439; Newell records that he went out on both the 16th and 17th but doesn't mention his Native traveling companions.
6. Drury, 1979, pp. 248–249
7. Recorded by McWhorter, 1952, p. 113
8. Quoted in McWhorter, 1959, pp. 113–114
9. McWhorter, 1959, p. 114
10. Alcorn 1983, p. 51
11. Newell, 1868, p. 26
12. Drury, 1979, pp. 250–253
13. Webb, 1972, p. 5.

CHAPTER 8

1. Drury, 1979, p. 50; West, 2009, p. 51
2. Drury, 1979, p. 50
3. Josephy, 1997, p. 191; Barid et al, 2015, p. 224
4. Drury, 1966, p. 181
5. Slickpoo and Walker, 1973, pp. 83–141; Josephy, 1997, pp. 315–316; West, 2009, p. 62
6. Josephy, 1997, pp. 348–355; Drury, 1979, pp. 137–138; Baird et al, 2015, pp. 417–429
7. Josephy, 1997, pp. 348–255; Drury, 1979, pp. 137–138
8. West, 2009, p. 70
9. Drury, 1979, p. 139
10. Josephy, 1997, pp. 356–357
11. Drury, 1979, pp. 138–139; Baird et al, 2015, pp. 417–429
12. Baird et al, 2015, pp. 425–426
13. Barid, et al, 2015, p. 426
14. Drury, 1979, pp. 140–141
15. Baird et al, 2015, p. 427
16. Slickpoo and Walker, 1973, p. 54
17. Baird et al, 2015, p. 427
18. Josephy, 1997, pp. 446–447
19. Josephy, 1997, pp. 450–455
20. Josephy, 1997, p. 455
21. Josephy, 1997, p. 456
22. Josephy, 1997, pp. 454–457; West, 2009, pp. 106–107
23. Josephy, 1997, pp. 454–466; West, 2009. p. 107
24. Josephy, 1997, pp. 466–467; West, 2009. Pp. 107–108
25. Josephy, 1997, pp. 473–487; West, 2009, p. 114
26. Paraphrased from Josephy, 1997, pp. 487–488
27. *Chief Joseph's Own Story*, 1879, pp. 10–11
28. Josephy, 1997, pp. 485–491
29. Josephy, 1997, p. 491; West, 2009, p. 115
30. Josephy, 1997, pp. 494–496; West, 2009, p. 115
31. West, 2009, p. 115
32. Josephy, 1997, pp. 496–497
33. Josephy, 1997, p. 501
34. Josephy, 1997, p. 504; West, 2009, p. 119
35. Josephy, 1997, pp. 505–506
36. Josephy, 1997, p. 507; West, 2009, p. 119
37. *Chief Joseph's Own Story*, 1879, p. 14
38. *Chief Joseph's Own Story*, 1879, p. 15
39. *Chief Joseph's Own Story*, 1879, p. 15

CHAPTER 9

1. *Chief Joseph's Own Story*, 1879, pp. 15–16; Josephy, 1997, p. 509
2. West, 2009, p. 123; Josephy, 1997, pp. 510–511; McWhorter, 1983, p. 41; McWhorter, 1952, p. 176
3. West, 2009, p123; Josephy, 1997, p. 511; McWhorter, 1952, pp. 177–187
4. McWhorter, 1983, pp. 41–42
5. West, 2009, p. 124; Josephy, 1997, p. 512
6. West, 2009, p. 124; Josephy, 1997, p. 513
7. West, 2009, pp. 124–125 Josephy, 1997, p. 514
8. West, 2009, p. 125; Josephy, 1997, p. 514
9. West, 2009, pp. 126–130; McWhorter, 1952, pp. 186–197
10. Josephy, 1997, pp. 515
11. Josephy, 1997, p. 518
12. West, 2009, p. 130; Josephy, 1997, pp. 513–518; McWhorter, 1952, pp. 194–206; McWhorter, 1983, pp. 45–50
13. McWhorter, 1952, p. 181
14. West, 2009, p. 134; Josephy, 1997, pp. 524–256; McWhorter, 1952, pp. 231–261; McWhorter, 1983, pp. 54–64
15. West, 2009, p. 134; Josephy, 1997, p. 524–526; McWhorter 1953, pp. 213–261; McWhorter, 1983, pp. 54–64
16. West, 2009, p. 134; McWhorter, 1952, p. 234; McWhorter, 1983, p. 55–56
17. McWhorter, 1952, pp. 262–274
18. McWhorter, 1983, p. 77
19. Trafzer, Sherman, 1986, p. 115
20. West, 2009, pp. 153–157; Greene, 2000, p. 373
21. West, 2009, pp. 165–166; Josephy, 1997, pp. 554–558
22. Josephy, 1997, p. 557
23. West, 2009, pp. 171–172; McWhorter, 1983, pp. 107–108
24. West, 2009, p. 182; McWhorter, 1983, p. 108
25. McWhorter, 1983, p. 109
26. West, 2009, pp. 182–183; Josephy, 1997, p. 577
27. West, 2009, p. 183; McWhorter, 1983, p. 111
28. West, 2009, p. 183; Josephy, 1997, pp. 576–577; McWhorter, 1952, pp. 368–369; McWhorter, 1983, pp. 109–110
29. West, 2009, p. 184; Josephy, 1997, pp. 578–579; McWhorter, 1952, pp. 369–370
30. Josephy, 1997, p. 581
31. Trafzer, Sherman, 1986, p. 116
32. McWhorter, 1983, p. 115
33. McWhorter, 1983, p. 376
34. West, 2009, p. 189; McWhorter, 1952, p. 381
35. West, 2009, p. 189; McWhorter, 1952, p. 132
36. West, 2009, pp. 190–191; McWhorter, 1983, p. 118
37. McWhorter, 1983, p. 120
38. McWhorter, 1952, p. 392
39. West, 2009, p. 196; McWhorter, 1952, p. 403
40. McWhorter, 1952, pp. 381–382
41. Pearson, 2008, p. 39

42. Pearson, 2008, p. 39
43. Pearson, 2008, p. 39
44. West, 2009, p. 196; McWhorter, 1983, pp. 155–156; McWhorter, 1952, pp. 392–393
45. West, 2009, p. 196
46. West, 2009. P. 202
47. Author was personal witness to hearing story shared at Big Hole commemoration, August 9, 2024

CHAPTER 10
1. McWhorter, 1952, pp. 404–477, McWhorter, 1983 pp. 161–203
2. Josephy, 1997, p. 616
3. Josephy, 1997 pp. 612–617; McWhorter, 1952, p. 474
4. Josephy, 1997, pp. 616–617
5. West, 2009, p.269; Josephy, 1997, p. 617
6. West, 2009, p. 269; McWhorter, 1983, p. 205
7. McWhorter, 1952, p. 479
8. McWhorter, 1952, p. 485
9. McWhorter, 1952, pp. 485–486
10. McWhorter, 1952, p. 484
11. McWhorter, 1952, p. 483
12. West, 2009, p. 276
13. McWhorter, 1983, p. 211
14. McWhorter, 1952, p. 486
15. McWhorter, 1983, pp. 214–216; McWhorter, 1952, pp. 487–490; Josephy, 1997, pp. 621–625
16. West, 2009, p.279, McWhorter, 1952, p. 625, McWhorter, 1983, p. 222
17. McWhorter, 1983, p. 224
18. West, 2009, p. 281; Josephy, 1997, p. 628; McWhorter, 1983, p. 224
19. West, 2009, p. 280; McWhorter, 1983, p. 224
20. West, 2009, p. 282
21. Josephy, 1997, p. 630
22. McWhorter, 1983, p. 225
23. Pearson, 2008, p. 52; Josephy, 1997, p. 631
24. West, 2009, p. 281; Pearson, 2008, p. 53; Josephy, 1997, p. 632
25. Pearson, 2008, pp. 53–58
26. West, 2009, p. 293; Josephy, 1997, p. 634
27. Josephy, 1997, p. 634
28. Josephy, 1997, p. 634
29. West, 2009, p. 293; Josephy, 1997, p. 635
30. Greene, 2000, pp. 334–335
31. West, 2009, p. 293; Josephy, 1997, p. 635
32. Trafzer, 1987, pp. ix–x
33. Bond, 1998, p. 12
34. Pearson, 2008, pp. 59–61
35. Pearson, 2008, pp. 62–63
36. Josephy, 1997, p. 636

37. Pearson, 2008, p. 65
38. Josephy, 1997, p. 636
39. Josephy, 1997, p. 636
40. Pearson, 2008, p. 66; Josephy, 1997, p. 637
41. Pearson, 2008, p. 69
42. McWhorter, 1983, p. 289
43. Pearson, 2008, pp. 71–74
44. Pearson, 2008, pp. 73–74
45. Pearson, 2008, p. 74
46. Pearson, 2008, pp. 74–76
47. Pearson, 2008, pp. 78–79; McWhorter, 1952, pp. 528–529
48. Pearson, 2008, p. 75
49. Josephy, 1997, p. 637

CHAPTER 11
1. The Bismarck *Tribune*, Bismarck, D.T., November 14, 1877
2. The Bismarck *Tribune*, Bismarck, D.T., November 26, 1877; Josephy, 1997, p. 637
3. The Bismarck *Tribune*, Bismarck, D.T., December 8, 1877
4. The Bismarck *Tribune*, Bismarck, D.T., December 1877
5. The Bismarck *Tribune*, Bismarck, D.T., November 14, 1877

CHAPTER 12
1. Pearson, 2008, p. 79
2. Pearson, 2008, pp. 79–80
3. Pearson, 2008, p. 80
4. Pearson, 2008, pp. 82–83
5. Pearson, 2008, p. 92
6. Pearson, 2008, pp. 92–93
7. Pearson, 2008, pp. 100–101
8. Clark, 1945, p. 214
9. Pearson, 2008, pp. 83–84
10. Pearson, 2008, pp. 116–117
11. Clark, 1945, p. 215
12. Trafzer, 1987, pp. 13–15
13. Clark, 1945, p. 216
14. Clark, 1945, p. 217
15. Wortman, Wortman, and Bottorff, 1999, p. 179
16. Clark, 1945, p. 217
17. Pearson, 2008, p. 120
18. Pearson, 2008, pp. 120–124
19. Pearson, 2008, pp. 138–139
20. Pearson, 2008, p. 244
21. Clark, 1945, p. 217
22. Clark, 1945, p. 217; McWhorter, 1953, p. 533
23. *Chief Joseph's Own Story*, 1879, pp. 29–31; Chief Joseph, "An Indian's View of Indian Affairs" *North American Review*, April 1879.
24. Pearson, 2008, pp. 171–177

25. Clark, 1945, p. 221
26. Clark, 1945, p. 222
27. Pearson, 2008, pp. 186–197
28. Pearson, 2008, p. 192
29. Pearson, 2008, pp. 182–184
30. Pearson, 2008, pp. 187–188
31. Pearson,2008, pp. 188–189
32. Pearson, 2008. p. 207
33. Pearson, 2008, p. 208
34. Clark, 1945, p. 222
35. Frankl, 1959, p. 109
36. Frankl, 1959, p. 9
37. Wortman et al., 1999, pp. 183–189
38. Wortman et al., 1999, pp. 187–188
39. Wortman, et al., 1999, p. 191
40. Pearson, 2008, p. 275
41. McWhorter, 1953, p. 537
42. Slickpoo and Walker, 1973, p. 200
43. McWhorter, 1953, p. 538
44. Pearson, 2008, pp. 277–279
45. Pearson, 2008, pp. 279–280
46. Pearson, 2008, p. 280
47. Pearson, 2008, p. 280
48. Trafzer, 1987, p. 63
49. Pearson, 2008, p. 276
50. Clark, 1945, p. 231
51. Pearson, 2008, pp. 286–288
52. Trafzer, 1987, p. 65
53. Pearson, 2008, p. 289
54. Pearson, 2008, p. 290; Slickpoo and Walker, 1973, p. 210
55. Slickpoo and Walker, 1973, p. 210
56. Pearson, 2008, p. 290, Trafzer, 1987, pp. 65–66
57. Trafzer, 1987, p. 66
58. Pearson, 2008, pp. 291–292
59. Pearson, 2008, p. 293

CHAPTER 13
1. Adams, 1995, pp. 5–7
2. Adams, 1995, p. 7
3. Adams, 1995, p. 8
4. Adams, 1995, p. 9
5. Adams, 1995, p. 11
6. Adams, 1995, p. 17
7. Adams, 1995, p. 17
8. Adams, 1995, p. 19
9. Adams, 1995, pp. 21–24
10. Adams, 1995, p. 29
11. Adams, 1995, p. 30
12. Witmer, 1993, p. 2
13. Pratt, 1964, p. 7
14. Pratt, 1964, pp. 7–8
15. Pratt, 1964, p. 116–117, Adams, 1995, pp. 36–38

16. Pratt, 1964, pp. 118–119
17. Pratt, 1964, pp. 155–166
18. Glancy, 2014, pp. 75–77
19. Crowe, F. Hilton: "Indian Prisoner–Students at Fort Marion: The Founding of Carlisle Was Dreamed in St. Augustine." *The Regionals Review* [National Park Service], vol. V, no. 6 (December 1940). Accessed August 13, 2025, from https://www.nps.gov/parkhistory/online_books/regional_review/vol5-6c.htm#:~:text=A%20school%20for%20the%20Indians,little%20money%20or%20outside%20aid.20. Hoxie, 1984, p. 42
21. Pratt, 1964, p. 335
22. Pratt, 1964, p. xv
23. NPR *Codeswitch*, https://www.npr.org/sections/codeswitch/2014/01/05/260006815/the-ugly-fascinating-history-of-the-word-racism, accessed September 7, 2021
24. Barrows, Isabel C., editor, 1892. "Proceedings of the National Conference of Charities and Correction: At the Nineteenth Annual Session Held in Denver, Colorado, June 23–29, 1892, p. 45
25. Witmer, 1993, p. 11
26. Witmer, 1993, p. 12
27. Witmer, 1993, p. 12
28. Pratt, 1964, p. 220
29. Pratt, 1964. p. 222
30. Pratt, 1964, pp. 222–223
31. Pratt, 1964, p. 223
32. Pratt, 1964, p. 222
33. Interview in October 2021 with Jim Gerencser, the Dickinson College archivist. The College is now the home of the Carlisle archives.
34. Pratt, 1964, pp. 228–229
35. Pratt, 1964, pp. 230–231
36. Pratt, 1964, p. 231
37. Pratt, 1964, pp. 231–232
38. Standing Bear, 1928, p. 141
39. Standing Bear, 1928, p. 142
40. Standing Bear, 1928, p. 142
41. Pratt, 1964, p. 233
42. Pratt, 1964, pp. 235–236
43. Pearson, 2008, pp. 228–229
44. Witmer, 1993, p. 25
45. *Eadle Keatah Toh*, April 1880, vol. 1, No. 2, p. 4
46. *Eadle Keatah Toh*, April 1880, vol. 1, No. 2, p. 2
47. Standing Bear, 1928, p. 137
48. Witmer, 1993, p. 26–27
49. Standing Bear, 1928, p. 145
50. Adams, 1996, p. 155
51. Witmer, 1993, p. 28

52. Adams, 1995, p. 155
53. *The Morning Star* Vol 7, No. 9, June 1887. Downloaded from https://carlisleindian.dickinson.edu/
54. Adams, 1995, p. 124
55. *The Morning Star*, Vol VIII. No. 5, January and February 1887. Downloaded from https://carlisleindian.dickinson.edu/
56. Witmer, 1993, p. 28
57. Standing Bear, 1928, p. 154
58. *The Indian Helper*, Vol. II, February 18, 1887, No. 28. Downloaded from https://carlisleindian.dickinson.edu.
59. *The Indian Helper*, Vol. III May 25, 1888, No. 41. Downloaded from https://carlisleindian.dickinson.edu/
60. Pratt, 1964, p. 194
61. Adams, 1995, p. 157
62. Adams, 1995, p. 157
63. Adams, 1995, p. 158
64. Adams, 1995, p. 234
65. Witmer, 1993, p. 35
66. Witmer, 1993, p. 29
67. Standing Bear, 1928, p. 174
68. Standing Bear, 1928, p. 175
69. Pratt, 1964, p. 280
70. Quoted in Pratt, 1964, p. 280
71. Lomawaima, 1994, p. 14
72. National Native American Boarding School Healing Coalition. https://boardingschool-healing.org/list/ Accessed August 26, 2021
73. National Native American Boarding School Healing Coalition. https://boardingschoolhealing.org/education/us-indian-boarding-school-history/ Accessed August 26, 2021
74. Federal Indian Boarding School Initiative Investigative Report Vol. II, July 2024, p. 9
75. Federal Indian Boarding School Initiative Investigative Report Vol. II, July 2024, p. 22

CHAPTER 14

1. Retrieved from the Carlisle archives which are now housed at Dickinson College, Carlisle, PA. https://carlisleindian.dickinson.edu/
2. *Indian Helper*, October 12, 1888, Vol. 4, No 9. Retrieved from https://carlisleindian.dickinson.edu. Accessed September 2, 2025.
3. Slickpoo and Walker, 1973, p. 219
4. Slickpoo and Walker, 1973, p. 223
5. Slickpoo and Walker, 1973, p. 223
6. Gay, 1981, p. xxx
7. Gay, 1981, p. xxxii
8. Slickpoo and Walker, 1973, p. 223
9. Gay, 1981, p. 49
10. Gay, 1981, p. 49
11. Gay, 1981, p. 50
12. Gay, 1981, p. 51
13. Gay, 1981, p. 55
14. Gay, 1981, p. 60
15. Tonkovich, 2012, p. 194
16. Gay, 1981, p. xxv
17. Slickpoo and Walker, 1973, p. 224
18. Slickpoo and Walker, 1973, p. 226
19. Slickpoo and Walker, 1973, p. 226

CHAPTER 15

1. Drury, 1936, pp. 398–401
2. Drury, 1936, p. 416
3. Morrill and Morrill, 1978, p. 15
4. Slickpoo and Walker, 1973, p. 202
5. Slickpoo and Walker, 1973, p. 202
6. Morrill and Morrill, 1978, p. 70
7. Morrill and Morrill, 1978, p. 177
8. Morrill and Morrill, 1978, pp. 177–178
9. Morrill and Morrill, 1978, p. 185
10. McBeth, 1908, p. 89
11. McBeth, 1908, p. 89
12. Slickpoo and Walker, 1973, pp. 210–211
13. Slickpoo and Walker, 1973, p. 209
14. Slickpoo and Walker, 1973, p. 215
15. Slickpoo and Walker, 1973, p. 215
16. The calling cards have been scanned and shared in an archive on the Washington State University Plateau Peoples' Web Portal, https://plateauportal.libraries.wsu.edu/people/paul-family.
17. Maxine Paul and Bruce Paul "The Paul Family" in Thompson, 1984, p. 152
18. Maxine Paul and Bruce Paul "The Paul Family" in Thompson, 1984, p. 154
19. Retrieved from the National Archives, July 2004
20. Sugden, 1972, p. 13
21. Slickpoo and Walker, 1973, p. 237
22. Slickpoo and Walker, 1973, p. 242
23. Slickpoo and Walker, 1973, p. 242
24. Slickpoo and Walker, 1973, pp. 253–284

CHAPTER 17

1. Aoki, 1994, p. 286
2. Lomawaima, 1994, p. 1
3. Lomawaima, 1994, p. 12
4. Lomawaima, 1994, p. 14
5. Lomawaima, 1994, p. 45
6. Lomawaima, 1994, p. 12, 13

CHAPTER 19

1. A fictionalized version of Susan's story is told by Loula Grace Erdman in the young adult novel *A Bluebird Will Do* (1973).
2. TRC Conference Report, 2006, p. 3

CHAPTER 20

1. Indian Health Service website, "Disparities," https://www.ihs.gov/newsroom/factsheets/disparities/, accessed February 17, 2022.
2. Briefs on the success of six former camp attendees are available on the WSU website, https://magazine.wsu.edu/web-extra/na-ha-shnee-profiles/.
3. Hodge, 2002, p. 6
4. McGuire 2021, p. xxi.
5. Bopp and Morris, 1989, p. 43

Bibliography

Adams, D.W. *Education for Extinction: American Indians and the Boarding School Experience 1875–1928.* Lawrence, KS: University Press of Kansas, 1995.

Alcorn, R. L.. *Timothy, a Nez Perce Chief, 1800–1891.* Fairfield, WA: Ye Galleon Press, 1985

Aoki, H., *Nez Perce Dictionary.* Berkeley, CA: University of California Press, 1994.

Baird, D., Mallickan, D., and Swagerty, W. R., eds. *The Nez Perce Nation Divided.* Moscow, ID: University of Idaho Press, 2002.

Baird, D., Mallickan, D., and Swagerty, W. R., eds. *Encounters with The People.* Pullman, WA: Washington State University Press, 2015.

Bopp, Judie, Michael Bopp, Lee Brown, Phil Lane, and Patricia Lucas. *The Sacred Tree.* 3rd edition. Wilmot, WI: Lotus Light, 1989.

Brave Heart, M. Y. H., Chase, J., Elkins, J., and Altschul, D. B. "Historical Trauma Among Indigenous Peoples of the Americas: Concepts, Research, and Clinical Considerations." *Journal of Psychoactive Drugs* 43, no. 4 (2011): 282–90.

Brouillet, J. B. A. *Authentic Account of the Murder of Dr. Whitman and Other Missionaries, by The Cayuse Indians of Oregon, in 1847, and the Causes Which Led to the Horrible Catastrophe.* 2d ed. Portland, OR: S. J. McCormick, 1869.

Carlisle Indian Industrial School. "Home Items." *Eadle Keahtah Toh* 12 (1880): 3.

Chemawa Indian School. *History of Chemawa Indian School.* Accessed August 13, 2025, from https://cis.bie.edu/our-school/our-history.

Clark, J. S. "The Nez Perces in exile." *Pacific Northwest Quarterly* 36, no. 3 (1945): 213–232.

Crowe, F. H. "Indian Prisoner-Students at Fort Marion: The Founding of Carlisle Was Dreamed in St. Augustine." *The Regional Review* V, no. 6 (1940). Accessed August 13, 2025, from https://www.nps.gov/parkhistory/online_books/regional_review/vol5-6c.htm#:~:text=A%20school%20for%20the%20Indians,little%20money%20or%20outside%20aid.

Drury, C.M. *Henry Harmon Spalding: Pioneer of Old Oregon.* Caldwell, ID: Caxton Press, 1936.

Drury, C. M., ed. *The Diaries and Letters of Henry H. Spalding and Asa Bowen Smith: Relating to the Nez Perce Mission, 1838–1842. With Introductions and Editorial Notes by Clifford Merrill Drury.* Glendale, CA: Arthur H. Clark Company, 1958.

Drury, C. M., ed. *First White Women Over The Rockies; Diaries, Letters, and Biographical Sketches of the Six Women of the Oregon Mission Who Made The Overland Journey in 1836 and 1838.* Glendale, CA: Arthur H. Clark Company, 1963.

Drury, C.M. *Chief Lawyer of the Nez Perce Indians 1796–1876.* Glendale, CA: Arthur H. Clark Company, 1979.

Frankl, V. E. *Man's Search for Meaning: An Introduction to Logotherapy.* 3d ed. New York: Simon & Schuster, 1984.

Gay, E. J., F. E. Hoxie, and J. T. Mark. *With the Nez Perces : Alice Fletcher in the Field, 1889–92.* Lincoln, NE: University of Nebraska Press, 1981.

Glancy, D. *Fort Marion Prisoners and the Trauma of Native Education.* Lincoln, NE: University of Nebraska Press, 2014

Greene, J.A. *Nez Perce Summer, 1877: The U.S. Army and the Nee-me-poo Crisis.* Helena, MT: Montana Historical Society Press, 2000.

Haines, F. *Red Eagles of the Northwest.* New York: AMS Press, 1980

Haines, F. *The Nez Perces: Tribesmen of the Columbia Plateau.* Norman, OK: University of Oklahoma Press, 1955.

Haskell Indian Nations University. "Haskell History." Accessed August 13, 2025, from https://haskell.edu/about/history/.

Hodge, F. S., A. Pasqua, C. A. Marguez, and B. Geishirt-Cantrell. "Utilizing Traditional Storytelling to Promote Wellness in American Indian Communities." *Journal of Transcultural Nursing* 13, no. 1 (2002): 6–11.

Hoxie, F.E.. *A Final Promise: The Campaign to Assimilate the Indians, 1880–1920*. Lincoln, NE: University of Nebraska Press, 1984

Indian Health Service. *Regional Differences*. Washington, DC: US Department of Health and Human Services. Accessed February 15, 2022, from https://www.ihs.gov/newsroom/factsheets/disparities/.

Joseph. *Chief Joseph's Own Story: As told by Chief Joseph in 1879*. Billings, MO: Montana Council for Indian Education, 1879

Josephy, A. M., Jr.. *The Nez Perce Indians and the Opening of the Northwest*. Boston: Houghton Mifflin Company, 1997

Karson, Jennifer, ed. *Wiyaxayxt / Wiyaakaa'awn / As Days Go By: Our History, Our Land, and Our People; The Cayuse, Umatilla, and Walla Walla*. Seattle: University of Washington Press, 2015.

Locke, J. *Two Treatises of Government and a Letter Concerning Toleration*. Ed. by I. Shapiro,. New Haven, CT: Yale University Press, 2003

Lomawaima, K. T.. *They Called It Prairie Light: The Story of Chilocco Indian School*. Lincoln, NE: University of Nebraska Press, 1994

Kip, L. *Army Life on the Pacific*. Fairfield, WA: Ye Galleon Press, 1989.

Mann, B. A. *The Tainted Gift: The Disease Method of Frontier Expansion*. Santa Barbara, CA: Praeger, 2009

Manring, B. F. *The Conquest of the Coeur d'Alenes, Spokanes and Palouses: The Expeditions of Colonels E. J. Steptoe and George Wright against the "Northern Indians" in 1858*. Spokane, WA: Inland Printing Company, 1912.

McBeth, K. *The Nez Perces Since Lewis and Clark*. University of Idaho Press reprint ed. Moscow, ID: University of Idaho Press, 1993.

McGhee, H. *The Sum of Us: What Racism Costs Everyone and How We Can Prosper Together*. New York: One World, 2021.

McWhorter, L. V. *Hear Me, My Chiefs! Nez Perce History and Legend*. Caldwell, ID: Caxton Printers, 1952.

Morrill, A. C., and E. D. Morrill. *Out of the Blanket: The Story of Sue and Kate McBeth, Missionaries to the Nez Perce*. Moscow, ID: University of Idaho Press, 1978

Morrill, A. and E. Morrill. "Talmaks." *Idaho Yesterdays* 8 (1964): 48–56.

National Native American Boarding School Healing Coalition. Accessed Aug. 26, 2021, from https://boardingschoolhealing.org/list/ and https://boardingschoolhealing.org/education/us-indian-boarding-school-history/.

National Park Service. "Educator's Guide." Accessed July 20, 2021, from https://www.nps.gov/nepe/learn/education/upload/isaaptakay-lesson-plan_web.pdf.

National Public Radio. *Codeswitch*. Accessed Sept. 7, 2021, from https://www.npr.org/sections/codeswitch/2014/01/05/260006815/the-ugly-fascinating-history-of-the-word-racism. 2014.

Paul, M. S. and B. Paul. "The Paul Family." In J. Thomason, ed., *1984 Highlands of Craig Mountain*. Craigmont, ID: Highland Press, 1984.

Pearson, J.D.. *The Nez Perces in Indian Territory: Nimiipuu Survival*. Norman, OK: University of Oklahoma Press, 2008

Pevar, S. L.. *The Rights of Indians and Tribes: The Basic ACLU Guide to Indian and Tribal Rights*. 2d ed. Carbondale, IL: Southern Illinois University Press, 1992.

Pinkham, A. V., and Evans, S. R. *Lewis and Clark Among the Nez Perce*. Pullman, WA: Washington State University Press. Originally published by The Dakota Institute Press of the Lewis & Clark Fort Mandan Foundation, 2013.

Pollock, W. J. *Eadle Keahtah Toh. 12 2*. Carlisle, PA: Carlisle Indian Industrial School, 1880.

Pratt, R. H. *Battlefield and Classroom Four Decades with the American Indians, 1867–1904*. R.M. Utley, ed.. Norman, OK: University of Oklahoma Press, 2003.

Prucha, F.P. *The Great Father: The United States Government and the American Indians*. Lincoln, NE: University of Nebraska Press, 1984

Richards, K. D. *Isaac I. Stevens: Young Man in a Hurry*. Pullman, WA: Washington State University Press, 1993.

Rogers, B. "A Path of Healing and Wellness for Native Families." *American Behavioral Scientist* 449 (2001): 1512–14.

Sherman Indian School. "Sherman Indian School History." Accessed August 13, 2025, from https://sih.bie.edu/our-school/our-history

Slickpoo, A. P., Sr., L. L. Seth, and D. E. Walker. *Nu Mee Poom Tit Wah Tit: Nez Perce Legends*. Lapwai, ID: Nez Perce Tribe, 1972

Slickpoo, A. P., Sr., and Walker, D. E.. *Noon Nee-Me-Poo: We, the Nez Perces*. Lapwai, ID: Nez Perce Tribe, 1973

Smith, D. K., ed. *The 1867 Nez Perce Treaty Council*. Northwest Historical Manuscript Series. Moscow, ID: University of Idaho Press, 2001

Standing Bear, Luther. *My People the Sioux*. Edited by E. A. Brininstool. Lincoln, NE: University of Nebraska Press, 1975.

Sugden, H. L. ed. *Seventy-five years Presbyterian camp meetings of the Nez Perce Indians 1897–1972*. Kamiah, ID: Nez Perce Presbyterian Churches, 1972.

Swayne, Z. L. *Do them no Harm! Lewis and Clark among the Nez Perce*. Caldwell, ID: Caxton Press, 2003

Tonkovich, N. *The Allotment Plot: Alice C. Fletcher, E. Jane Gay, and Nez Perce Survivance*. Lincoln, NE: University of Nebraska Press, 2012.

Trafzer, C. ed. *Northwestern Tribes in Exile, Modoc, Nez Perce, and Palouse Removal to the Indian Territory*. Sacramento, CA: Sierra Oaks Publishing Co, 1987.

Trafzer, C., and R. D. Scheuerman. *Renegade Tribe: The Palouse Indians and the Invasion of the Inland Pacific Northwest*. Pullman, WA: Washington State University Press, 1993.

Treaties: Nez Perce Perspectives. Nez Perce Tribe in association with the United States Department of Energy. Winchester, ID: Confluence Press, 2003.

Truth and Reconciliation Commission. "Memory, Narrative and Forgiveness: Reflecting on Ten Years of South Africa's Truth and Reconciliation Commission, University of Cape Town, 23–27 November 2006 Conference Report." Farmington Hills, MI: Borderlands, The Gale Group, 2006.

Webb, S. *Nez Perce Songs of Historical Significance, as Sung by "Sol" Web*. Lapwai, ID: Nez Perce Tribe of Idaho in cooperation with the Music Department of Washington State University Pullman, WA, 1972.

West, Elliott. *The Last Indian War; The Nez Perce Story*. New York: Oxford University Press, 2009.

Witmer, Linda F. *The Indian Industrial School, Carlisle, Pennsylvania 1879–1918*. Carlisle, PA: Cumberland County Historical Society, 1993.

Wortman, R. K., Wortman, M. A., & Battorff, W. W., eds. *History of Cowley County Kansas, Volume II the Indians*. Winfield, KS: Arkansas City Historical Society, 1999.

Yellow Wolf and L. V. McWhorter. *Yellow Wolf: His Own Story*. Caldwell, ID: Caxton Printers, Ltd., 1983

Roberta Tawlitkitsanmay' Paul

Roberta Tawlikitsanmay' Paul is a mother, wife, grandmother, great-grandmother, and an enrolled Nez Perce Tribal member who grew up on the reservation in the small town of Craigmont, Idaho. She is the founding director of Native American Health Sciences for Washington State University. Among her awards are Woman of Distinction from Washington State University and Woman of Courage from the University of Washington. She received her doctorate from Gonzaga University. Her research focus is intergenerational traumas and healing.